Android
Application Development
FOR
DUMMIES®

APR   2011

Android™ Application Development FOR DUMMIES®

by Donn Felker with Joshua Dobbs

WILEY

Wiley Publishing, Inc.

Android™ Application Development For Dummies®

Published by
Wiley Publishing, Inc.
111 River Street
Hoboken, NJ 07030-5774
www.wiley.com

Copyright © 2011 by Wiley Publishing, Inc., Indianapolis, Indiana

Published by Wiley Publishing, Inc., Indianapolis, Indiana

Published simultaneously in Canada

For general information on our other products and services, please contact our Customer Care Department within the U.S. at 877-762-2974, outside the U.S. at 317-572-3993, or fax 317-572-4002.

For technical support, please visit www.wiley.com/techsupport.

Wiley also publishes its books in a variety of electronic formats. Some content that appears in print may not be available in electronic books.

Library of Congress Control Number: 2010939962

ISBN: 978-0-470-77018-4

Manufactured in the United States of America

10 9 8 7 6 5 4 3 2

WILEY

About the Authors

Donn Felker is a recognized leader in the development and consultation of state-of-the-art, cutting-edge software in the mobile and Web fields. He is an independent consultant with over 10 years of professional experience in various markets that include entertainment, health, retail, insurance, financial, and real estate. He is a mobile junkie, serial entrepreneur, and creative innovator in all things mobile and Web. He is the founder of Agilevent, an innovative creative development firm that has done work for small startups as well as Fortune 500 companies. He is a Microsoft ASP Insider, an MCTS for .NET Framework 2.0 and 3.5 Web Applications, and a certified ScrumMaster. He's a national speaker on topics that include Android, .NET, and software architecture. He is the author of the TekPub.com Introduction to Android video series. He is a writer, presenter, and consultant on various topics ranging from architecture to development in general, agile practices, and patterns and practices. Follow Donn on Twitter (@donnfelker) or read his blog here: http://blog.donnfelker.com.

Joshua Dobbs is a senior lead Web application developer for a large electronics manufacturer in Southern California. He has more than ten years' experience in Web and desktop application development. Josh was an early adopter of the Android platform and creates Android apps in his spare time. His apps have been downloaded more than 6 million times, and he was selected by Google as top Android developer for its Device Seeding Program. His Web site is www.joshdobbs.com.

Dedication

To my dogs, Lulu and Macho, and my cat, Vito: Thanks for keeping me company in the cold basement while I cranked out page after page in the wee hours of the morning while everyone else was asleep. Writing is a lonely gig, and your company helped the time pass much easier (and kept my feet and lap warm too).

To my dearest daughter, Sophia, who made even the toughest days brighter through her contagious, infectious laughter and antics. I love you.

Most of all, to my gorgeous wife, Ginamarie, who has always been very supportive of all my crazy, harebrained ideas over the years. I would not have gotten where I am in my life if it were not for your support. I love you.

Author's Acknowledgments

Thanks to coauthor Joshua Dobbs for writing the couple of chapters that I needed help with. May we both have many more successful books in the future!

Thanks to Wiley Acquisitions Editor Kyle Looper for giving me a shot at writing this book. I really appreciate the help, support, and insight into everything publishing-related. You've been a life saver on this project. Thank you.

Project Editor Kathy Simpson pushed me beyond what I thought would be possible in terms of the organization of the content and readability. Thank you for being a diligent editor.

Copy Editor John Edwards helped find some of my most subtle mistakes, which allowed me to polish the book content even more. Thank you.

Technical Editor Andre Taddeini is one of the few technical individuals I trust wholeheartedly. I'm glad you were my second pair of eyes on this project. Your sanity check of the technical accuracy of the book was outstanding. Thank you.

Finally, thank you to my friend John Benda for contributing by being supportive of me and my family during this process. It's been a long road. Now it's your turn to write a book!

Publisher's Acknowledgments

We're proud of this book; please send us your comments at http://dummies.custhelp.com. For other comments, please contact our Customer Care Department within the U.S. at 877-762-2974, outside the U.S. at 317-572-3993, or fax 317-572-4002.

Some of the people who helped bring this book to market include the following:

Acquisitions and Editorial

Project Editor: Kathy Simpson

Acquisitions Editor: Kyle Looper

Copy Editor: John Edwards

Technical Editor: Andre Taddeini

Editorial Manager: Jodi Jensen

Editorial Assistant: Amanda Graham

Sr. Editorial Assistant: Cherie Case

Cartoons: Rich Tennant (www.the5thwave.com)

Composition Services

Project Coordinator: Sheree Montgomery

Layout and Graphics: Nikki Gately, Laura Westhuis

Proofreaders: Laura Bowman, Rebecca Denoncour

Indexer: BIM Indexing & Proofreading Services

Publishing and Editorial for Technology Dummies

> **Richard Swadley,** Vice President and Executive Group Publisher
>
> **Andy Cummings,** Vice President and Publisher
>
> **Mary Bednarek,** Executive Acquisitions Director
>
> **Mary C. Corder,** Editorial Director

Publishing for Consumer Dummies

> **Diane Graves Steele,** Vice President and Publisher

Composition Services

> **Gerry Fahey,** Vice President of Production Services
>
> **Debbie Stailey,** Director of Composition Services

Contents at a Glance

Table of Contents

Introduction

*W*elcome to *Android Application Development For Dummies,* the first *For Dummies* book that covers Android application development. When I was contacted to write this book, I was ecstatic about the opportunity to spread the wealth of knowledge that I'd picked up over the past year and a half of Android development. I hope you enjoy finding out about how to program for the Android platform from this book as much as I enjoyed writing it!

When Android was acquired by Google in 2005 (yes, Android was a start-up company at one point), I'll be honest, I didn't have much interest in it. I heard that Google might be entering the mobile space, but as with anything in the technology industry, I didn't believe it until I saw it firsthand. Fast-forward to a few years later, when Google announced its first Android phone: the G1. When I heard this news, I was glued to the computer, reading reviews, watching videos, and researching the product as much as I could. I knew that this product would be the start of something huge.

I got my start in Android development about a week after my wife received her first G1 Android device. The G1 was the first publicly released Android device. It didn't match the rich feature set of the iPhone at the time, but I desperately believed in the platform. As soon as Donut (Android 1.6) was released, it was evident that Google was putting some effort into the product. Immediately after version 1.6 was released, talk of 2.0 was already on the horizon.

Today, we're on version 2.2 of the Android platform, and 3.0 is just around the corner. The platform is barely two years old, and I see no sign of the platform development slowing down. Without doubt, this is an exciting time in Android development. I hope that your excitement carries through as you read this book and later as you release your own applications on the market.

About This Book

Android Application Development For Dummies is a beginner's guide to developing Android applications. You don't need any Android application development experience under your belt to get started. I expect you to approach this material as a blank slate because the Android platform accomplishes various mechanisms by using different paradigms that most programmers aren't used to using — or developing with — on a day-to-day basis. I expect you to be familiar with the Java programming language, however. You don't have to be a Java guru, but you should understand the syntax, basic data structures, and language constructs. XML is also used in developing Android applications, so I advise understanding XML as well.

The Android platform is a *device-independent* platform, which means that you can develop applications for various devices. These devices include but aren't limited to phones, e-book readers, netbooks, and GPS devices. Soon, television sets will join the list. Yes, you read it correctly — TV! Google has announced plans to include a Google TV offering in the Android platform.

Finding out how to develop for the Android platform opens a large variety of development options for you. This book distills hundreds, if not thousands, of pages of Android documentation, tips, tricks, and tutorials into a short, digestible format that allows you to springboard into your future as an Android developer. This book isn't a recipe book, but it gives you the basic knowledge to assemble various pieces of the Android framework to create interactive and compelling applications.

Conventions Used in This Book

Throughout the book, you use the Android framework classes, and you will be creating Java classes and XML files.

Code examples in this book appear in a monospace font so that they stand out from other text in the book. This means that the code you'll see looks like this:

```
public class MainActivity
```

Java is a high-level programming language that is case-sensitive, so be sure to enter the text into the editor *exactly* as you see it in the book. I also use the standard Java conventions in this book. Therefore, you can transition easily between my examples and the example code provided by the Android Software Development Kit (SDK). All class names, for example, appear in `PascalCase` format, and all class-scoped variables start with `m`.

All the URLs in the book appear in monospace font as well:

```
http://d.android.com
```

If you're ever unsure about anything in the code, you can download the full source code from my GitHub account, located at `http://github.com/donnfelker`. From time to time, I provide code updates to the source. You can also find other examples in my other source repositories stored on the same site. Finally, you can find the same material on the *For Dummies* Web site at `www.dummies.com/go/androidappdevfd`.

Foolish Assumptions

To begin programming with Android, you need a computer that runs one of the following operating systems:

- ✔ Windows XP (32 bit), Vista (32 or 64 bit), or Windows 7 (32 or 64 bit)
- ✔ Mac OS X (Intel) 10.5.8 (x86 only)
- ✔ Linux (i386)

You also need to download the Android SDK (which is free) and the Java Development Kit (or JDK, which is also free), if you don't already have them on your computer. I explain the entire installation process for all the tools and frameworks in Chapter 2.

As I state earlier in this introduction, because Android applications are developed in the Java programming language, you need to understand the Java language. Android also uses XML quite heavily to define various resources inside the application, so you should understand XML too. I don't expect you to be an expert in these languages, however. I started in Android with a background in C#, having done Java only in college nearly 10 years earlier, and I fared just fine.

You don't need a physical Android device, because all the applications you build in this book work on the emulator. I highly recommend developing on a real device, however, because it allows you to interact with your applications as real users would.

How This Book Is Organized

Android Application Development For Dummies has four parts, which I describe in the following sections.

Part I: The Nuts and Bolts of Android

Part I introduces the tools and frameworks that you use to develop Android applications. It also introduces the various SDK components and shows you how they're used in the Android ecosystem.

Part II: Building and Publishing Your First Android Application

Part II introduces you to building your first Android application: the Silent Mode Toggle application. After you build the initial application, I show you how to create an app widget for the application that you can place on the home screen of the Android device. I tie everything together by demonstrating how to publish your application to the Android Market.

Part III: Creating a Feature-Rich Application

Part III takes your development skills up a notch by walking you through the construction of the Task Reminder application, which allows users to create various tasks with reminders. I cover the implementation of an SQLite database in this multiscreen application. You also see how to use the Android status bar to create notifications that can help increase the usability of your application.

Part IV: The Part of Tens

Part IV brings together the prizes that I've found through my trials and tribulations in Android development. I give you a tour of sample applications that prove to be stellar launching pads for your Android apps, and I introduce useful Android libraries that can make your Android development career a lot easier.

Icons Used in This Book

This icon indicates a useful pointer that you shouldn't skip.

This icon represents a friendly reminder about a vital point you should keep in mind while proceeding through a particular section of the chapter.

This icon signifies that the accompanying explanation may be informative but isn't essential to understanding Android application development. Feel free to skip these snippets, if you like.

 This icon alerts you to potential problems that you may encounter along the way. Read and remember these tidbits to avoid possible trouble.

Where to Go from Here

It's time to explore the Android platform! If you're a bit nervous, let me assure you that you don't have to worry; you should be nervous only because you're excited.

Part I
The Nuts and Bolts of Android

The 5th Wave   By Rich Tennant

"Frankly, the idea of an entirely wireless future scares me to death."

In this part . . .

Part I introduces you to the Android platform and describes what makes a spectacular Android application. I briefly explore various parts of the Android software development kit (SDK) and explain how you can use them in your applications. I also guide you through the process of installing the tools and frameworks necessary to develop Android applications.

Chapter 1

Developing Spectacular Android Applications

In This Chapter

▶ Seeing reasons to develop Android apps

▶ Starting with the basics of Android programming

▶ Working with the hardware

▶ Getting familiar with the software

Google rocks! Google acquired the Android project in 2005 (see the sidebar "The roots of Android" later in this chapter) to ensure that a mobile operating system (OS) could be created and maintained in an open platform. Google continues to pump time and resources into the Android project, which has already proved to be beneficial. As of July 2010, 160,000 Android handsets have been activated daily, which is good considering that handsets have been available only since October 2008. That's less than two years, and Android has already made a huge impact!

It has never been easier for a developer to be able to make money on his own. Android users may not know who you are, but they know what Google is, and they trust Google. Because your app resides in the Android Market — which Google controls — Google assumes that your application is okay too.

Why Develop for Android?

Well, the real question should be "Why not?" Do you want your app to be available to millions of users worldwide? Do you want to publish apps as soon as you're done writing and testing them? Do you like developing on open platforms? If you answered yes to any of these questions, I think you have your answer, but in case you're still undecided, keep reading, and I'll explain what I mean.

Market share

As a developer, you have an opportunity to develop apps for a fairly new market that is booming on a daily basis. Android is currently set to outpace many other carriers in market share in the industry in coming months. With so many users, it's never been easier to write an application that can be downloaded and used by real people! The Android Market puts your app right into your users' hands easily! Users don't have to go searching the Internet to find an app to install. They just simply go to the Android Market that is preinstalled on their device, and they have access to all *your* apps. Because the Android Market comes preinstalled on most Android devices (I discuss a few exceptions later), users typically search the Android Market for all of their app needs. It's not hard to see an app's number of downloads soar in just a few days.

Time to market

With all the application programming interfaces (APIs) that Android comes packed with, it's easy to develop full-featured applications in a relatively short time frame. After you've signed up with the Android Market, just upload your apps and publish them. "Wait," you may say, "are you sure?" Why, yes, I am! Unlike other mobile marketplaces, the Android Market has no app-approval process. All you have to do is write apps and publish them.

Technically, anyone can publish anything, but it's good karma to keep within Google's terms of service and keep your apps family-friendly. Remember that Android users come from diverse areas of the world and are in all age categories.

Open platform

The Android operating system is *open platform,* meaning that it's not tied to one hardware manufacturer and/or one provider. As you can imagine, the openness of Android is allowing it to gain market share quickly. All hardware manufacturers and providers can make and sell Android devices. The Android source code is available at `http://source.android.com` for you to view and/or modify. Nothing is holding you back from digging into the source code to see how a certain task is handled. The open-source code allows phone manufacturers to create custom user interfaces (UIs) and add built-in features to some devices. This also puts all developers on an even playing field. Everyone can access the raw Android source code.

The roots of Android

Most people don't know this, but Google didn't start the Android project. The initial Android operating system was created by a small start-up company in Silicon Valley known as Android, Inc., which was purchased by Google in July 2005. The founders of Android, Inc., came from various Internet technology companies such as Danger, Wildfire Communications, T-Mobile, and WebTV. Google brought them into the Google team to help create what is now the full-fledged Android mobile operating system.

Cross-compatibility

Android can run on many devices with different screen sizes and resolutions. Besides being cross-compatible, Android comes with the tools that help you develop cross-compatible applications. Google allows your apps to run only on compatible devices. If your app requires a front-facing camera, for example, only phones with a front-facing camera will be able to see your app in the Android Market. This arrangement is known as *feature detection*. (For more information on publishing your apps to the Android Market, see Chapter 8.)

For Android devices to be certified compatible (devices have to be compatible to have access to the Android Market), they must follow certain hardware guidelines. These guidelines include but are not limited to the following:

- Camera
- Compass
- GPS (Global Positioning System) feature
- Bluetooth transceiver

See the Compatibility Program Overview page at http://source.android.com/compatibility/overview.html for specific device configurations that are considered to be compatible. Compatibility ensures that your apps can run on all devices.

Mashup capability

A *mashup* combines two or more services to create an application. You can create a mashup by using the camera and Android's location services, for example, to take a picture with the exact location displayed on the image! It's easy to make a ton of apps by combining services or libraries in new and exciting ways.

With all the APIs that Android includes, it's easy to use two or more of these features to make your own app. You can use a maps API with the contact list to show all your contacts on a map, for example (see "Google APIs," later in this chapter).

Here are a few other mashups to get your brain juices pumping. All this stuff is included for you to use, and it's completely legal and free!

✔ **Geolocation and social networking:** Social networking is the "in" thing right now. Suppose you want to write an app that tweets your current location every 10 minutes throughout the day. You can, and it's easy. Use Android's location services and a third-party Twitter API (such as iTwitter), and you can do just that.

✔ **Geolocation and gaming:** Location-based gaming is gaining popularity. It's a great way to really put your users into the game. A game might run a background service to check your current location and compare it with the locations of other users of the game in the same area. If another user is within 1 mile of you, for example, you could be notified, and you could challenge her to a battle. None of this would be possible without a strong platform such as Android and GPS technology.

✔ **Contacts and Internet:** With all these cool APIs at your disposal, it's easy to make full-featured apps by combining the functionality of two or more APIs. You can combine contacts and the Internet to create a greeting-card app, for example. Or you may just want to add an easy way for your users to contact you from an app or enable users to send the app to their friends. This is all possible with the built-in APIs.

The sky is the limit. All this cool functionality is literally in the palm of your hand. If you want to develop an app that records the geographic location of the device, you can with ease. Android really opens the possibilities by allowing you to tap into these features easily. It's up to you, as the developer, to put them together in a way that can benefit your users.

Developers can do just about anything they want with Android, so be careful. Use your best judgment when creating and publishing apps for mass consumption. Just because you want a live wallpaper that shows you doing the hula in your birthday suit doesn't mean that anyone else wants to see it.

Also, keep privacy laws in mind before you harvest your users' contact info for your own marketing scheme.

Android Programming Basics

You don't have to be a member of Mensa to program Android applications. I'm glad, because otherwise, I wouldn't be writing them! Programming for Android is simple because the default programming language of Android is Java. Although writing Android applications is fairly easy, programming in itself can be a difficult task to conquer.

If you've never programmed before, this book may not be the best place to start. I advise that you pick up a copy of *Beginning Programming with Java For Dummies,* by Barry Burd (Wiley Publishing), to learn the ropes. After you have a basic understanding of Java under your belt, you should be ready to tackle this book.

Although the majority of Android is Java, small parts of the framework aren't. Android also encompasses the XML language as well as basic Apache Ant scripting for build processes. I advise you to have a basic understanding of XML before delving into this book.

If you need an introduction to XML, check out *XML For Dummies,* by Lucinda Dykes and Ed Tittel (Wiley).

If you already know Java and XML, congratulations — you're ahead of the curve!

Java: Your Android programming language

Android applications are written in Java — not the full-blown Java that J2EE developers are used to, but a subset of Java that is sometimes known as the *Dalvik virtual machine.* This smaller subset of Java excludes classes that don't make sense for mobile devices. If you have any experience in Java, you should be right at home.

It may be a good idea to keep a Java reference book on hand, but in any case, you can always Google what you don't understand. Because Java is nothing new, you can find plenty of examples on the Web that demonstrate how to do just about anything.

In Java source code, not all libraries are included. Verify that the package is available to you. If it's not, an alternative is probably bundled with Android that can work for your needs.

Activities

Android applications are made up of one or more activities. Your app must contain at least one activity, but an Android application can contain several. Think of an activity as being a container for your UI, holding your UI as well as the code that runs it. It's kind of like a form, for you Windows programmers out there. I discuss activities in more detail in Chapters 3 and 5.

Intents

Intents make up the core message system that runs Android. An intent is composed of an action that it needs to perform (View, Edit, Dial, and so on) and data. The action is the general action to be performed when the intent is received, and the data is the data to operate on. The data might be a contact item, for example.

Intents are used to start activities and to communicate among various parts of the Android system. Your application can either broadcast an intent or receive an intent.

Sending messages with intents

When you broadcast an intent, you're sending a message telling Android to make something happen. This intent could tell Android to start a new activity from within your application, or it could start a different application.

Registering intent receivers

Just because you send a message doesn't mean that something will happen automatically. You have to register an *intent receiver* that listens for the intent and then tells Android what to do, whether the task is starting a new activity or starting a different app. If many receivers can accept a given intent, a chooser can be created to allow the user to pick the app she wants to use. A classic example is long-pressing an image in an image gallery. *Long-pressing* means clicking something for a long time to bring up a context menu.

By default, various registered receivers handle the image-sharing intents. One of many is e-mail, and another is the messaging application (among various other installed applications). Because you find more than one possible intent receiver, the user is presented with a chooser asking him what he should do: use e-mail, messaging, or another application, as shown in Figure 1-1.

Figure 1-1:
A chooser.

If the Android system cannot find a match for the intent that was sent, and a chooser was not created manually, the application will crash due to a *run-time exception:* an unhandled error in the application. Android expects developers to know what they're doing. If you send an intent that a user's Android device doesn't know how to handle, the device crashes. It's best practice to create choosers for intents that don't target other activities within your application.

Cursorless controls

Unlike PCs, which let you use a mouse to move the cursor across the screen, Android devices let you use your fingers to do just about anything a mouse can do. But how do you right-click? Instead of supporting right-clicking, Android has implemented the long press. Press and hold a button, icon, or screen for an extended period of time, and a context menu appears. As a developer, you can create and manipulate context menus. You can allow users to use two fingers on an Android device instead of just one mouse cursor, for example. Keep in mind that fingers come in all sizes, however, and design your user interface accordingly. Make the buttons large enough, with enough spacing, so that even users with large fingers can interact with your apps easily.

Views and widgets

What the heck is a view? A *view* is a basic UI element — a rectangular area on the screen that is responsible for drawing and event handling. I like to think of views as being basic controls, such as a label control in HTML. Here are a few examples of views:

- ✔ ContextMenu
- ✔ Menu
- ✔ View
- ✔ Surface view

Widgets are more-advanced UI elements, such as check boxes. Think of them as being the controls that your users interact with. Here are a few widgets:

- ✔ Button
- ✔ CheckBox
- ✔ DatePicker
- ✔ DigitalClock
- ✔ Gallery
- ✔ FrameLayout
- ✔ ImageView
- ✔ RelativeLayout
- ✔ PopupWindow

Many more widgets are ready for you to use. Check out the android. widget package in the Android documentation at http://developer. android.com/reference/android/widget/package-summary.html for complete details.

Asynchronous calls

Who called? I don't know anybody named Asynchronous, do you?

The AsyncTask class in Android allows you to run multiple operations at the same time without having to manage a separate thread yourself. AsyncTask not only lets you start a new process without having to clean up after yourself, but also returns the result to the activity that started it. This allows you to have a clean programming model for asynchronous processing.

A *thread* is a process that runs separately from and simultaneously with everything else that's happening.

When would you use asynchronous processing? I'm glad you asked! You'd use asynchronous processing for tasks that take a long time — network communication (Internet), media processing, or anything else that might make the user wait. If the user has to wait, you should use an asynchronous call and some type of UI element to let him know that something is happening.

Failing to use an asynchronous programming model can cause users of your application to believe that your application is buggy. Downloading the latest Twitter messages via the Internet takes time, for example. If the network gets slow, and you're not using an asynchronous model, the application will lock up, and the user will assume that something is wrong because the application isn't responding to her interactions. If the application doesn't respond within a reasonable time that the Android OS defines, Android presents an "application not responding" (ANR) dialog box, as shown in Figure 1-2. At that time, the user can decide to wait or to close the application.

Figure 1-2:
An ANR
dialog box.

> **⚠ Sorry!**
>
> Activity Hello, Android (in application Hello, Android) is not responding.
>
> | Force close | Wait |

It's best practice to run CPU-expensive or long-running code inside another thread, as described in the Designing for Responsiveness page on the Android developer site (`http://developer.android.com/guide/practices/design/responsiveness.html`).

Background services

If you're a Windows user, you may already know what a *service* is: an application that runs in the background and doesn't necessarily have a UI. A classic example is an antivirus application that usually runs in the background as a service. Even though you don't see it, you know that it's running.

Most music players that can be downloaded from the Android Market run as background services. This is how you can listen to music while checking your e-mail or performing another task that requires the use of the screen.

Hardware Tools

Google exposes a plethora of functionality in Android, thus giving developers (even the independent guys) the tools needed to create top-notch, full-featured mobile apps. Google has gone above and beyond by making it simple to tap into and make use of all the devices' available hardware.

To create a spectacular Android app, you should take advantage of all that the hardware has to offer. Don't get me wrong: If you have an idea for an app that doesn't need hardware assistance, that's okay too.

Android phones come with several hardware features that you can use to build your apps, as shown in Table 1-1.

Table 1-1	Android Device Hardware
Functionality Required	*Hardware*
Where am I?	GPS radio
Which way am I walking?	Built-in compass
Is my phone facing up or down?	Proximity sensor
Is my phone moving?	Accelerometer
Can I use my Bluetooth headphones?	Bluetooth radio
How do I record video?	Camera

Most Android phones are released with the hardware that I discuss in the following sections, but not all devices are created equal. Android is free for hardware manufacturers to distribute, so it's used in a wide range of devices, including some made by small manufacturers overseas (and it's not uncommon for some of these phones to be missing a feature or two).

Also, as the technology advances, phone manufacturers are starting to add features that aren't yet natively supported by Android. But don't worry; manufacturers that add hardware usually offer a software development kit (SDK) that lets developers tap into the device's unique feature. At this writing, HTC's Evo 4G, available from Sprint, is the only Android phone that comes with a front-facing camera. Because this device is the first of its kind, Sprint has released an SDK that developers can use to access this cool new feature, as well as sample code that lets them implement the feature easily.

Android devices come in all shapes and sizes: phones, tablet computers, and e-book readers. You will find many other implementations of Android in the future, such as Google TV — an Android-powered home appliance — as well as cars with built-in Android-powered touchscreen computers. The engineers behind Android provide tools that let you easily deploy apps for multiple screen sizes and resolutions. Don't worry — the Android team has done all the hard work for you. I cover the basics of screen sizes and densities in Chapter 4.

Touchscreen

Android phones have touchscreens, a fact that opens a ton of possibilities and can enhance users' interaction with your apps. Users can swipe, flip, drag, and pinch to zoom, for example, by moving a finger or fingers on the touchscreen. You can even use custom gestures for your app, which opens even more possibilities.

Android also supports *multitouch,* which means that the entire screen is touchable by more than one finger at a time.

Hardware buttons are old news. You can place buttons of any shape anywhere on the screen to create the UI that's best suited for your app.

GPS

The Android OS combined with a phone's GPS radio allows developers to access a user's location at any given moment. You can track a user's movement as she changes locations. The Foursquare social-networking app is a good example; it uses GPS to determine the phone's location and then accesses the Web to determine which establishment or public place the user is in or near.

Another great example is the Maps application's ability to pinpoint your location on a map and provide directions to your destination. Android combined with GPS hardware gives you access to the phone's exact GPS location. Many apps use this functionality to show you where the nearest gas station, coffeehouse, or even restroom is located. You can even use the maps API to pinpoint the user's current location on a map.

Accelerometer

Android comes packed with accelerometer support. An *accelerometer* is a device that measures acceleration. That sounds cool and all, but what can you do with it? If you want to know whether the phone is moving or being shaken, or even the direction in which it's being turned, the accelerometer can tell you.

You may be thinking, "Okay, but why do I care whether the phone is being shaken or turned?" Simple! You can use that input as a way to control your application. You can do simple things like determine whether the phone has been turned upside down and do something when it happens. Maybe you're making a dice game and want to immerse your users in the game play by having them shake the phone to roll the dice. This is the kind of functionality that is setting mobile devices apart from typical desktop personal computers.

SD Card

Android gives you the tools you need to access (save and load) files on the device's *SD Card* — a portable storage medium that you can insert into various phones and computers. If a device is equipped with an SD Card, you can use it to store and access files needed by your application. Android 2.2 allows you to install apps on the SD Card, but maybe your users have phones that don't get Android 2.2. Just because some users don't have the option of installing apps on the SD Card doesn't mean that you have to bloat your app with 20MB of resources and hog the phone's limited built-in memory. You can download some or all of your application's resources from your Web host and save them to the phone's SD Card. This makes your users happy and less likely to uninstall your app when space is needed.

Not all devices come with an SD Card installed, although most do. Always make sure that the user has an SD Card installed and that adequate space is available before trying to save files to it.

Software Tools

Various Android tools are at your disposal while writing Android applications. In the following sections, I outline some of the most popular tools that you will use in your day-to-day Android development process.

Internet

Thanks to the Internet capabilities of Android devices, real-time information is easy to obtain. As a user, you can use the Internet to see what time the next movie starts or when the next commuter train arrives. As a developer, you can use the Internet in your apps to access real-time, up-to-date data such as weather, news, and sports scores. You can also use the Web to store some of your application's assets, which is what Pandora and YouTube do.

Don't stop there. Why not offload some of your application's intense processes to a Web server when appropriate? This can save a lot of processing time in some cases and also helps keep your Android app streamlined. This arrangement is called *client–server computing* — a well-established software architecture in which the client makes a request to a server that is ready and willing to do something. The built-in Maps app is an example of a client accessing map and GPS data from a Web server.

Audio and video support

The Android OS makes including audio and video in your apps a breeze. Many standard audio and video formats are supported. Including multimedia content in your apps couldn't be any easier. Sound effects, instructional videos, background music, streaming video, and audio from the Internet can all be added to your app with little to no pain. Be as creative as you want to be. The sky is the limit.

Contacts

Your app can access user contacts that are stored on the phone. You can use this feature to display the contacts in a new or different way. Maybe you don't like the built-in Contacts application. With the ability to access the contacts stored on the phone, nothing is stopping you from writing your own. Maybe you write an app that couples the contacts with the GPS system and alerts the user when she is close to one of the contacts' addresses.

Use your imagination, but be responsible. You don't want to use contacts in a malicious way (see the next section).

Security

Android allows your apps to do a lot! Imagine if someone released an app that went through the contact list and sent the entire list to a server somewhere for malicious purposes. This is why most of the functions that modify the user's device or access its protected content need to have permissions to work. Suppose that you want to download an image from the Web and save it to the SD Card. To do so, you need to get permission to use the Internet so that you can download the file. You also need permission to save files to the SD Card. Upon installation of the application, the user is notified of the permissions that your app is requesting. At that point, the user can decide whether he wants to proceed with the installation. Asking for permission is as easy as implementing one line of code in your application's manifest file, which I cover in Chapter 3.

Google APIs

The Android OS isn't limited to making phone calls, organizing contacts, or installing apps. You have much more power at your fingertips. As a developer, you can integrate maps into your application. To do so, you have to use the maps APIs that contain the map widgets.

Pinpointing locations on a map

Perhaps you want to write an app that displays your current location to your friends. You could spend hundreds of hours developing a mapping system — or you could just use the Android Maps API. Google provides the Android Maps API, which you can use in your app, and just like everything else in Android, it's free! You can embed and use the API in your application to show your friends where you are; it won't take hundreds of hours or cost you a cent. Imagine all the juicy map goodness with none of the work developing it. Using the maps API, you can find just about anything with an address; the possibilities are endless. Display your friend's location, the nearest grocery store, or the nearest gas station — anything or anyplace with an address.

Getting around town with navigation

Showing your current location to your friends is cool, but wait — there's more! The Android Maps API can also access the Google Navigation API. Now you can pinpoint your location and also show your users how to get to that location.

The KISS principle

It's easy to overthink and overcomplicate things when developing applications. The hardest part is to remember the KISS (Keep It Simple, Stupid) principle. One way to overly complicate your code is to just dive in without understanding all the built-in APIs and knowing what they do. You can go that route, but doing so may take more time than just glossing over the Android documentation. You don't have to memorize it, but do yourself a favor and take a look at the documentation. You'll be glad you did when you see how easy it is to use the built-in functionality and how much time it can save you. You can easily write multiple lines of code to do something that takes only one line. Changing the volume of the media player or creating a menu is a simple process, but if you don't know the APIs, you may end up rewriting them and in the end causing yourself problems.

When I started with my first app, I just dived in and wrote a bunch of code that managed the media player's volume. If I'd just looked into the Android documentation a little more, I'd have known that I could handle this with one line of code that's strategically placed inside my application. The same thing goes for the menu. I wrote a lot of code to create a menu, and if I'd only known that a menu framework already existed, it would have saved me several hours.

Another way to really muck things up is to add functionality that isn't needed. Most users want the easiest way to do things, so don't go making some fancy custom tab layout when a couple of menu items will suffice. Android comes with enough built-in controls (widgets) that you can use to accomplish just about anything. Using the built-in controls makes your app that much easier for your users to figure out because they already know and love these controls.

Messaging in the clouds

You may be thinking — clouds, I don't see a cloud in the sky! Well, I'm not talking about those kinds of clouds. The Android Cloud to Device Messaging framework allows you to send a notification from your Web server to your app. Suppose that you store your application's data in the cloud and download all the assets the first time your app runs. But what if you realize after the fact that one of the images is incorrect? For the app to update the image, it needs to know that the image changed. You can send a cloud-to-device message (a message from the Web to the device) to your app, letting it know that it needs to update the image. This works even if your app is not running. When the device receives the message, it dispatches a message to start your app so that it can take the appropriate action.

Chapter 2

Prepping Your Development Headquarters

*A*ll the software that you need to develop Android applications is *free!* That's where the beauty of developing Android applications lies. You'll be happy to find out that the basic building blocks you need to develop rich Android applications — the tools, the frameworks, and even the source code — are free. No, you don't get a free computer out of it, but you do get to set up your development environment and start developing applications for free, and you can't beat free. Well, maybe you can — such as someone paying you to write an Android application, but you'll get there soon enough.

In this chapter, I walk you through the necessary steps to get the tools and frameworks installed so that you can start building kick-butt Android applications.

Developing the Android Developer Inside You

Becoming an Android developer isn't a complicated task. Actually, it's a lot simpler than you probably think. To see what's involved, ask yourself these questions:

> ✔ Do I want to develop Android applications?
>
> ✔ Do I like free software development tools?
>
> ✔ Do I like to pay no developer fees?
>
> ✔ Do I have a computer to develop on?

If you answered yes to all these questions, today is your lucky day; you're ready to become an Android developer. You may be wondering about the "no fees" part. Yep, you read that correctly: You pay no fees to develop Android applications.

There's always a catch, right? You can develop for free to your heart's content, but as soon as you want to publish your application to the Android Market — where you upload and publish your apps — you need to pay a small nominal registration fee. At this writing, the fee is $25.

Just to ease your mind about fees, it's important to note that if you're developing an application for a client, you can publish your application as a redistributable package that you can give him. Then your client can publish the application to the Android Market, using his Market account. This ensures that you don't have to pay a fee for client work — which means that you can be a bona fide Android developer and never have to pay a fee. Now, that's cool.

Assembling Your Toolkit

Now that you know you're ready to be an Android developer, grab your computer and get cracking on installing the tools and frameworks necessary to build your first blockbuster application.

Android source code

You should be aware that the full Android source code is open source, which means that it's not only free to use, but also free to modify. If you'd like to download the Android source code and create a new version of Android, you're free to do so. Check the Android Git repository. You can also download the source code at `http://source.android.com`.

Linux 2.6 kernel

Android was created on top of the open-source Linux 2.6 kernel. The Android team chose to use this kernel because it provided proven core features to develop the Android operating system on. The features of the Linux 2.6 kernel include (but aren't limited to) the following:

- ✔ **Security model:** The Linux kernel handles security between the application and the system.

- ✔ **Memory management:** The kernel handles memory management for you, leaving you free to develop your app.

- ✔ **Process management:** The Linux kernel manages processes well, allocating resources to processes as they need them.

- ✔ **Network stack:** The Linux kernel also handles network communication.

- ✔ **Driver model:** The goal of Linux is to ensure that everything works. Hardware manufacturers can build their drivers into the Linux build.

You can see a good sampling of the Linux 2.6 feature set in Figure 2-1.

Figure 2-1:
Some of the
Linux kernel
features.

Android framework

Atop the Linux 2.6 kernel, the Android framework was developed with various features. These features were pulled from numerous open-source projects. The output of these projects resulted in the following:

- ✔ **The Android run time:** The Android run time is composed of Java core libraries and the Dalvik virtual machine.

- ✔ **Open GL (graphics library):** This cross-language, cross-platform application program interface (API) is used to produce 2D and 3D computer graphics.

- ✔ **WebKit:** This open-source Web browser engine provides the functionality to display Web content and simplify page loading.

✔ **SQLite:** This open-source relational database engine is designed to be embedded in devices.

✔ **Media frameworks:** These libraries allow you to play and record audio and video.

✔ **Secure Sockets Layer (SSL):** These libraries are responsible for Internet security.

See Figure 2-2 for a list of common Android libraries.

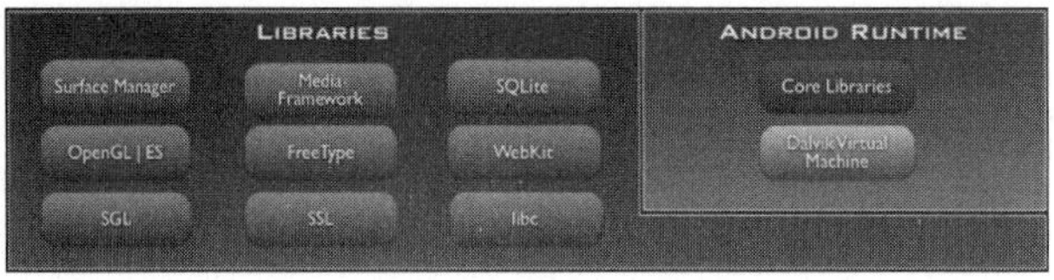

Figure 2-2:
Android and other third-party libraries sit atop the Linux 2.6 kernel.

Application framework

You're probably thinking, "Well, that's all nice and well, but how do these libraries affect me as a developer?" It's simple: All these open-source frameworks are available to you through Android. You don't have to worry about how Android interacts with SQLite and the surface manager; you just use them as tools in your Android tool belt. The Android team has built on a known set of proven libraries and has given them to you, all exposed through Android interfaces. These interfaces wrapped up the various libraries and made them useful to the Android platform as well as useful to you as a developer. Android has all these libraries built in the background and exposes these features to you without your having to build any of the functionality that they provide:

✔ **Activity manager:** Manages the activity life cycle.

✔ **Telephony manager:** Provides access to telephony services as well as some subscriber information, such as phone numbers.

✔ **View system:** Handles the views and layouts that make up your user interface (UI).

✔ **Location manager:** Finds out the device's geographic location.

Take a look at Figure 2-3 to see the libraries that make up the application framework.

Figure 2-3:
A glimpse at part of the Android application framework.

From kernel to application, the Android operating system has been developed with proven open-source technologies. This allows you, as a developer, to build rich applications that have been fostered in the open-source community. See Figure 2-4 for a full picture of how the Android application framework stacks up.

Figure 2-4:
How the Android application framework stacks up. The Applications section is where your application sits.

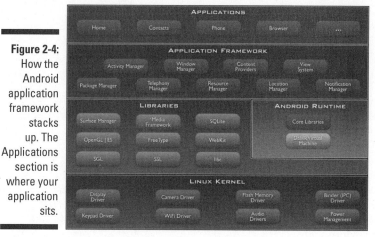

Sometimes when developing an Android application, you'd like to use the same resource as in the core Android system. A good example would be an icon for a Settings menu option. By accessing the Android source code, you can browse the various resources and download the resources you need for your project. Having access to the source code also allows you to dig in and see exactly how Android does what it does.

Open Handset Alliance libraries

Huh? I didn't join any "alliance"; what's this about? Don't worry; you're not going to have to use the force to battle the unwieldy Darth Vader. It's not that big of a deal, and actually it's kind of cool. It's kind of like a bunch of really smart companies combining efforts to achieve the same goal.

The Open Handset Alliance (OHA) was announced in November 2007. At the time, the alliance consisted of 34 members, led by Google.

The OHA currently has 71 members. It's a group of technology and mobile companies that have come together to pursue innovation in the mobile field. The goal is to provide users comprehensive, compelling, and useful handsets. You can read more about the group at www.openhandsetalliance.com.

Now that's cool! The alliance has a lot of brilliant companies that are combining their efforts to make the mobile world a better place. They include T-Mobile, Sprint, LG, Motorola, HTC, NVidia, and Texas Instruments.

You should be aware of the OHA because all the libraries that comprise the Android operating system (OS) are based on open-source code. Each member contributes in its own special way. Chip manufacturers ensure that chipsets support the platform; hardware manufacturers build devices; and other companies contribute intellectual property (code, documentation, and so on). The goal is to make Android a commercial success.

As these members contribute, they also start to innovate on the Android platform. Some of this innovation makes it back into the Android source code, and some of it remains the intellectual property of the alliance members as decided by the OHA.

Just because one device has a fancy doohickey on it doesn't mean that another device will. The only thing that you can count on as a developer is the core Android framework. OHA members may have added an extra library to help facilitate something on a device, but there's no guarantee that this library will be available on another device in, say, Turkey or England. An exception occurs if you're developing for a particular device, and only that device, such as an e-book reader. If that hardware has the sole function of reading books, you can program it for just such a purpose. A real-world example of an e-book reader is the Barnes & Noble Nook, which is powered by Android. It has special Forward and Back buttons that other Android devices don't have. Therefore, you'd program for these buttons because this device is a special case (if you're developing for the Nook), but you can't expect these buttons to be used on other devices.

Java knowledge

The Java programming language is one of the glorious tools that make programming Android a breeze compared with programming for other mobile platforms. Whereas other languages insist that you manage memory, deallocate and allocate bytes, and then shift bits around like a game of dominoes, Java has a little buddy called the Java Virtual Machine (JVM) that helps take care of that for you. The JVM allows you to focus on writing code to solve a business problem by using a clean, understandable programming language (or to build that next really cool first-person shooter game you've been dreaming of) instead of focusing on the plumbing just to get the screens to show up.

You're expected to understand the basics of the Java programming language before you write your first Android application. If you're feeling a bit rusty and need a refresher course on Java, you can visit the Java tutorials site at `http://java.sun.com/docs/books/tutorial`.

I cover some Java in this book, but you may want to spend some time with a good book like *Java All-in-One For Dummies,* by Doug Lowe (Wiley), if you don't have any Java experience.

Tuning Up Your Hardware

You can develop Android applications on various operating systems, including Windows, Linux, and Mac OS X. I do the development in this book on a Windows 7 operating system, but you can develop using Mac OS X or Linux instead.

Operating system

Android supports all the following platforms:

- ✔ Windows XP (32-bit), Vista (32- or 64-bit), and 7 (32- or 64-bit)
- ✔ Mac OS X 10.5.8 or later (x86 only)
- ✔ Linux (tested on Linux Ubuntu Hardy Heron)

Note that 64-bit distributions must be capable of running 32-bit applications.

Throughout the book, the examples use Windows 7 64-Bit Edition. Therefore, some of the screen shots may look a little different from what you see on your machine. If you're using a Mac or Linux machine, your paths may be different. Paths in this book look similar to this:

```
c:\path\to\file.txt
```

If you're on a Mac or Linux machine, however, your paths will look similar to this:

```
/path/to/file.txt
```

Computer hardware

Before you start installing the required software, make sure that your computer can run it adequately. I think it's safe to say that just about any desktop or laptop computer manufactured in the past four years will suffice. I wish I could be more exact, but I can't; the hardware requirements for Android simply weren't published when I wrote this book. The slowest computer that I have run Eclipse on is a laptop with a 1.6-GHz Pentium D processor with 1GB of RAM. I've run this same configuration under Windows XP and Windows 7, and both operating systems combined with that hardware can run and debug Eclipse applications with no problems.

To ensure that you can install all the tools and frameworks you'll need, make sure that you have enough disk space to accommodate them. The Android developer site has a list of hardware requirements, outlining how much hard drive space each component requires, at `http://developer.android.com/sdk/requirements.html`.

To save you time, I've compiled my own statistics from personal use of the tools and software development kits (SDKs). I've found that if you have about 3GB of free hard-drive space, you can install all the tools and frameworks necessary to develop Android applications.

Installing and Configuring Your Support Tools

Now it's starting to get exciting. It's time to get this Android going, but before you can do so, you need to install and configure a few tools, including SDKs:

✔ **Java JDK:** Lays the foundation for the Android SDK.

✔ **Android SDK:** Provides access to Android libraries and allows you to develop for Android.

✔ **Eclipse IDE (integrated development environment):** Brings together Java, the Android SDK, and the Android ADT (Android Development Tools), and provides tools for you to write your Android programs.

✔ **Android ADT:** Does a lot of the grunt work for you, such as creating the files and structure required for an Android app.

In the following sections, I show you how to acquire and install all these tools.

A benefit of working with open-source software is that most of the time, you can get the tools to develop the software for free. Android is no exception to that rule. All the tools that you need to develop rich Android applications are free of charge.

Getting the Java Development Kit

For some reason, the folks responsible for naming the Java SDK decided that it would be more appropriate to name it the Java Development Kit, or JDK for short.

Installing the JDK can be a somewhat daunting task, but I guide you through it one step at a time.

Downloading the JDK

Follow these steps to install the JDK:

1. **Point your browser to `http://java.sun.com/javase/downloads/index.jsp`.**

   The Java SE downloads page appears.

2. **Click the JDK link under the Java Platform (JDK) heading (see Figure 2-5).**

   This link is on the `http://java.sun.com/javase/downloads/index.jsp` page at this writing.

   If you're on a Mac, install the JDK through Software Update panel.

A new Java SE downloads page appears, asking you to specify which platform (Windows, Linux, or Mac) you'll be using for your development work.

Figure 2-5:
Select JDK.

Choose JDK.

3. **Using the Platform drop-down list, confirm your platform, and then click the Download button.**

   An optional Log in for Download screen appears.

4. **Click the Skip This Step link at the bottom of the page.**

5. **Click `JDK-6u20-windows-i586.exe` to download the file.**

   Windows opens a message box with a security warning, as shown in Figure 2-6.

6. **In the Save As dialog box, select the location where you want to save the file, and click Save.**

Figure 2-6:
The security
warning.

The Web page shown in Figure 2-5 may look different in the future. To ensure that you're visiting the correct page, visit the Android SDK System Requirements page in the online Android documentation for a direct link to the Java SDK download page. View the requirements page at `http://developer.android.com/sdk/requirements.html`.

 You must remember what version of the Java SDK you need to install. At this writing, Android 2.2 supports Java SDK versions 5 and 6. If you install the wrong version of Java, you'll get unexpected results during development.

Installing the JDK

When the download is complete, double-click the file to install the JDK. You are prompted by a dialog box that asks whether you want to allow the program to make changes to your computer. Click the Yes button. If you click the No button, the installation is stopped. When you're prompted to do so, read and accept the license agreement.

That's all there is to it! You have the JDK installed and are ready to move to the next phase. In this section, I show you how to install the Android SDK step by step.

Acquiring the Android SDK

The Android SDK is composed of a debugger, Android libraries, a device emulator, documentation, sample code, and tutorials. You can't develop Android apps without it.

Downloading the Android SDK

To download the Android SDK, follow these steps:

1. **Point your browser to `http://developer.android.com/sdk/index.html`.**

2. **Choose the latest version of the SDK starter package for your platform.**

3. **Extract the SDK.**

   I recommend extracting to `c:\android` because I reference this location later in this chapter.

   You've just downloaded the Android SDK.

4. Navigate to the directory where you extracted the SDK, and double-click SDK Setup, as shown in Figure 2-7.

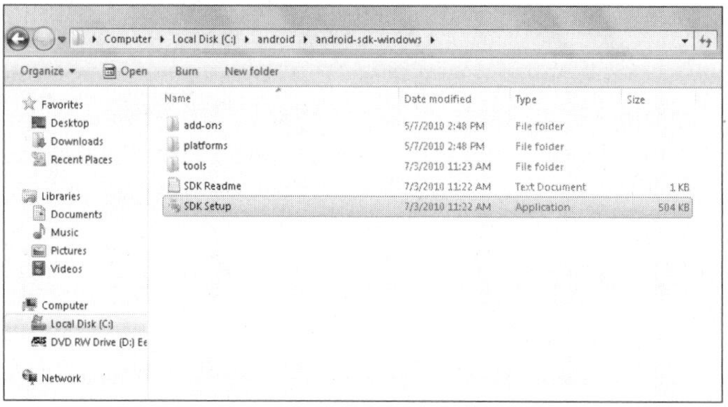

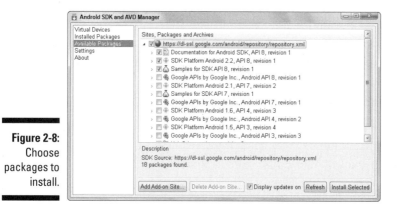

Figure 2-7:
Double-click
SDK Setup.

5. If you're prompted to accept the authenticity of the file, click Yes.

The Android SDK and AVD Manager dialog box opens.

6. Select the SDK Platform Android 2.2 check box.

For the purposes of this book, select version 2.2, as shown in Figure 2-8. At this writing, 2.2 is the latest and greatest version of Android. You should also check the boxes for the documentation and samples that correspond with Android version 2.2 (API 8).

Figure 2-8:
Choose
packages to
install.

Every time a new version of the Android OS is released, Google also releases an SDK that contains access to the added functionality in that version. If you want to include Bluetooth functionality in your app, for example, make sure that you have Android SDK version 2.0 or later, because this functionality isn't available in earlier versions.

7. Click Install Selected.

The Choose Packages to Install dialog box opens.

8. Select the Accept radio button to accept the license and then click Install (see Figure 2-9).

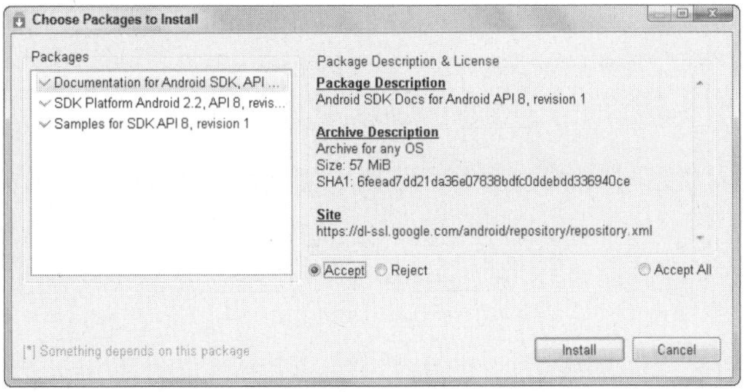

Figure 2-9:
The Choose
Packages
to Install
dialog box.

9. In the next dialog box, select Accept and click Install.

The Installing Archives dialog box opens, displaying a progress bar (see Figure 2-10).

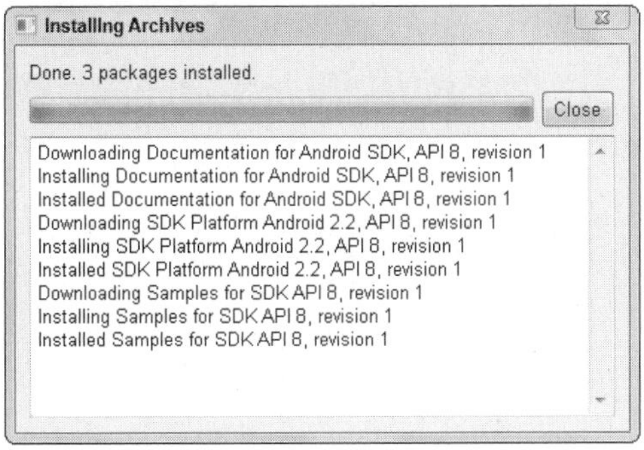

Figure 2-10:
The
Installing
Archives
dialog box.

10. When the archives installation is complete, click the Close button.

While the Android SDK is attempting to connect to the servers to obtain the files, you may occasionally receive a `Failure to fetch URL` error. If this happens to you, navigate to Settings, select Force https://... Sources to be Fetched Using http://, and then attempt to download the available packages again.

Adding the Android NDK

The Android Native Development Kit (NDK) is a set of tools that allows you to embed components that use native code — code that you've written in a native language such as C or C++.

If you decide to take on the NDK, you still have to download the SDK. The NDK isn't a replacement for the SDK; it's an added functionality set that complements the SDK.

Following and setting your tools path

This step is optional, but I highly recommend setting the tools path because it saves you from having to remember and type the full path when you're accessing the Android Debug Bridge (adb) via the command line.

The adb lets you manage the state of an emulator or Android device so that you can debug your application or interact with the device at a high level. The adb tool is very in-depth, so I don't go into a lot of detail about it here; for detailed information, see the Android documentation.

To add the Android tools to your system-path variable, follow these steps:

1. **Open Control Panel, and double-click the System icon to open System Preferences.**

2. **Click the Advanced System Settings link (see Figure 2-11) to open the System Properties window.**

Figure 2-11: The Advanced System Settings link.

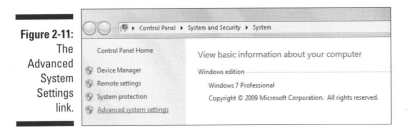

3. **Click the Environment Variables button (see Figure 2-12) to bring up the Environment Variables dialog box.**

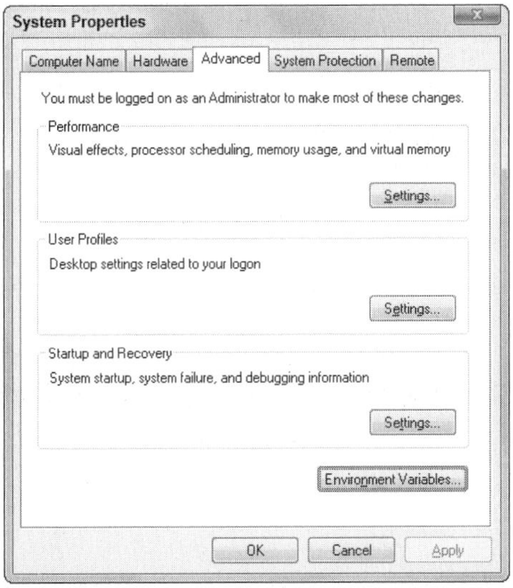

Figure 2-12:
Click the
Environment
Variables
button.

4. **Click the New button (see Figure 2-13).**

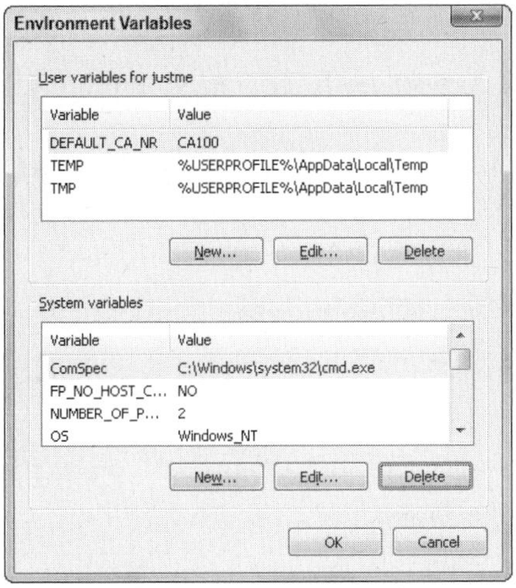

Figure 2-13:
The
Environment
Variables
window.

5. **In the Variable Name field, type** ANDROID.

6. **Type the full path to the tools directory (c:\android\android-sdk-windows\tools) in the Variable Value field (see Figure 2-14).**

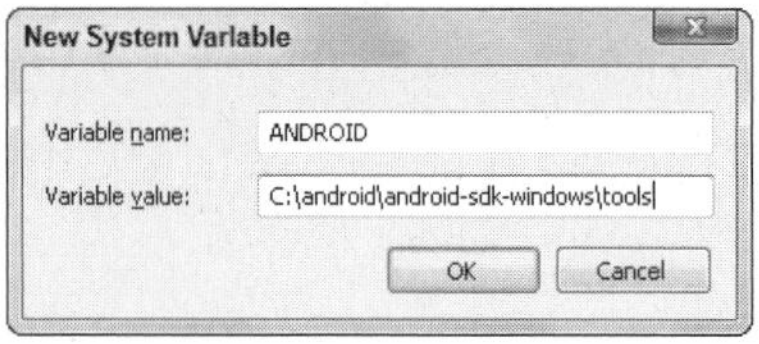

Figure 2-14:
Setting
up a new
environment
variable.

New System Variable

Variable name: ANDROID

Variable value: C:\android\android-sdk-windows\tools

OK　Cancel

7. **Click OK.**

8. **In the System Variables window of the resulting dialog box (see Figure 2-15), select the PATH variable.**

Environment Variables

User variables for justme

Variable	Value
DEFAULT_CA_NR	CA100
TEMP	%USERPROFILE%\AppData\Local\Temp
TMP	%USERPROFILE%\AppData\Local\Temp

New...　Edit...　Delete

System variables

Variable	Value
NUMBER_OF_P...	4
OS	Windows_NT
Path	C:\Windows\system32;C:\Windows;C:\...
PATHEXT	.COM;.EXE;.BAT;.CMD;.VBS;.VBE;.JS;....

New...　Edit...　Delete

OK　Cancel

Figure 2-15:
Editing the
PATH
variable.

9. **Click Edit and then type the following text at the end of the Variable Value field:**

```
;%ANDROID%
```

That's it; you're done. Now any time you access the Android tools directory, just use your newly created system variable.

In most operating systems, your system PATH variable won't be updated until you log out of and log back on to your operating system. If you find that your PATH variable values aren't present, try logging out of and logging back on to your computer.

Getting the Total Eclipse

Now that you have the SDK, you need an integrated development environment (IDE) to use it. It's time to download Eclipse!

Choosing the right Eclipse version

Downloading the correct version of Eclipse is very important. At this writing, Android doesn't support Eclipse Helios (version 3.6). Check the Android System Requirements page at http://developer.android.com/sdk/requirements.html. If you're still unsure, download Eclipse Galileo (version 3.5). When you download the file, you'll probably need to find the Older Versions link on the download page and select the latest Galileo version.

To download the correct version, navigate to the Eclipse downloads page (www.eclipse.org/downloads); select the Older Versions link; and then select Eclipse IDE for Java Developers. Eclipse IDE for JAVA EE Developers works as well.

Installing Eclipse

Eclipse is a self-contained executable file; after you unzip it, the program is installed. Even though you could stop here, it's best to pin a shortcut to your Start menu so that Eclipse is easy to find when you need it.

To install Eclipse, you need to extract the contents of the Eclipse .zip file to the location of your choice. For this example, I'll be using C:\Program Files\Eclipse.

To install Eclipse, follow these steps:

1. **Double-click the shortcut that you just created to run Eclipse.**

   If you're running a recent version of Windows, the first time you run Eclipse, a Security Warning dialog box may appear, as shown in Figure 2-16. This dialog box tells you that the publisher has not been verified and asks whether you still want to run the software. Clear the Always Ask Before Opening This File check box, and click the Run button.

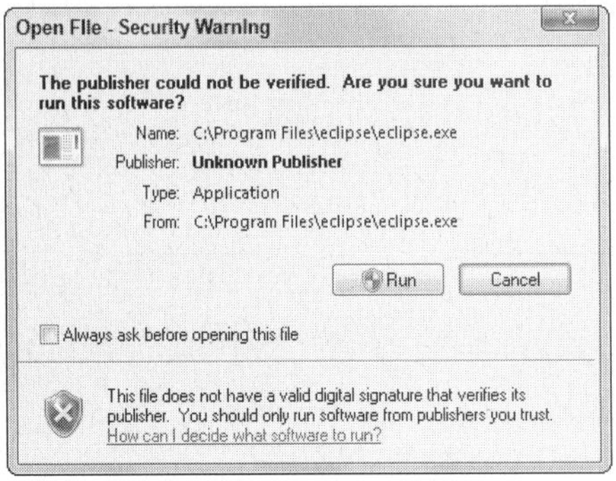

Figure 2-16:
The
Windows
security
warning.

2. **Set your workspace.**

   When Eclipse starts, the first thing you see is the Workspace Launcher dialog box, as shown in Figure 2-17. Here, you can modify your workspace if you want, but for this book, I'm sticking with the default:

   ```
   c:\users\<username>\workspace
   ```

   Leave the Use This as the Default and Do Not Ask Again check box deselected, and click the OK button.

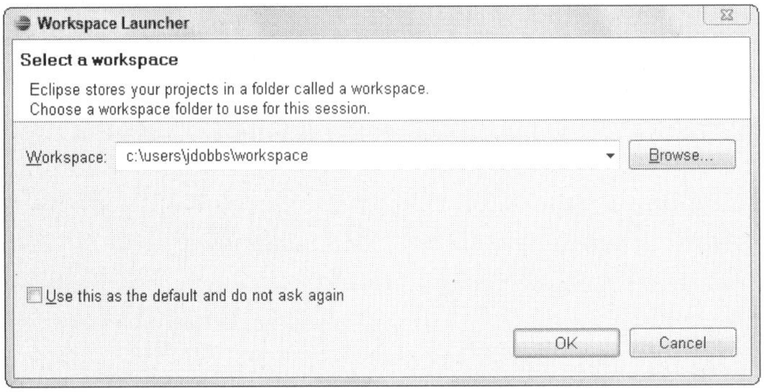

Figure 2-17:
Set your
workspace.

   If you plan to develop multiple applications, I recommend using a separate workspace for each project. If you store multiple projects in one workspace, it gets difficult to keep things organized, and it's easy to change a similarly named file in a different project. Keeping projects in their own workspaces makes it easier to find the project when you have to go back to it to fix bugs.

   When Eclipse finishes loading, you see the Eclipse welcome screen, shown in Figure 2-18.

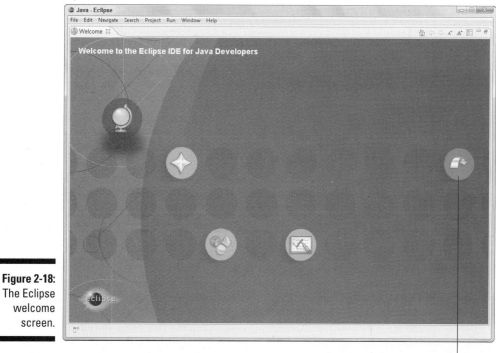

Figure 2-18:
The Eclipse
welcome
screen.

Click the arrow to go to the workbench.

3. Click the curved-arrow icon on the right side of the screen to go to the workbench.

Eclipse is installed and easily accessible. I show you how to add the Android Development Tools in the next section.

Configuring Eclipse

Android Development Tools (ADT) adds functionality to Eclipse to do a lot of the work for you. The ADT allows you to create new Android projects easily; it creates all the necessary base files so that you can start coding your application quickly. It also allows you to debug your application using the Android SDK tools. Finally, it allows you to export a signed application file, known as an Android Package (APK), right from Eclipse, eliminating the need for some command-line tools. In the beginning, I had to use various command-line utilities to build an APK. Although that wasn't hard, it was tedious and sometimes frustrating. The ADT eliminates this frustrating process by guiding you through it "wizard style" from within Eclipse. I show you how to export a signed APK in Chapter 8.

Setting up Eclipse with the ADT

To set up Eclipse with the ADT, follow these steps:

1. **Start Eclipse, if it's not already running.**

2. **Choose Help⇨Install New Software.**

   The Install window pops up (see Figure 2-19). This window allows you to install new plug-ins in Eclipse.

3. **Click the Add button to add a new site that will display the Add Repository window (see Figure 2-20).**

   Sites are the Web addresses where the software is hosted on the Internet. Adding a site to Eclipse makes it easier for you to update the software when a new version is released.

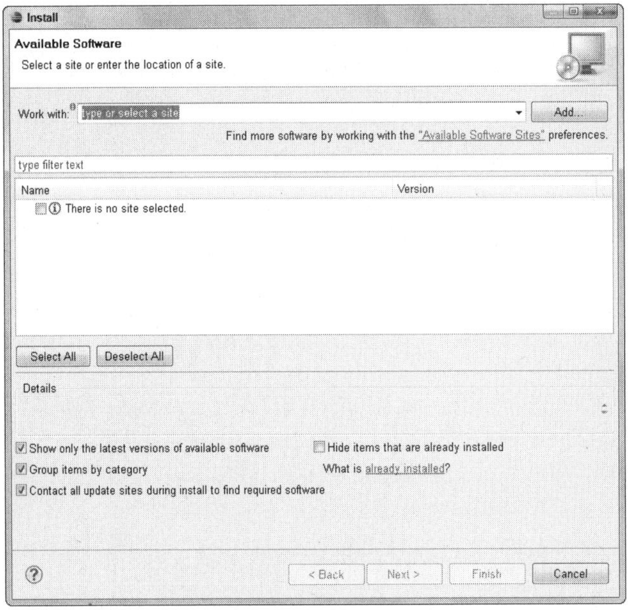

Figure 2-19:
Click the Add button to add a new site.

4. **Type a name in the Name field.**

   I recommend using Android ADT, but it can be anything you choose.

5. **Type** https://dl-ssl.google.com/android/eclipse/ **in the Location field.**

Figure 2-20:
Enter the
name and
location of
the site.

6. **Click the OK button.**

   Android ADT is selected in the Work With drop-down menu, and the available options are displayed in the Name and Version window of the Install Details dialog box.

7. **In the Install dialog box, select the check box next to Developer Tools, and click the Next button (see Figure 2-21).**

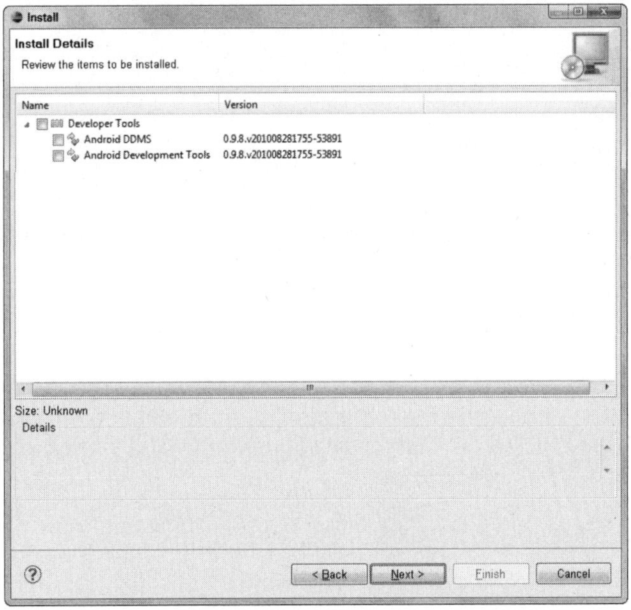

Figure 2-21:
Select
Developer
Tools.

The Install Details dialog box should list both the Android Dalvik Debug Monitor Server (DDMS; see "Get physical with a real Android device," later in this chapter) and the ADT (see Figure 2-22).

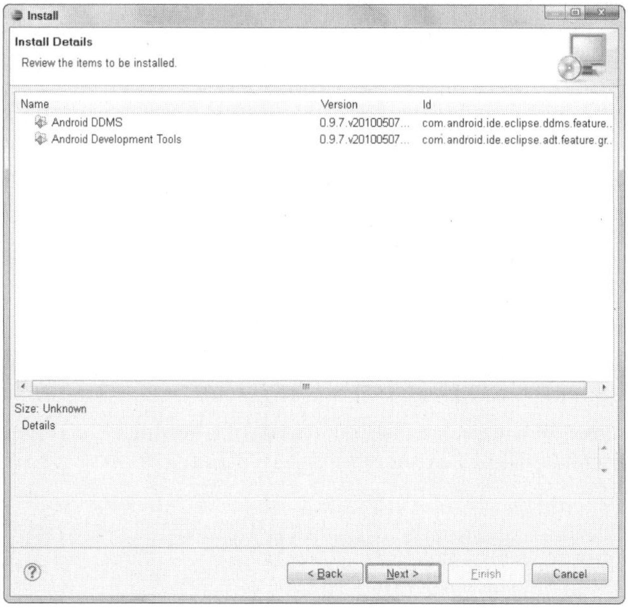

Figure 2-22:
DDMS and
ADT listed
in the Install
Details dia-
log box.

8. **Click the Next button to review the software licenses.**

9. **Click the Finish button.**

10. **When you're prompted to do so, click the Restart Now button to restart Eclipse.**

    The ADT plug-in is installed.

Setting the location of the SDK

In this section, I guide you through the configuration process. I know that this seems like a lot to do, but you're almost done, and you have to do this work only once. Follow these steps:

1. **Choose Window⇨Preferences.**

   The Preferences dialog box opens (see Figure 2-23).

2. **Select Android in the left pane.**

3. **Set the SDK Location to** `C:\android\android-sdk-windows`.

4. **Click OK.**

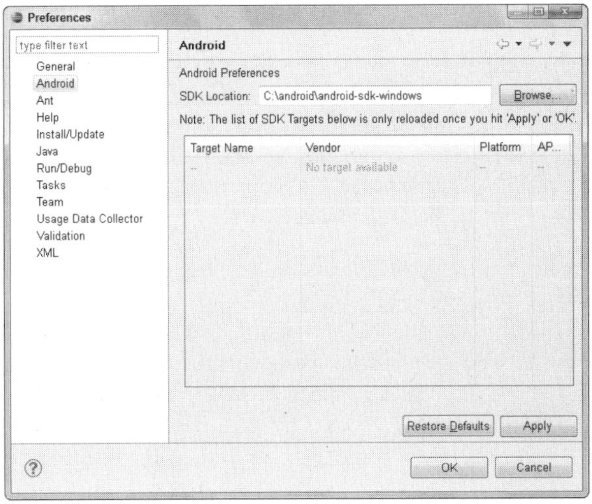

Figure 2-23:
Specify
the loca-
tion of the
SDK in the
Preferences
dialog box.

Eclipse is configured, and you're ready to start developing Android apps.

If you're having difficulty downloading the tools from `https://dl-ssl.google.com/android/eclipse`, try removing the *s* from `https://`, as follows: `http://dl-ssl.google.com/android/eclipse`.

Getting Acquainted with the Android Development Tools

Now that the tools of the trade are installed, I introduce you to the SDK and some of the tools that are included with it.

Navigating the Android SDK

Whoa! You find a lot of folders in the SDK! Don't worry; the folder structure of the Android SDK is pretty easy to understand when you get the hang of it. You need to understand the structure of the SDK for you to fully master it. Table 2-1 outlines what each folder is and what it contains.

Table 2-1	Folders in the Android SDK
SDK Folder	*Description*
`usb_driver`	Contains the drivers for Android devices. If you connect your Android device to the computer, you need to install this driver so that you can view, debug, and push applications to your phone via the ADT.
	The `usb_driver` folder won't be visible until you install the USB driver.
`tools`	Contains various tools that are available for use during development — debugging tools, view-management tools, and build tools, to name a few.
`temp`	Provides a temporary swap for the SDK. At times, the SDK may need a temporary space to perform some work. This folder is where that work takes place.
`samples`	Contains a bunch of sample projects for you to play with. Full source code is included.
`platforms`	Contains the platforms that you target when you build Android applications, such as folders named `android-8` (which is Android 2.2), `android-4` (which is Android 1.6), and so on.
`docs`	Contains a local copy of the Android SDK documentation.
`add-ons`	Contains additional APIs that provide extra functionality. This folder is where the Google APIs reside; these APIs include mapping functionality. This folder remains empty until you install any of the Google Maps APIs.

Targeting Android platforms

Android platform is just a fancy way of saying *Android version*. At this writing, seven versions of Android are available, ranging from version 1.1 through version 2.2. You can target any platform that you choose.

Keep in mind that several versions of Android are still widely used on phones. If you want to reach the largest number of users, I suggest targeting an earlier version. If your app requires functionality that older platforms can't support, however, by all means target the new platform. It wouldn't make any sense to write a Bluetooth toggle widget targeting any platform earlier than 2.0 because earlier platforms can't use Bluetooth.

Figure 2-24 shows the percentage of each platform in use as of July 1, 2010. To view the current platform statistics, visit `http://developer.android.com/resources/dashboard/platform-versions.html`.

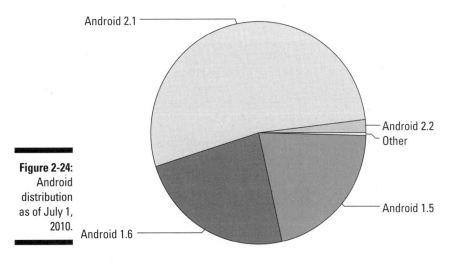

Android 2.1

Android 2.2

Other

Android 1.5

Android 1.6

Figure 2-24:
Android
distribution
as of July 1,
2010.

Using SDK tools for everyday development

You just installed the SDK tools. Now I introduce you to these tools so that
they can work for you. The SDK tools are what you use to develop your
Android apps. They allow you to develop applications easily as well as give
you the ability to debug them. New features packed into every release enable
you to develop for the latest version of Android.

Say hello to my little emulator

The emulator has to be my favorite tool of all. Not only does Google provide
the tools you need to develop apps, but it also gives you this awesome little
emulator that allows you to test your app! The emulator does have some
limitations, however — it cannot emulate certain hardware components such
as the accelerometer, but not to worry. Plenty of apps can be developed and
tested using only an emulator.

When you're developing an app that uses Bluetooth, for example, you should
use an actual device that has Bluetooth. If you develop on a speedy computer, testing on an emulator is fast, but on slower machines, the emulator
can take a long time to do a seemingly simple task. When I develop on an
older machine, I usually use an actual device, but when I use my newer, faster
machine, I typically use the emulator because I don't notice much lag, if any.

The emulator comes in handy for testing your app at different screen sizes
and resolutions. It's not always practical or possible to have several devices
connected to your computer at the same time, but you can run multiple emulators with varying screen sizes and resolutions.

Get physical with a real Android device

The emulator is awesome, but sometimes you need an actual device to test on. The DDMS allows you to debug your app on an actual device, which comes in handy for developing apps that use hardware features that aren't or can't be emulated. Suppose that you're developing an app that tracks the user's location. You can send coordinates to the device manually, but at some point in your development, you probably want to test the app and find out whether it in fact displays the correct location. Using an actual device is the only way to do this.

If you develop on a Windows machine and want to test your app on a real device, you need to install a driver. If you're on a Mac or Linux machine, you can skip this section, because you don't need to install the USB driver.

To download the Windows USB driver for Android devices, follow these steps:

1. **In Eclipse, choose Window⇨Android SDK and AVD Manager.**

   The Android SDK and AVD Manager dialog box opens (see Figure 2-25).

2. **In the left pane, select Available Packages.**

3. **Expand the Android repository, and select the USB Driver package.**

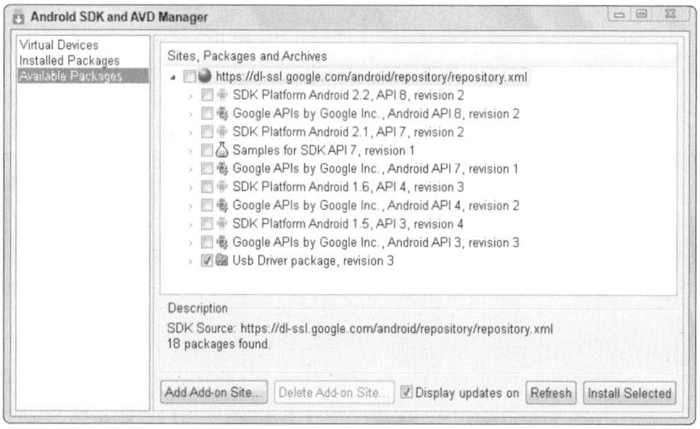

Figure 2-25:
The
available
packages.

4. **Click the Install Selected button.**

   The Choose Packages to Install dialog box opens.

5. **Select the Accept radio button to accept the license and then click the Install button (see Figure 2-26).**

   The Installing Archives dialog box opens, displaying a progress bar.

Figure 2-26:
Click the
Install
button.

6. **When the package finishes downloading and installing, click the Close button.**

7. **Exit the Android SDK and AVD Manager dialog box.**

Debug your work

The DDMS equips you with the tools you need to find those pesky bugs, allowing you to go behind the scenes as your app is running to see the state of hardware such as wireless radios. But wait. There's more! It also simulates actions that you normally need an actual device to do, such as sending Global Positioning System (GPS) coordinates manually, simulating a phone call, or simulating a text message. I recommend getting all the DDMS details at `http://developer.android.com/guide/developing/tools/ ddms.html`.

Try out the API and SDK samples

The API and SDK samples are provided to demonstrate how to use the functionality provided by the API and SDK. If you ever get stuck and can't figure out how to make something work, you should visit `http://developer. android.com/resources/samples/index.html`. Here, you can find samples of almost anything from using Bluetooth to making a two-way text application or a 2D game.

You also have a few samples in your Android SDK. Simply open the Android SDK and navigate to the `samples` directory, which contains various samples that range from interacting with services to manipulating local databases. You should spend some time playing with the samples. I've found that the best way to learn Android is to look at existing working code bases and then play with them in Eclipse.

Give the API demos a spin

The API demos inside the `samples` folder in the SDK are a collection of apps that demonstrate how to use the included APIs. Here, you can find sample apps with a ton of examples, such as these:

- ✔ Notifications
- ✔ Alarms
- ✔ Intents
- ✔ Menus
- ✔ Search
- ✔ Preferences
- ✔ Background services

If you get stuck or just want to prep yourself for writing your next spectacular Android application, check out the complete details at `http://developer.android.com/resources/samples/ApiDemos/index.html`.

Part II
Building and Publishing Your First Android Application

"He seemed nice, but I could never connect with someone who had a ring tone like his."

In this part . . .

In Part II, I walk you through developing a useful Android application. I start with the basics of the Android tools and then delve into developing the screens and home-screen widgets that users will interact with. When the application is complete, I demonstrate how to sign your application digitally so that you can deploy it to the Android Market. I finish the part with an in-depth view of publishing your application to the Android Market.

Chapter 3

Your First Android Project

*Y*ou're excited to get started building the next best Android application known to man, right? Good! But before you create that next blockbuster application, I'm going to walk you through how to create your first Android application to help solidify a few key aspects in the Android project creation process. You will be creating a very simple "Hello Android" application that requires no coding whatsoever. What? No coding? How's that possible? Follow along; I'll show you.

Starting a New Project in Eclipse

First things first: You need to start Eclipse. After it's started, you should see something that looks similar to Figure 3-1. Now you're ready to start cooking with Android.

Remember setting up your development environment in the previous chapter? I'm sure you do! In that chapter, you set up all the tools and frameworks necessary to develop Android applications, and in the process of doing so, the Eclipse Android Development Tools (ADT) plug-in was installed. The ADT plug-in gives you the power to generate new Android applications directly from within the Eclipse File menu. That's exactly what you're about to do; I think you're ready to create your first Android Application project. Follow these steps:

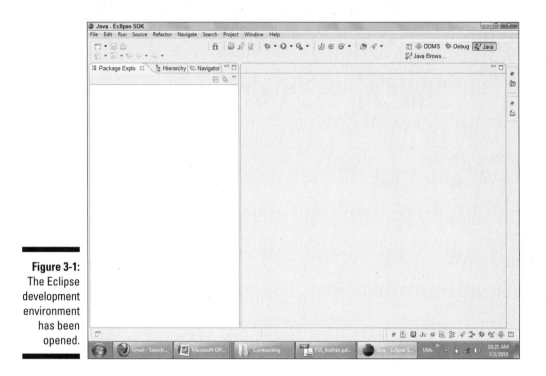

Figure 3-1:
The Eclipse development environment has been opened.

1. **In Eclipse, choose File⇨New⇨Project.**

   The New Project/Select a Wizard dialog box opens, as shown in Figure 3-2.

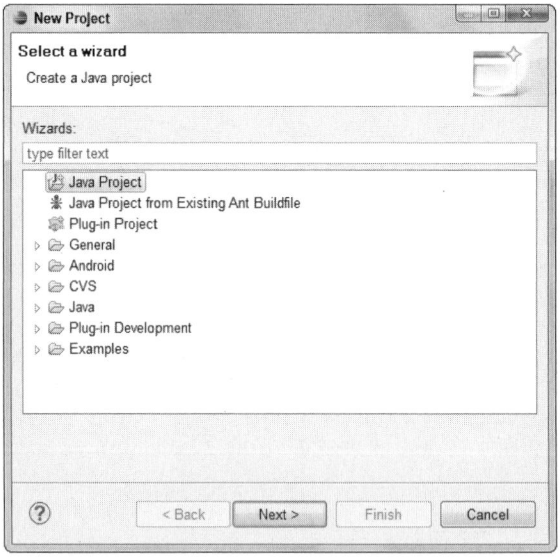

Figure 3-2:
The New Project/ Select a Wizard dialog box.

2. **From the New Project/Select a Wizard dialog box, expand the Android item by clicking the Android folder.**

3. **After the Android folder is expanded, click Android Project and then click the Next button.**

   The New Android Project dialog box appears, as shown in Figure 3-3.

4. **In the Project Name field, type** Hello Android.

   The Project Name field is very important, the descriptive name that you provide identifies your project in the Eclipse workspace. After your project is created, a folder in the workspace is named with the project name you define here.

5. **In the Contents panel, leave the default radio button Create New Project in Workspace and the check box Use Default Location selected.**

   These defaults are selected automatically when a new project is created. The Contents panel identifies where the contents of your Eclipse projects are going to be stored in the file system. The contents are the source files that make up your Android project.

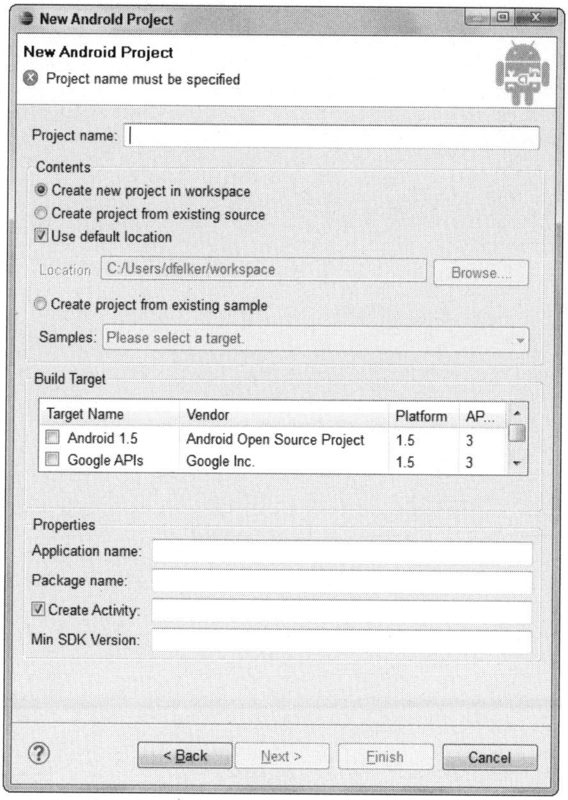

Figure 3-3:
The New
Android
Project
dialog box.

When you set up Eclipse in Chapter 2, the Eclipse system asked you to set your default workspace. The workspace usually defaults to your home directory. A *home directory* is where the system places files pertinent to you. Figure 3-4 shows my home directory.

If you would rather store your files in a location other than the default workspace location, deselect the Use Default Location check box. This enables the Location text box. Click the Browse button, and select a location where you'd like your files to be stored.

6. In the Build Target section, select Android 2.2.

The Build Target section identifies which application programming interface (API) you want to develop under for this project. By selecting Android 2.2, you have elected to use the Android 2.2 framework. Doing so allows you to develop with the Android 2.2 APIs, which include new features such as the Backup Manager and new speech-recognition APIs. If you selected Android 1.6 as the target, you would not be able to use any features supported by version 2.2 (or 2.1). Only the features in the targeted framework are supported. If you installed other software development kits (SDKs) in Chapter 2, you might have the option of selecting them at this point. If you selected version 1.6, you'd have access only to version 1.6 APIs.

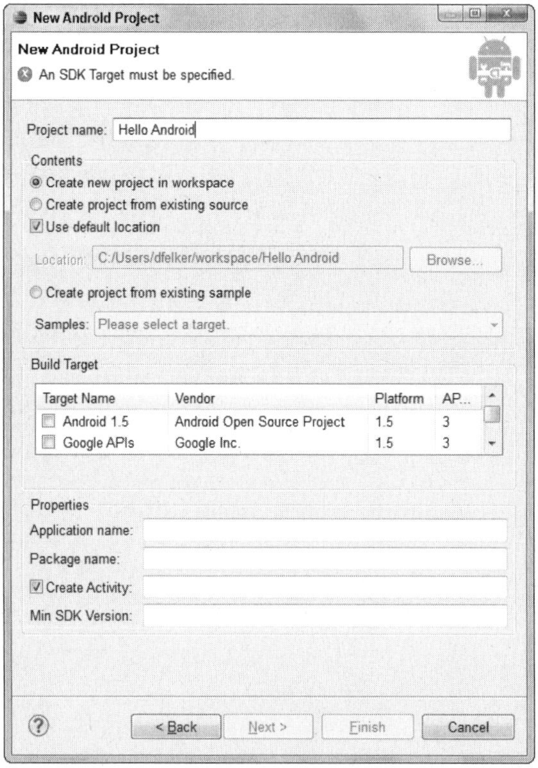

Figure 3-4:
My default workspace location for the Hello Android project is C : / Users/ dfelker/ work space.

New Android Project
New Android Project
An SDK Target must be specified.

Project name: Hello Android

Contents
- ⦿ Create new project in workspace
- ○ Create project from existing source
- ☑ Use default location

Location: C:/Users/dfelker/workspace/Hello Android   Browse...

- ○ Create project from existing sample

Samples: Please select a target.

Build Target

Target Name	Vendor	Platform	AP...
☐ Android 1.5	Android Open Source Project	1.5	3
☐ Google APIs	Google Inc.	1.5	3

Properties

Application name:

Package name:

☑ Create Activity:

Min SDK Version:

⑦   < Back   Next >   Finish   Cancel

For more information, see the section "Understanding the Build Target and Min SDK Version settings," later in this chapter.

7. In the Properties section, type Hello Android **in the Application Name box.**

The application name is the name of the application as it pertains to Android. When the application is installed on the emulator or physical device, this name will appear in the application launcher.

8. In the Package Name box, type com.dummies.android.helloandroid.

This is the name of the Java package (see the nearby sidebar "Java package nomenclature").

9. In the Create Activity box, type MainActivity.

The Create Activity section defines what the initial activity will be called. This is the entry point to your application. When Android runs your application, this is the first file that gets accessed. A common naming pattern for the first activity in your application is `MainActivity.java` (how creative, right?).

10. In the Min SDK Version box, type 8.

Your screen should now look similar to Figure 3-5.

Java package nomenclature

A *package* in Java is a way to organize Java classes into namespaces similar to modules. Each package must have a unique name for the classes it contains. Classes in the same package can access one another's package-access members.

Java packages have a naming convention defined as the hierarchical naming pattern. Each level of the hierarchy is separated by periods. A package name starts with the highest-level domain name of the organization; then the subdomains are listed in reverse order. At the end of the package name, the company can choose what it would like to call the package. The package name `com.dummies.android.helloandroid` is the name you will use for this example.

Notice that the highest-level domain is at the front of the package name (`com`). Subsequent subdomains are separated by periods. The package name traverses down through the subdomains to get to the final package name of `helloandroid`.

A great example of another use for a package would be having a Java package for all your Web-related communications. Any time you needed to find one of your Web-related Java classes, you could open that Java package and work on your Web-related Java classes. Packages allow you to keep your code organized.

Understanding Android versioning

Version codes are not the same as version names. Huh? Android has version names and version codes. Each version name has one and only one version code associated with it. The following table outlines the version names and their respective version code.

Version Name (Platform Level)	Version Code (API Level)
1.5	3
1.6	4
2.0	5
2.0.1	6
2.1	7
2.2	8

You can also find this information in the Build Target section of the New Android Project dialog box.

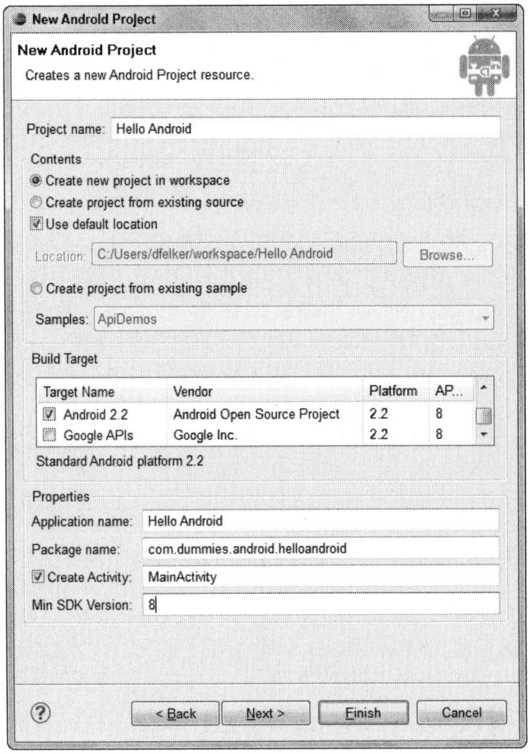

Figure 3-5:
A completed New Android Project wizard.

The Min SDK Version defines the minimum version code of Android that the user must have before he can run your application. Note that this field is not required to create your app.

For more information, see the section "Understanding the Build Target and Min SDK Version settings," later in this chapter.

11. **Click the Finish button.**

You're done! You should see Eclipse with a single project in the Package Explorer, as shown in Figure 3-6.

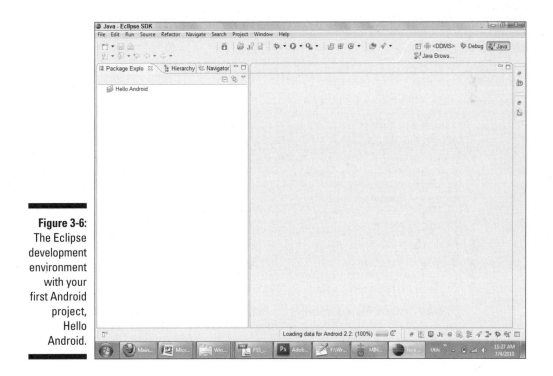

Figure 3-6:
The Eclipse development environment with your first Android project, Hello Android.

Deconstructing Your Project

The Android project generated by Eclipse is a fresh clean project with no compiled binary sources. Sometimes, it takes a second for Eclipse to catch up to how fast you are, so you may notice little oddities about the system. You also need to understand what happens under the hood of Eclipse at a high level; I cover this information in the next sections.

Responding to error messages

If you were quick enough to look (or if your computer runs on the slower edge of the spectrum), you may have noticed a little red icon that hovered over the Hello Android folder icon in the Package Explorer in your Eclipse window right after you clicked the Finish button. If you didn't see it, you can see an example in Figure 3-7. That icon is Eclipse's way of letting you know that something is wrong with the project in the workspace.

Figure 3-7:
A project
with errors
in Eclipse.

Package Explo ⊠	🏛 Hierarchy	⌸ Navigator

📁 Hello Android

A project with errors in Eclipse

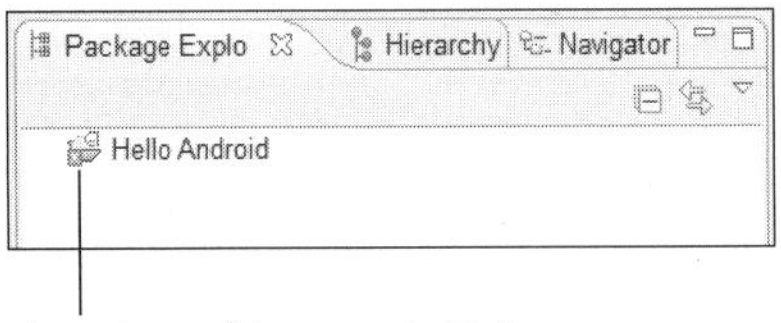

By default, Eclipse is set up to let you know when an error is found within a project with this visual queue. How can you have an error with this project? You just created the project through the New Android Project wizard; what gives? Behind the scenes, Eclipse and the Android Development Tools are doing a few things for you:

- ✔ **Providing workspace feedback:** This feedback lets you know when a problem exists with any of the projects in the workspace. You receive notification in Eclipse via icon overlays, such as the one shown in Figure 3-7. Another icon overlay you may see often is a small yellow warning icon, which alerts you to some warnings in the contents of the project.

- ✔ **Automatically compiling:** By default, Eclipse autocompiles the applications in your workspace when any files within them are saved after a change.

If you don't want automatic recompilation turned on, you can turn it off by choosing Project➪Build Automatically. This disables the automatic building of the project. If this option is deselected, you need to build your project manually by pressing Ctrl+B each time you change your source code.

So why are you getting an error with the first build? When the project was added to your workspace, Eclipse took over, and in conjunction with the ADT, it determined that the project in the workspace had an error. The issue that raised the error in Eclipse was that the gen folder and all its contents were not present. (I cover the gen folder in "Understanding Project Structure," later in this chapter.)

The gen folder is automatically generated by Eclipse and the ADT when the compilation takes place. As soon as the New Android Project wizard was completed, a new project was created and saved in Eclipse's workspace. Eclipse recognized this fact and said, "Hey! I see some new files in my workspace. I need to report any errors I find as well as compile the project." Eclipse reported the errors by placing an error icon over the folder. Immediately thereafter, the compilation step took place. During the compilation step, the gen folder was created by Eclipse, and the project was successfully built. Then Eclipse recognized that the project did not have any more errors. At that time, it removed the error icon from the folder, leaving you with a clean workspace and a clean folder icon, as shown in Figure 3-8.

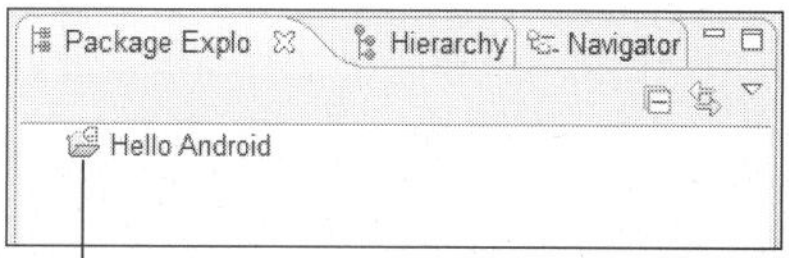

Figure 3-8:
A project in
the Package
Explorer
that has
no errors.
Notice the
folder icon;
it has no
error icon
overlay
on it.

A project without any errors

Understanding the Build Target and Min SDK Version settings

So how does the Build Target setting differ from the Min SDK Version setting?

The *build target* is the operating system you're going to write code with. If you choose 2.2, you can write code with all the APIs in version 2.2. If you choose 1.6, you can write code only with the APIs that are in version 1.6. You can't use the Bluetooth APIs in version 1.6, for example, because they weren't introduced until version 2.0. If you're targeting 2.2, you can write with the Bluetooth APIs.

Know which version you want to target before you start writing your Android application. Identify which Android features you need to use to ensure that your app will function as you expect. If you're positive that you're going to need Bluetooth support, you need to target at least version 2.0. If you're not sure which versions support the features you're looking for, you can find that information on the platform-specific pages in the SDK section of http://d.android.com. The Android 2.2 platform page is at http://d.android.com/sdk/android-2.2.html.

Version codes and compatibility

The Min SDK Version is also used by the Android Market (which I cover in detail in Chapter 8) to help identify which applications to show you based on which version of Android you're running. If your device is running version code 3 (Android 1.6), you would want to see the apps pertinent to your version, not version code 8 (Android 2.2) apps. The Android Market manages which apps to show to each user through the Min SDK Version setting.

If you're having trouble deciding which version to target, the current version distribution chart can help you decide. That chart is located here: `http://developer.android.com/resources/dashboard/platform-versions.html`.

A good rule of thumb is to analyze the distribution chart on `at://developer.android.com` to determine which version will give your app the best market share. The more devices you can target, the wider the audience you will have, and the more installs you have, the better your app is doing.

Android operating-system (OS) versions are backward-compatible. If you target Android version 1.6, for example, your application can run on Android 2.2, 2.1, 2.0, and of course 1.6. The benefit of targeting the 1.6 framework is that your application is exposed to a much larger market share. Your app can be installed on 1.6, 2.0, 2.1, and 2.2 devices (and future versions, assuming that no breaking framework changes are introduced in future Android OS releases). Selecting an older version doesn't come without consequences, however. By targeting an older framework, you're limiting the functionality that you have access to. By targeting 1.6, for example, you won't have access to the Bluetooth APIs.

The Min SDK Version setting is the minimum version of Android that the user must be running for the application to run properly on his or her device. This field isn't required to build an app, but I highly recommend that you fill it in. If you don't indicate the Min SDK Version, a default value of 1 is used, indicating that your application is compatible with all versions of Android.

If your application is *not* compatible with all versions of Android (such as if it uses APIs that were introduced in version code 5 — Android 2.0), and you haven't declared the Min SDK Version, when your app is installed on a system with an SDK version code of less than 5, your application will crash at run time when it attempts to access the unavailable APIs. As best practice, always set the Min SDK Version in your application to prevent these types of crashes.

Setting Up an Emulator

Aw, shucks! I bet you thought you were about to fire up this bad boy. Well, you're almost there. You have one final thing to cover, and then you get to see all of your setup work come to life in your Hello Android application. To see this application in a running state, you need to know how to set up an emulator through the various different launch configurations.

First, you need to create an Android Virtual Device (AVD), also known as an emulator. An AVD is a virtual Android device that looks, acts, walks, and talks (well, maybe not walks and talks) just like a real Android device. AVDs can be configured to run any particular version of Android as long as the SDK for that version is downloaded and installed.

It's time to get reacquainted with your old buddy the Android SDK and AVD Manager. Follow these steps to create your first AVD:

1. **To open the Android SDK and AVD Manager, click the icon on the Eclipse toolbar shown in Figure 3-9.**

   When the Android SDK and AVD Manager is open, you should see a dialog box similar to Figure 3-10.

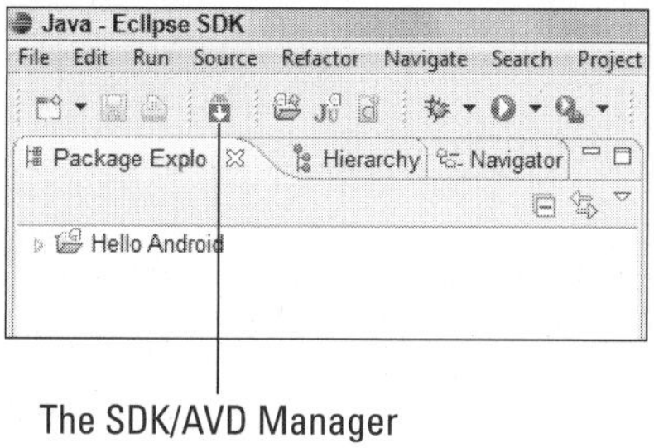

Figure 3-9:
The Android
SDK and
AVD
Manager
icon on
the Eclipse
toolbar.

The SDK/AVD Manager

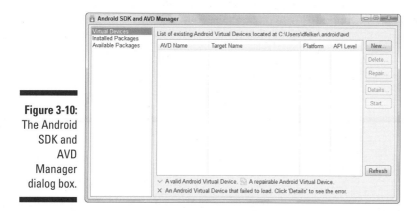

Figure 3-10:
The Android
SDK and
AVD
Manager
dialog box.

2. **Click the New button.**

   The Create New Android Virtual Device (AVD) dialog box opens, as shown in Figure 3-11.

3. **For this AVD, in the Name field, type** 2_2_Default_HVGA**.**

   For more information on naming your AVDs, see the nearby sidebar "AVD nomenclature."

4. **In the Target box, select Android 2.2 — API Level 8.**

5. **In the SD Card section, leave the fields blank.**

   You have no use for an SD Card in your application. You would use the SD Card option if you needed to save data to the SD Card. If you want to have an emulator in the future, insert the size of the SD Card in megabytes (MB) that you would like to have created for you. At that time, an emulated SD Card will be created and dropped in your local file system.

6. **Leave the Skin option set to Default (HVGA).**

7. **Don't select any new features in the Hardware section.**

   The Hardware section outlines the hardware features your AVD should emulate. You don't need any extra hardware configuration for your first application.

AVD nomenclature

Be careful when naming your AVDs. Android is available on many devices in the real world, such as phones, e-book readers, and netbooks. A time will come when you have to test your app on various configurations; therefore, adhering to a common nomenclature when creating your AVDs can later help you recognize which AVD is for what purpose. The nomenclature I tend to follow is the following:

```
{TARGET_VERSION}_{SKIN}_
    {SCREENSIZE}[{_Options}]
```

In Step 3 of the example in this section, you used the name of 2_2_Default_HVGA. This AVD will have a TARGET_VERSION of Android 2.2. The version name 2.2 is transformed into 2_2.

The underscores are used in place of periods to keep the name of the AVD combined. Creating an AVD name as a single combined word helps when you're working in advanced scenarios with AVDs via the command line.

The SKIN is the name of the skin of the emulator. Emulators can have various skins that make them look like actual devices. The default skin is provided by the Android SDK.

The SCREENSIZE value is the size of the screen with regard to the Video Graphics Array (VGA) size. The default is HVGA. Other options include QVGA and WVVGA800.

8. **Click the Create AVD button.**

   The Android SDK and AVD Manager dialog box should now look like Figure 3-12.

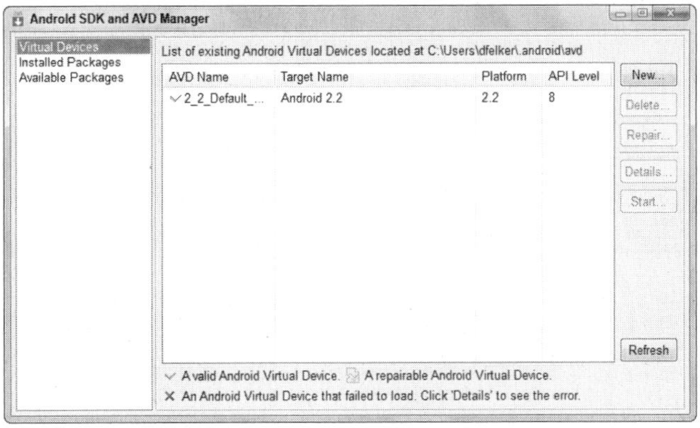

Figure 3-12: The recently created AVD in the Android SDK and AVD Manager dialog box.

9. **Close the Android SDK and AVD Manager dialog box.**

You may receive an error message after you create your AVD. This message may say `Android requires .class compatibility set to 5.0. Please fix project properties`. If this happens to you, you can fix it by right-clicking the project in Eclipse and choosing Android Tools⇨Fix Project Properties from the context menu.

You've created your first Android virtual device. Congratulations!

Creating Launch Configurations

You're almost at the point where you can run the application. A run configuration specifies the project to run, the activity to start, and the emulator or device to connect to. Whoa! That's a lot of stuff happening real quickly. Not to worry; the ADT can help you by automating a lot of the key steps so that you can get up and running quickly.

The Android ADT gives you two options for creating launch configurations:

- **Run configuration:** Used when you need to run your application on a given device. You'll use run configurations most of the time during your Android development career.
- **Debug configuration:** Used for debugging your application while it's running on a given device.

 When you first run a project as an Android application by choosing Run⇨Run, the ADT automatically creates a run configuration for you. The Android Application option is visible when you choose Run⇨Run. After the run configuration is created, it's the default run configuration, used each time you choose Run⇨Run menu from then on.

Creating a debug configuration

You shouldn't worry about debugging your application at this point because you'll be debugging it in the near future.

Creating a run configuration

Now it's your turn to create a run configuration for your application.

If you're feeling ambitious and decide that you'd like to create a run configuration manually, follow along here. Don't worry; it's very simple. Follow these steps:

1. **Choose Run⇨Run Configurations.**

   The Run Configurations dialog box opens, as shown in Figure 3-13. In this dialog box, you can create many types of run configurations. The left side of the dialog box lists many types of configurations, but the ones that you should pay attention to are as follows:

   • Android Application

   • Android JUnit Test

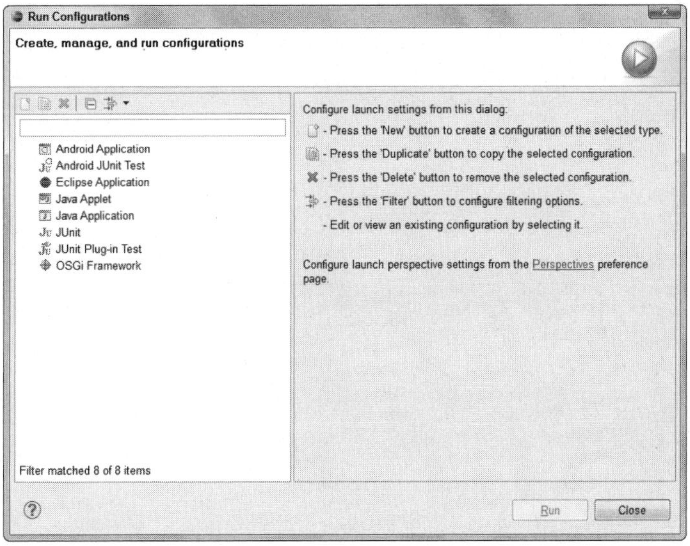

Figure 3-13:
The Run
Configura-
tions
dialog box.

2. **Select the Android Application item, and click the New Launch Configuration icon, shown in Figure 3-14 (or right-click Android Application and choose New from the context menu).**

   The New Launch Configuration window opens.

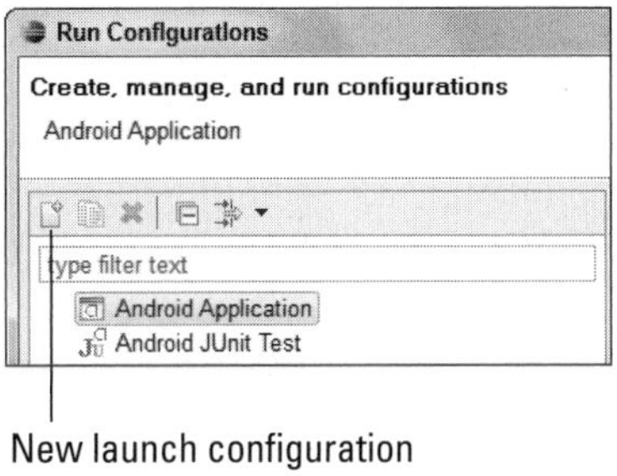

Figure 3-14:
The New
Launch
Configuration
icon.

New launch configuration

3. **Type** ExampleConfiguration **in the Name field.**

4. **On the Android tab, select the project you are creating this launch configuration for, and click the Browse button.**

   The Project Selection dialog box opens.

5. **Select Hello Android and click the OK button (see Figure 3-15).**

   The Run Configurations dialog box reopens.

Figure 3-15:
Selecting
the project
for the new
launch
configuration.

6. **On the Android tab, leave the Launch Action option set to Launch Default Activity.**

   In this case, the default activity is MainActivity, which you set up in "Starting a New Project in Eclipse," earlier in this chapter.

7. **On the Target tab (see Figure 3-16), leave Automatic selected.**

   Notice that an AVD is listed in the Select a Preferred Android Virtual Device for Deployment section.

8. **Select the 2_2_Default_HVGA device.**

   This device is the AVD that you created previously. By selecting it, you're instructing this launch configuration to launch this AVD when a user runs the app by choosing Run⇨Run. This view has both manual and automatic options. The manual option allows you to choose which device to connect to when using this launch configuration. Automatic sets a predefined AVD to use when launching in this current launch configuration.

9. **Leave the rest of the settings alone, and click the Apply button.**

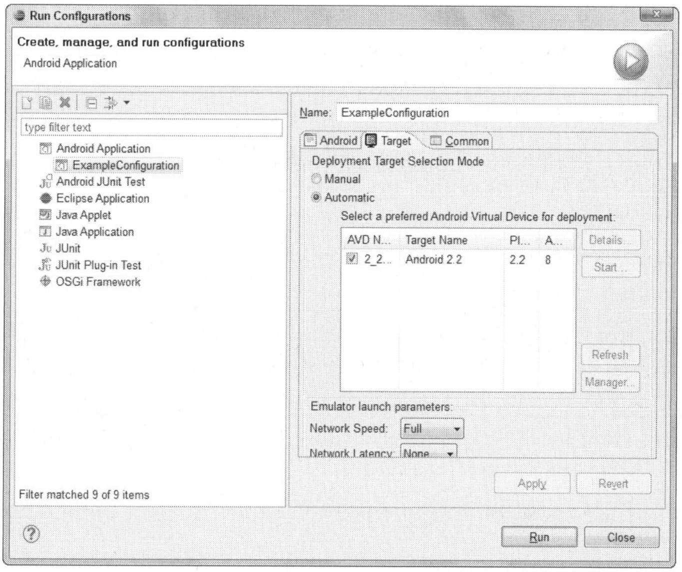

Figure 3-16:
A new,
manually
created
launch
configura-
tion named
`Example`
`Config-`
`uration.`

Congratulations! You've created your first launch configuration by hand.

Duplicating your launch configuration for quick setup

At some point, during your very successful and lucrative Android development career, one of your applications may have a problem on one particular
device. Launch configurations are designed to help you launch into a particular environment quickly. Setting up many launch configurations can be a
time-consuming task, however — especially if the launch configuration needs
to be altered only slightly from an existing launch configuration. Fortunately,
the ADT has included functionality that duplicates existing launch configurations, which allows you to quickly create various launch configurations that
are set up independently with their own configuration in mind.

To duplicate an existing launch configuration, follow these steps:

1. **Make sure that the launch configuration window is open.**

   If it's not, choose Run⇨Run Configurations to open the launch configuration window.

2. **In the left panel, right-click ExampleConfiguration, and choose Duplicate from the context menu.**

   This step creates a new launch configuration that's an exact copy of ExampleConfiguration. Its name will be `ExampleConfiguration (1)`.

3. **Change the name of the run configuration by typing** DuplicateTest **in the Name field near the top of the window.**

   You have created a duplicate launch configuration, and now you can change various settings to give the launch configuration a unique configuration.

   You don't need the `DuplicateTest` launch configuration; it was created to illustrate how to duplicate an existing launch configuration.

4. **To delete this configuration, select `DuplicateTest` in the left panel and click the Delete button on the toolbar, or right-click it and choose Delete from the context menu.**

5. **Click the Close button to close the Run Configurations dialog box.**

Running the Hello Android App

Congratulations! You've made it! Understanding the basics of how to get an Android application up and running has been a simple yet detailed process. You're now ready to see your hard work in action. You've created a launch configuration and Android Virtual Device; now it's time for you to get the application running. Finally!

Running the app in the emulator

Running the application is simple. Upon your instruction, the ADT will launch an emulator with the default launch configuration you built earlier in this chapter. Starting your application is as simple as choosing Run⇨Run or pressing Ctrl+F11. Either action launches the application in an emulator using the default launch configuration — in this case, ExampleConfiguration. The ADT compiles your application and then deploys it to the emulator.

If you didn't create a launch configuration, you see the Run As dialog box, shown in Figure 3-17. Choose Android Application, and a launch configuration is created for you.

Figure 3-17:
The Run As
dialog box
appears
when a
launch
configura-
tion hasn't
been set up
for the proj-
ect you're
attempting
to run.

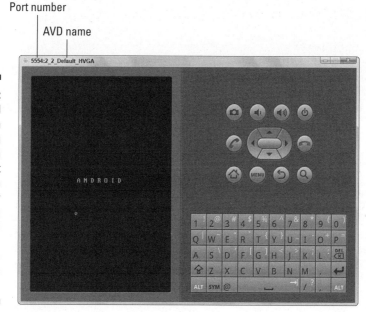

If you created the `ExampleConfiguration`, you see the emulator loading, as shown in Figure 3-18.

Port number

AVD name

Figure 3-18:
The initial
emulator in
a loading
state, with
the port
number the
emulator
is running
under and
the AVD
name in the
window's
title bar.

 Help! My emulator never loads! It stays stuck on the ANDROID screen(s)! No need to worry, comrade. The first time the emulator starts, the system could take upwards of 10 minutes for the emulator to finally finish loading. This is because you're running a virtual Linux system in the emulator. The emulator has to boot up and initialize. The slower your computer, the slower the emulator will be in its boot process.

The emulator has many boot screens. The first is shown in Figure 3-18. The window's title bar contains the port number that the emulator is running on your computer (5554) and the AVD name (2_2_Default_HVGA). Roughly one half of boot time is spent in this screen.

The second boot screen shows the Android logo (see Figure 3-19). This logo is the same one that default Android OS users see when they boot their phones (if a device manufacturer hasn't installed its own user-interface customizations, as on the HTC Sense).

The third and final screen you see is the loaded emulator, shown in Figure 3-20.

Figure 3-19:
The default loading screen for the Android OS.

Figure 3-20:
The loaded 2_2_Default_HVGA emulator.

Save valuable time by leaving the emulator running. The emulator doesn't have to be loaded each time you want to run your application. After the emulator is running, you can change your source code and then rerun your application. The ADT will find the running emulator and deploy your application to the emulator.

When the emulator completes its loading phase, the default locked home screen appears. To unlock the home screen, click and drag the Lock icon to the right side of the screen. When the icon reaches the far side of the Android screen, release the icon. During the drag, the icon's background turns green, and its label changes to `Unlock`, as shown in Figure 3-21.

Figure 3-21:
Unlocking
a locked
home
screen.

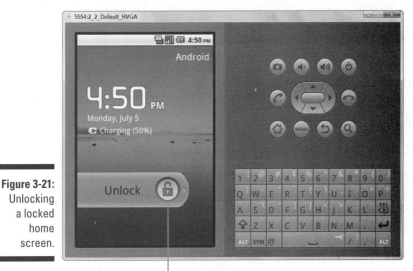

Click and drag to the right side of the screen.

After the emulator is unlocked, the home screen appears, as shown in Figure 3-22.

Figure 3-22:
The
emulator
home
screen.

Immediately thereafter, the ADT starts the Hello Android application for you. You should see a black screen containing the words `Hello World, MainActivity!`, as shown in Figure 3-23. Congratulations! You just created and started your first Android application.

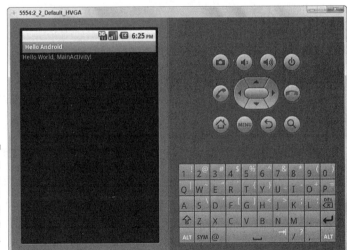

Figure 3-23:
The Hello
Android
application
in the
emulator.

If you don't unlock the screen when the emulator starts, the ADT won't be able to start the application. If you unlock the home screen and your application doesn't started within five to ten seconds, simply run the application from Eclipse again by choosing Run⇨Run. The application is redeployed to the device, and it starts running. You can view the status of the installation via the Console view in Eclipse, as shown in Figure 3-24.

The Console

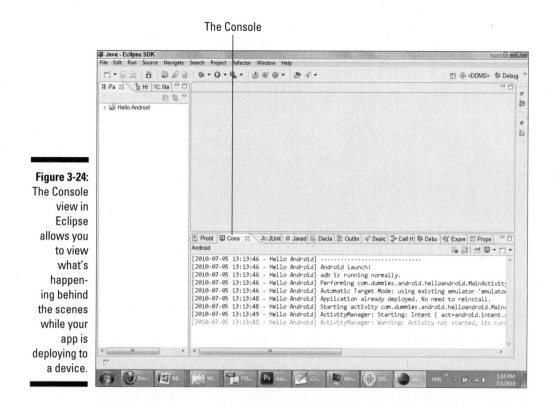

Figure 3-24:
The Console
view in
Eclipse
allows you
to view
what's
happen-
ing behind
the scenes
while your
app is
deploying to
a device.

Checking deployment status

Inside Console view, you can see information regarding the state of your application deployment. Here's the full text of that information:

```
[2010-07-05 13:13:46 - Hello Android] -----------------------------
[2010-07-05 13:13:46 - Hello Android] Android Launch!
[2010-07-05 13:13:46 - Hello Android] adb is running normally.
[2010-07-05 13:13:46 - Hello Android] Performing com.dummies.android.
          helloandroid.MainActivity activity launch
[2010-07-05 13:13:46 - Hello Android] Automatic Target Mode: using existing
          emulator 'emulator-5554' running compatible AVD '2_2_Default_HVGA'
[2010-07-05 13:13:48 - Hello Android] Application already deployed. No need to
          reinstall.
[2010-07-05 13:13:48 - Hello Android] Starting activity com.dummies.android.
          helloandroid.MainActivity on device
[2010-07-05 13:13:49 - Hello Android] ActivityManager: Starting: Intent {
          act=android.intent.action.MAIN cat=[android.intent.category.
          LAUNCHER] cmp=com.dummies.android.helloandroid/.MainActivity }
[2010-07-05 13:13:49 - Hello Android] ActivityManager: Warning: Activity not
          started, its current task has been brought to the front
```

The Console view provides valuable information on the state of the application deployment. It lets you know it's launching an activity; shows what device the ADT is targeting; and shows warning information, as presented in the last line of the Console view:

```
[2010-07-05 13:13:49 - Hello Android] ActivityManager: Warning: Activity not
                started, its current task has been brought to the front
```

ADT informs you that the activity — `MainActivity`, in this case — hasn't been started because it was already running. Because the activity was already running, ADT brought that task to the foreground (the Android screen) for you to see.

Understanding Project Structure

Congratulations again! You created your first application. You even did it without coding. It's nice that the ADT provides you with the tools to fire up a quick application, but that's not going to help you create your next blockbuster application. The beginning of this chapter walked you through how to create a boilerplate Android application with the New Android Project wizard. From here on, you will use the file structure that the Android wizard created for you.

The following sections aren't ones that you should skim (trust me, they're important!), because you'll spend your entire Android development career navigating these folders. Understanding what they're for and how they got there is a key aspect of understanding Android development.

Navigating the app's folders

In Eclipse, the Package Explorer expands the Hello Android project so that it resembles Figure 3-25.

After the Hello Android project is expanded, the list of subfolders includes

- ✔ src
- ✔ gen
- ✔ Android version (such as `Android 2.2`)
- ✔ assets
- ✔ res

Package Explorer

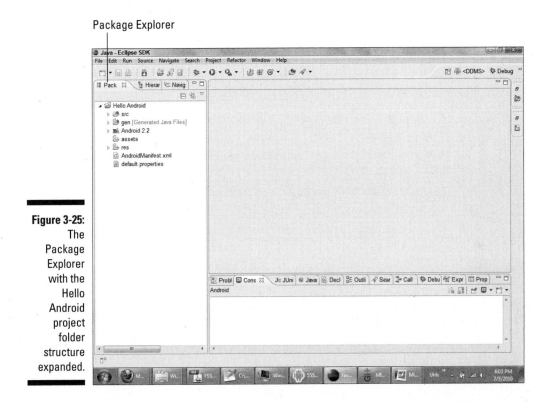

Package Explorer

Figure 3-25:
The
Package
Explorer
with the
Hello
Android
project
folder
structure
expanded.

These folders aren't the only ones that you can have inside an Android project, but they're the default folders created by the New Android Project wizard. Other folders include `bin`, `libs`, and `referenced libraries`.

You won't see the `bin` folder initially, because it's hidden from view in the latest version of the ADT (which may change in future versions of the ADT). The `libs` and `referenced libraries` folders don't show up until you add a third-party library and reference it in your project. I cover this process in detail later in this chapter.

The two other files in the project are `AndroidManifest.xml` and `default.properties`. The `AndroidManifest.xml` file helps you identify the components that build and run the application, whereas the `default.properties` file helps you identify the default properties of the Android project (such as Android version).

I discuss all these folders and files in the following sections.

Source (src) folder

The source folder — known as the `src` folder in Android projects — includes your stub `MainActivity.java` file, which you created in the New Android Project wizard earlier in this chapter. To inspect the contents of the `src` folder, you must expand it. Follow these steps:

1. **Select the `src` folder, and click the small arrow to the left of the folder to expand it.**

   You see your project's default package: `com.dummies.android. helloandroid`.

2. **Select the default package, and expand it.**

   This step exposes the `MainActivity.java` file within the `com. dummies.android.helloandroid` package, as shown in Figure 3-26.

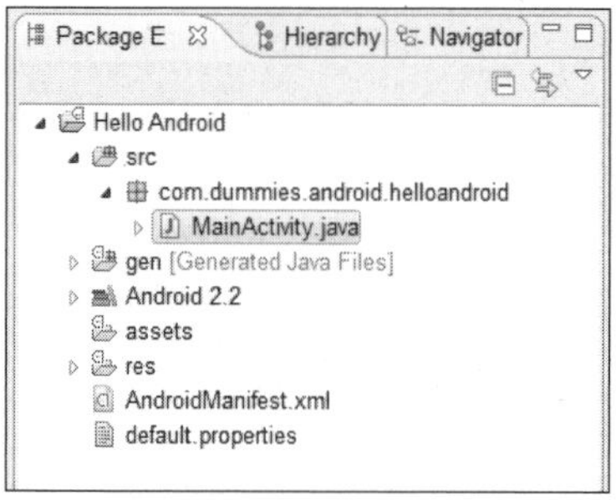

Figure 3-26:
The `src` folder expanded and showing the stub `Main Activity. java` file inside the default `com. dummies. android. hello android` Java package.

Package E	Hierarchy	Navigator

```
▲ 📁 Hello Android
   ▲ 📂 src
      ▲ ⊞ com.dummies.android.helloandroid
         ▷ 🗋 MainActivity.java
   ▷ 🗁 gen [Generated Java Files]
   ▷ ▥ Android 2.2
      🗁 assets
   ▷ 🗁 res
      🗋 AndroidManifest.xml
      🗋 default.properties
```

You aren't limited to a single package in your Android applications. In fact, separating different pieces of core functionality in your Java classes into packages is considered to be a best practice. An example would be if you had a class whose responsibility was to communicate with a Web API through eXtensible Markup Language (XML). Also, your application might have `Customer` objects that represent a customer domain model, and those customers are retrieved via the Web API classes. At this point, you might have two extra Java packages that contain the additional Java classes:

✔ com.dummies.android.helloandroid.models

✔ com.dummies.android.helloandroid.http

These packages would contain their respective Java components. com. dummies.android.helloandroid.models would contain the domain model Java classes, and com.dummies.android.helloandroid.http would contain the HTTP-related Java classes (Web APIs). An Android project set up this way would look similar to Figure 3-27.

Figure 3-27:
An example
of having
multiple
packages
under the
src folder
that contain
their own
respec-
tive Java
classes.

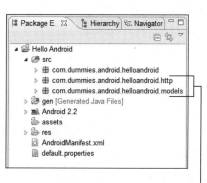

New packages containing models
and HTTP (Web API) components

Target Android Library folder

Wait a second; I skipped the gen folder! I delve into that folder when I reach the res folder. But for now, I want to focus on the Target Android Library folder. This isn't really a folder per se, but is more along the lines of an item in Eclipse presented through the ADT.

This item includes the android.jar file that your application builds against. The version of this file was determined by the build target that you chose in the New Android Project wizard. Expanding the Android 2.2 item in the project exposes the android.jar file and the path to where it's installed, as shown in Figure 3-28.

You may notice that the SDK is installed in the c:\SDK\ folder, which illustrates the fact that you don't have to install the SDK in any given location. It can go anywhere in your file system.

Figure 3-28:
The Android
2.2
version
of the
`android.`
`jar` file
with its
location.

```
Package E  ⋈      Hierarchy   Navigator
                                          ▤ ▯
                                      ▤ ▤ ▽

▲ 🗁 Hello Android
  ▷ 📂 src
  ▷ 📂 gen [Generated Java Files]
  ▲ ▣ Android 2.2
    ▷ 🗋 android.jar - C:\SDK\android-sdk-windows\p─┐
    🗁 assets                                        │
  ▷ 🗁 res                                           │
    🗋 AndroidManifest.xml                           │
    🗋 default.properties                            │
```

The `android.jar` file for version 2.2

Assets (assets) folder

The `assets` folder is empty by default. This folder is used to store raw asset files.

A *raw asset file* could be one of many assets you may need for your application to work. A great example would be a file that contains data in a proprietary format for consumption on the device. Android has the Asset Manager, which can return all the assets currently in the `assets` directory. Upon reading an asset, your application could read the data in the file. If you were to create an application that had its own dictionary for word lookups (for autocomplete, perhaps), you may want to bundle the dictionary into the project by placing the dictionary file (usually, an XML or binary file such as a SQLite database) in the `assets` directory.

Android treats assets as a raw approach to resource management. You aren't limited in what you can place in the `assets` directory. Note, however, that working with assets can be a little more tedious than working with resources, because you're required to work with streams of bytes and convert them to the objects you're after — audio, video, text, and so on.

Assets don't receive resource IDs like resources in the `res` directory. You have to work with bits, bytes, and streams manually to access the contents.

Resources (res) folder

The `res` folder contains the various resources that your application can consume. You should always externalize any resources that your application needs to consume. Classic examples of such resources include strings and images. As an example, you should avoid placing strings inside your code. Instead, create a string resource and reference that resource from within code. I show you how to do this later in the book. Such resources should be grouped in the `res` subdirectory that suits them best.

You should also provide alternative resources for specific device configurations by grouping them in specifically named resource directories. At run time, Android determines which configuration the application is running in and chooses the appropriate resource (or resource folder) to pull its resources from. You may want to provide a different user interface (UI) layout depending on the screen size or different strings depending on the language setting, for example.

After you externalize your resources, you can access them in code through resource IDs that are generated by the ADT in the R class (see "The mysterious gen folder," later in this chapter).

You should place each resource in a specific subdirectory of your project's res directory. The subdirectories listed in Table 3-1 are the most common types of resource folders under the parent res directory.

Table 3-1	Supported Subdirectories of the res Directory
Directory	**Resource Type**
anim/	XML files that define animations.
color/	XML files that define a list of colors.
drawable/	Bitmap files (.png, .9.png, .jpg, .gif) or XML files that are compiled into the following drawable resources.
drawable-hdpi/	Drawables for high-resolution screens. The hdpi qualifier stands for high-density screens. This is the same as the drawable/ resource folder except that all bitmap or XML files stored here are compiled into high-resolution drawable resources.
drawable-ldpi/	Drawables for low-resolution screens. The ldpi qualifier stands for low-density screens. This is the same as the drawable/ resource folder except that all bitmap or XML files stored here are compiled into low-resolution drawable resources.
drawable-mdpi/	Drawables for medium-resolution screens. The mdpi qualifier stands for medium-density screens. This is the same as the drawable/ resource folder except that all bitmap or XML files stored here are compiled into medium-resolution drawable resources.
layout/	XML files that define a user interface layout.
menu/	XML files that represent application menus.

(continued)

Table 3-1 *(continued)*

Directory	Resource Type
raw/	Arbitrary files to save in their raw form. Files in this directory aren't compressed by the system.
values/	XML files that contain simple values, such as strings, integers, and colors. Whereas XML resource files in other res/ folders define a single resource based on the XML filenames, files in the values/ directory define multiple resources for various uses. There are a few filename conventions for the resources you can create in this directory: * arrays.xml for resource arrays (storing like items together such as strings or integers) * colors.xml for resources that define color values. Accessed via the R.colors class. * dimens.xml for resources that define dimension values. For example, 20px equates 20 pixels. Accessed via the R.dimens class. * strings.xml for string values. Accessed via the R.strings class. * styles.xml for resources that represent styles. A style is similar to a Cascading Style Sheet in HTML. You can define many different styles and have them inherit from each other. Accessed via the R.styles class.

Never save resource files directly in the res directory. If you do, a compiler error occurs.

The resources that you save in the resource folders listed in Table 3-1 are known as *default resources* — that is, they define the default design and layout of your Android application. Different types of Android-powered devices may need different resources, however. If you have a device with a larger-than-normal screen, for example, you need to provide alternative layout resources to account for the difference.

Naming resources in the values directory

There are a few filename conventions for the resources you can create in the `values` directory:

✔ `arrays.xml` for resource arrays (storing like items, such as strings or integers, together)

✔ `colors.xml` for resources that define color values; accessed via the `R.colors` class.

✔ `dimens.xml` for resources that define dimension values (`20px` equals 20 pixels, for example); accessed via the `R.dimens` class.

✔ `strings.xml` for string values; accessed via the `R.strings` class.

✔ `styles.xml` for resources that represent styles; accessed via the `R.styles` class. A style is similar to a cascading style sheet in HTML. You can define many styles and have them inherit from one another.

The `resource/` mechanism inside Android is very powerful, and I could easily write a chapter on it alone, but I'm going to cover only the basics in this book to get you up and running. The `resource/` mechanism can help with internationalization (enabling your app for different languages and countries), device size and density, and even resources for the mode that the phone may be in. If you'd like to dive into the ocean that is resources, you can find out more about them by reviewing the "Providing Resources" section in the Dev Guide of the Android documentation, located at `http://d.android.com/guide/topics/resources/providing-resources.html`.

Bin, Libs, and Referenced Libraries folders

Did I say ribs? No! I said *libs,* as in libraries. Though these folders aren't shown in your Hello Android application, you should be aware of a couple of extra folders, one of which is the `libs/` directory. The `libs/` directory contains private libraries and isn't created by default. If you need it, you need to create it manually by right-clicking the project in the Package Explorer and choosing Folder from the context menu. Eclipse asks you for the name of the folder and the name of the parent folder. Choose Hello Android, type **libs**, and click Finish.

Private who? I'm not in the military; what gives? Private libraries usually are third-party libraries that perform some function for you. An example would be jTwitter, a third-party Java library for the Twitter API. If you were to use jTwitter in your Android application, the `jtwitter.jar` library would need to be placed in the `libs` directory.

After a library is placed in the `libs` directory, you need to add it to your Java build path — the class path that's used for building a Java project. If your project depends on another third-party or private library, Eclipse should know where to find that library, and setting the build path through

Eclipse does exactly that. Assuming that you added `jtwitter.jar` to your `libs` directory, you can add it to your build path easily by right-clicking the `jtwitter.jar` file and choosing Build Path➪Add to Build Path from the context menu.

In the action of adding jTwitter to your build path, you may have noticed that the `Referenced Libraries` folder was created, as shown in Figure 3-29. This folder exists to let you know what libraries you have referenced in your Eclipse project.

You can find out more about jTwitter at `www.winterwell.com/software/ jtwitter.php`.

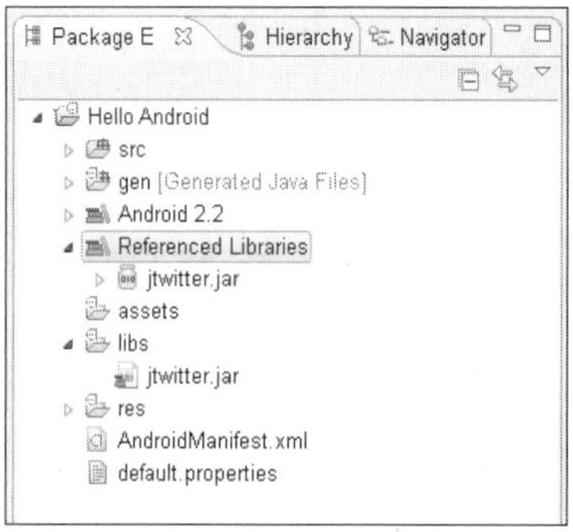

Figure 3-29: The Refer- enced Libraries folder with jtwitter. jar.

I don't use the `libs` directory in this book. But developers — myself included — commonly use third-party libraries in Android applications. I wanted to include this information in the book in case you need to reference a library in your own Android project.

The mysterious gen folder

Ah, you finally get to witness the magic that is the `gen` folder. When you create your Android application, before the first compilation, the `gen` folder doesn't exist. Upon the first compilation, ADT generates the `gen` folder and its contents.

The `gen` folder contains Java files generated by ADT. The ADT creates an `R.java` file (more about which in a moment). I covered the `res` folder before the `gen` folder because the `gen` folder contains items that are generated from the `res` directory. Without a proper understanding of what the `res` folder is and what it contains, you have no clue what the `gen` folder is for. But because you're already an expert on the `res` folder, I'm going to dive right into the `gen` folder now.

When you write Java code in Android, you will come to a point when you need to reference the items in the res folder. You do this by using the R class. The R.java file is an index to all the resources defined in your res folder. You use this class as a shorthand way to reference resources you've included in your project. This is particularly useful with the code-completion features of Eclipse because you can quickly identify the proper resource through code completion.

Expand the gen folder in the Hello Android project and the package name contained within the gen folder. Now open the R.java file by double-clicking it. You can see a Java class that contains nested Java classes. These nested Java classes have the same names as some of the res folders defined in the preceding res section. Under each of those subclasses, you can see members that have the same names as the resources in their respective res folders (excluding their file extensions). The Hello Android project's R.java file should look similar to the following code:

```
/* AUTO-GENERATED FILE.   DO NOT MODIFY.
 *
 * This class was automatically generated by the
 * aapt tool from the resource data it found.   It
 * should not be modified by hand.
 */

package com.dummies.android.helloandroid;

public final class R {
    public static final class attr {
    }
    public static final class drawable {
        public static final int icon=0x7f020000;
    }
    public static final class layout {
        public static final int main=0x7f030000;
    }
    public static final class string {
        public static final int app_name=0x7f040001;
        public static final int hello=0x7f040000;
    }
}
```

Whoa, what's all that 0x stuff? I'm happy to tell you that you don't need to worry about it. The ADT tool generates this code for you so that you don't have to worry about what's happening behind the scenes. As you add resources and the project is rebuilt, ADT regenerates the R.java file. This newly generated file contains members that reference your recently added resources.

You should never edit the `R.java` file by hand. If you do, your application may not compile, and then you're in a whole world of hurt. If you accidentally edit the `R.java` file and can't undo your changes, you can delete the `gen` folder and build your project. At this point, ADT regenerates the `R.java` file for you.

Viewing the application's manifest file

You keep track of everything you own and need through lists, don't you? Well, that's exactly what the Android manifest file does. It keeps track of everything your application needs, requests, and has to use to run.

The Android manifest file is stored at the root of your project and is named `AndroidManifest.xml`. Every application must have an Android manifest file in its root directory.

The application manifest file provides all the essential information to the Android system — information that it must have before it can run any of your application's code. The application manifest file also provides the following:

- ✓ The name of your Java package for the application, which is the unique identifier for your application in the Android system as well as in the Android Market
- ✓ The components of the application, such as the activities and background services
- ✓ The declaration of the permissions your application requires to run
- ✓ The minimum level of the Android API that the application requires

The Android manifest file declares the version of your application. You *must* version your application. How you version your application is very similar to how the Android OS is versioned. It's important to determine your application's versioning strategy early in the development process, including considerations for future releases of your application. The versioning requirements are that each application have a version code and version name. I cover these values in the following sections.

Version code

The *version code* is an integer value that represents the version of the application code relative to other versions of your application. This value is used to help other applications determine their compatibility with your application. Also, the Android Market uses it as a basis for identifying the application internally and for handling updates.

You can set the version code to any integer value you like, but you should make sure that each successive release has a version code greater than the previous one. The Android system doesn't enforce this rule; it's a best practice to follow.

Typically, on your first release, you set your version code to 1. Then you monotonically increase the value in a given order with each release, whether the release is major or minor. This means that the version code doesn't have a strong resemblance to the application release version that's visible to the user, which is the version name (see the next section). The version code typically isn't displayed to users in applications.

Upgrading your application code and releasing the app without incrementing your version code causes different code bases of your app to be released under the same version. Consider a scenario in which you release your application with version code 1. This is your first release. A user installs your application via the Android Market and notices a bug in your application, and she lets you know. You fix the bug in the code, recompile, and release the new code base without updating the version code in the Android manifest file. At this point, the Android Market doesn't know that anything has changed because it's inspecting your version code in the application manifest. If the version code had changed to a value greater than 1, such as 2, the Market would recognize that an update had been made and would inform users who installed the version-code 1 app that an update is available. If you didn't update the version code, users would never get the update to your code base, and they would be running a buggy app. No one likes that!

Version name

The *version name* is a string value that represents the release version of the application code as it should be shown to users. The value is a string that follows a common release-name nomenclature that describes the application version:

```
<major>.<minor>.<point>
```

An example of this release-name nomenclature is 2.1.4 or, without the `<point>` value (4, in this case), 2.1.

The Android system doesn't use this value for any purpose other than to enable applications to display it to users.

The version name may be any other type of absolute or relative version identifier. The Foursquare application, for example, uses a version-naming scheme that corresponds to the date. An example of the version application name is 2010-06-28, which clearly represents a date. The version name is left up to you. You should plan ahead and make sure that your versioning strategy makes sense to you and your users.

Permissions

Assume that your application needs to access the Internet to retrieve some data. Android restricts Internet access by default. For your application to have access to the Internet, you need to ask for it.

In the application manifest file, you must define which permissions your application needs to operate. Table 3-2 lists some of the most commonly requested permissions.

Table 3-2	Commonly Requested Application Permissions
Permission	**Description**
Internet	The application needs access to the Internet.
Write External Storage	The application needs to write data to the Secure Digital Card (SD Card).
Camera	The application needs access to the camera.
Access Fine Location	The application needs access to the Global Positioning System (GPS) location.
Read Phone State	The application needs to access the state of the phone (such as ringing).

Viewing the default.properties file

The `default.properties` file is used in conjunction with ADT and Eclipse. It contains project settings such as the build target. This file is integral to the project, so don't lose it!

The `default.properties` file should never be edited manually. To edit the contents of the file, use the editor in Eclipse. You can access this editor by right-clicking the project name in the Package Explorer and choosing Properties from the context menu. This opens the Properties editor, shown in Figure 3-30.

This editor allows you to change various properties of the project by selecting any of the options on the left. You could select the Android property and change the path to the Android SDK, for example.

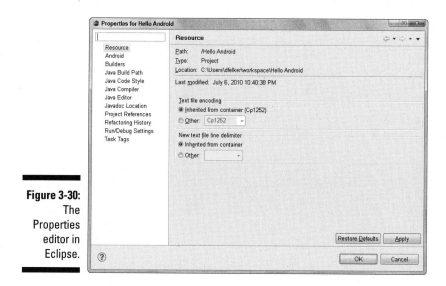

Chapter 4

Designing the User Interface

● ●

In This Chapter

▶ Setting up the Silent Mode Toggle application

▶ Designing the layout

▶ Developing the user interface

▶ Adding an image and a button widget

▶ Making a launcher icon

▶ Previewing your work

● ●

Congratulations! You discovered what Android is and how to build your first application. I'm happy to say that you are now getting into the fun stuff. You're going to build a real application that you can use and publish to the Android Market.

The application you're going to build allows the user to toggle the mode of his or her phone's ringer with a simple press of a button. This application seems simple, but it solves a real-world problem.

Imagine that you're at work and you're about to go to a meeting. You can turn your phone volume down, all the way to silence, and then attend the meeting. You'd never be "that guy" whose phone rings during a meeting, would you? The problem is that you like your ringer loud, but not too loud. You never keep it on the loudest setting, only the second-to-loudest setting. When you leave your meeting, you remember to turn your phone ringer volume back up, but you always have to go all the way to the max volume, and then down one setting, just to make sure that you have the correct setting. While this isn't a life-changing event, it's kind of a nuisance having to do this each time you need to silence your phone's ringer.

It would be great if you had an application that would allow you to touch a button to turn the ringer off, and then, when you leave the meeting, you could touch the button again and the ringer would return to the last state that it was in. You'd never have to readjust your ringer again. That's the application you're about to build.

Creating the Silent Mode Toggle Application

Your task at hand is to create the Silent Mode Toggle application, and because you're already an expert on setting up new Android applications, I'm not going to walk you through it step by step. If you need a brief refresher on how to create a new Android app in Eclipse, review Chapter 3.

Before you create the new application, you need to close all the files you already have open in Eclipse. You can do this by closing each file individually or by right-clicking the files and choosing Close All from the shortcut menu.

After you have closed all the files, you need to close the current project (Hello Android) in which you're working. In Eclipse, in the Package Explorer, right-click the Hello Android project and choose Close Project. By closing the project, you are telling Eclipse that you currently do not need to work with that project. This frees resources that Eclipse uses to track the project state, therefore speeding up your application.

You're now ready to create your new Silent Mode Toggle application.

Create the new application by choosing File↔New Project. Choose Android Project from the list, and then click the Next button. Use Table 4-1 for your project settings.

Table 4-1	Project Settings for Silent Mode Toggle
Setting	*Value*
Application Name	Silent Mode Toggle
Project name	Silent Mode Toggle
Contents	Leave the default selected (create new project in workspace)
Build target	Android 2.2
Package name	`com.dummies.android.silentmodetoggle`
Create activity	`MainActivity`
Min SDK Version	8

Click the Finish button. You should now have the Silent Mode Toggle application in your Package Explorer, as shown in Figure 4-1.

If you receive an error that looks similar to this — "The project cannot be built until build path errors are resolved" — you can resolve it by right clicking on the project and choosing Android Tools⇨Fix Project Properties. This realigns your project with the IDE workspace.

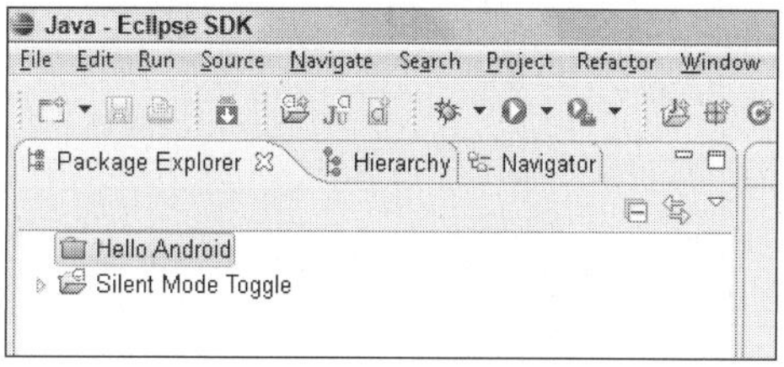

Figure 4-1:
The Silent
Mode Toggle
application
in Eclipse.

Notice how you selected the build target of Android 2.2, and a Min SDK Version of 8. What you have done is told Android that your code can run on any device that is running at least a version code of 8 (Android 2.2). If you were to change this to version code 4, you would be saying that your app can run on any device running version 4 or higher. How do I know which version this app can run on? I've already tested it, before I wrote the book! When creating a new application, you should check to see whether it can run on older versions.

Laying Out the Application

Now that you have the Silent Mode Toggle application created inside Eclipse, it's time for you to design the application's user interface. The user interface is the part of your application where your users interact with your app. It is of prime concern to make this area of the application as snappy as possible in all regards.

Your application is going to have a single button centered in the middle of the screen to toggle the silent mode. Directly above the button will be an image for visual feedback, letting the user know whether the phone is in silent or regular ringer mode. A picture is worth a thousand words, so take a look at Figures 4-2 and 4-3 to see what your application will look like.

Figure 4-2:
The Silent
Mode
Toggle
application
in regular
ringer mode.

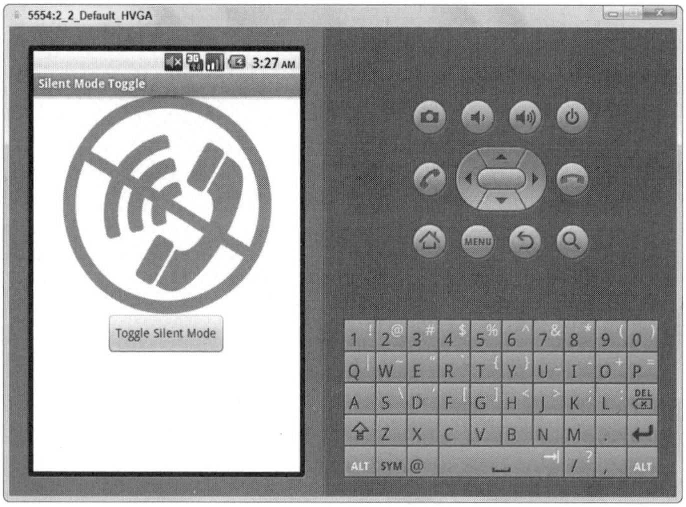

Figure 4-3:
The Silent
Mode
Toggle
application
in silent
ringer mode.

Using the XML layout file

All layout files for your application are stored in the res/layouts directory
of your Android project in Eclipse. When you created the Silent Mode Toggle
application a moment ago, the Android Development Tools (ADT) created
a file named main.xml in the res/layouts directory. This is the default
layout file that the ADT creates for you when you create a new application.

Open that file by double-clicking it, and you should see some XML in the Eclipse editor window, as shown in Figure 4-4.

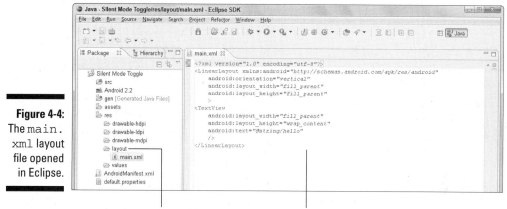

Figure 4-4:
The main.
xml layout
file opened
in Eclipse.

Layouts are stored here.   The main.xml layout file

What you see in Figure 4-4 is a simple layout in which you have a text value in the middle of the screen. Just to be sure that you're on the same page, your code should look like this:

```xml
<?xml version="1.0" encoding="utf-8"?>
<LinearLayout xmlns:android="http://schemas.android.com/apk/res/android"
    android:orientation="vertical"
    android:layout_width="fill_parent"
    android:layout_height="fill_parent"
    >
<TextView
    android:layout_width="fill_parent"
    android:layout_height="wrap_content"
    android:text="@string/hello"
    />
</LinearLayout>
```

This XML file defines exactly what your view is to look like. In the following sections, I break this file down for you element by element.

Default XML declaration

The first element provides the default XML declaration, letting text editors like Eclipse and consumers like Android know what type of file it is:

```xml
<?xml version="1.0" encoding="utf-8"?>
```

Layout type

The next element defines the layout type. In this case, you're working with a LinearLayout. I give you more info about LinearLayouts in a moment, but for now, be aware that a LinearLayout is a container for other items known as views that show up on the screen. Notice how I am not showing the closing </LinearLayout> tag; this is because this tag is a container of other items. The close tag is inserted after all the view items have been added to the container:

```
<LinearLayout xmlns:android="http://schemas.android.com/apk/res/android"
    android:orientation="vertical"
    android:layout_width="fill_parent"
    android:layout_height="fill_parent"
    >
```

Views

The "other items" I mention previously are known as views. Views in Android are the basic building blocks for user interface components. The following code shows TextView, which is responsible for displaying text to the screen:

```
<TextView
    android:layout_width="fill_parent"
    android:layout_height="wrap_content"
    android:text="@string/hello"
    />
```

A view occupies a rectangular space on the screen and is responsible for drawing and event handling. All items that can show up on a device's screen are all views. The View class is the superclass that all items inherit from in Android.

At the end of it all, you have the closing tag for the LinearLayout. This closes the container:

```
</LinearLayout>
```

In the following section, I describe the forest that is filled with different types of layouts.

Using the Android SDK's layout tools

When creating user interfaces, you sometimes have to lay components out relative to each other or in a table, or even under certain circumstances, using absolute positioning. Thankfully the engineering geniuses at Google who created Android thought of all this and provided you with the tools necessary to create those types of layouts. Table 4-2 gives you a brief introduction to the common types of layouts that are available in the Android Software Development Kit (SDK).

Table 4-2	Android SDK Layouts
Layout	*Description*
LinearLayout	A layout that arranges its children in a single row.
RelativeLayout	A layout where the positions of the children can be described in relation to each other or to the parent.
FrameLayout	This layout is designed to block out an area on the screen to display a single item. You can add multiple children to a FrameLayout, but all children are pegged to the upper left of the screen. Children are drawn in a stack, with the most recently added child at the top of the stack. This layout is commonly used as a way to lay out views in an absolute position.
TableLayout	A layout that arranges its children into rows and columns.

Other different types of layout tools exist, such as a TabHost for creating tabs and a Sliding Drawer for finger-swiping motions of hiding and displaying views. I'm not going to get into those at this point because they are only used in special-case scenarios. The items in Table 4-2 outline the layouts that you will use most commonly.

Using the visual designer

I have some good news for you: Eclipse includes a visual designer. I also have some bad news: The designer is limited in what it can do (as are all visual designers).

Opening the visual designer

To view the visual designer, with the main.xml file open in the Eclipse editor, click the Layout button (see Figure 4-5).

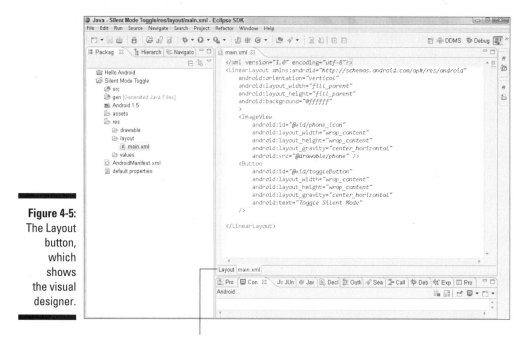

Figure 4-5:
The Layout button, which shows the visual designer.

Visual designer

You should now see the visual designer, as shown in Figure 4-6.

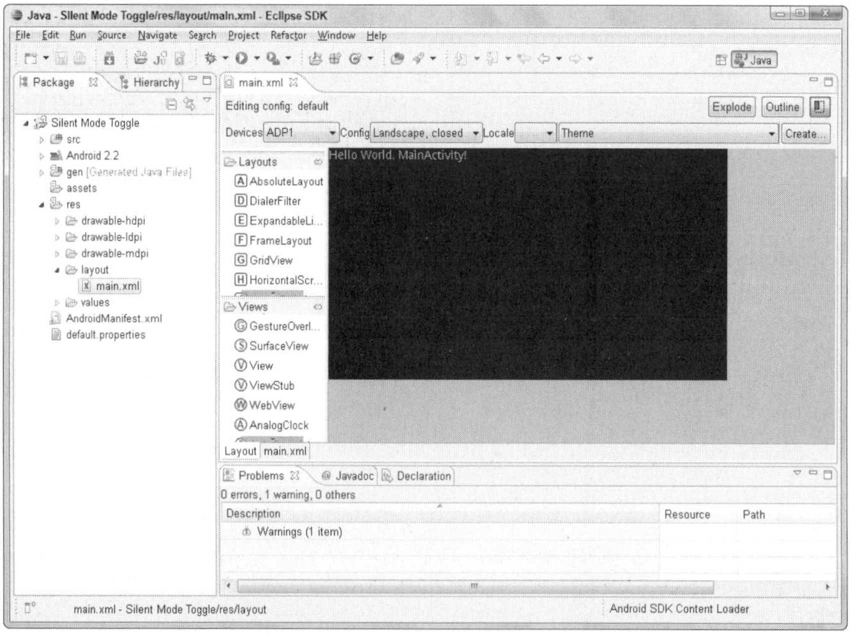

Figure 4-6:
The visual designer.

From here, you can drag and drop items from the Layouts or Views toolboxes.

Inspecting a view's properties

A feature I really like about the designer is the ability to view the properties of a given view, just by clicking it. Most likely, your Properties panel is hidden. To show it, follow these steps:

1. **Choose Window➪Show View➪Other.**

2. **Expand Java and choose Properties.**

   This opens the Properties view in Eclipse, as shown in Figure 4-7. To use the Properties window, simply select a view in the visual designer. The view has a red border around it, and the properties show up in the Properties window below. Scroll through the list of properties to examine what can be changed in the view.

Red line around selected view

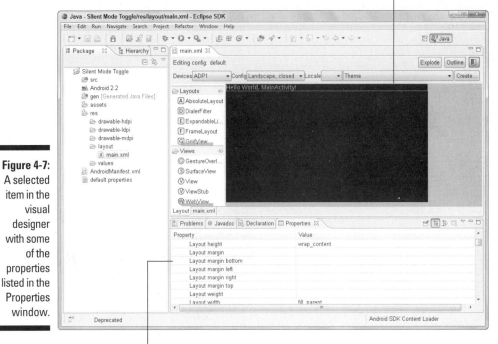

Figure 4-7: A selected item in the visual designer with some of the properties listed in the Properties window.

View properties

If you're not sure what properties a view has, open the visual designer, click the Properties Tab, and inspect the Properties view. This gives you a quick glance into what the view has to offer. If the Properties tab is not visible, enable it by choosing Windows➪Show View➪Other➪General➪Properties.

A view's available properties can change depending on its parent layout. For example, if a `TextView` is inside a `LinearLayout`, it has a different set of properties (for layout) than if it is inside a `RelativeLayout`.

The visual designer works well for simple scenarios where your contents are static in nature. But what happens when you need to draw items on the screen dynamically based on user input? That's where the designer falls down. It cannot help you in those scenarios. It is best suited for static content scenarios. A *static content scenario* occurs when you create your layout once and it does not update dynamically. The text of `TextViews` or images might change, but the actual layout of the views inside the layout would not change.

Developing the User Interface

Okay, it's time to start developing your user interface.

The first thing to do is to return to the XML view of your layout by clicking the `main.xml` tab, which is directly next to the Layout tab that you clicked to get to the visual designer. When you are in the XML view, delete the `TextView` of your layout. Your layout should now look like this:

```xml
<?xml version="1.0" encoding="utf-8"?>
<LinearLayout xmlns:android="http://schemas.android.com/apk/res/android"
    android:orientation="vertical"
    android:layout_width="fill_parent"
    android:layout_height="fill_parent"
    >

</LinearLayout>
```

Viewing XML layout attributes

Before I go any further, let me explain the Android layout XML that you are currently working with. See Table 4-3.

Table 4-3	XML Layout Attributes
Layout	*Description*
`xmlns:android="..."`	This defines the XML namespace that you will use to reference part of the Android SDK.

Layout	Description
`orientation="vertical"`	This informs Android that this view is to be laid out in a vertical fashion (like portrait format in printing).
`android:layout_width="fill_parent"`	This informs the view that it should fill as much horizontal space as it can, up to its parent. In short, it should make the width as wide as it can be within the parent.
`android:layout_height="fill_parent"`	This informs the view that it should fill as much vertical space as it can, up to its parent. In short, it should make the height as tall as it can be within the parent.

At this point, you have defined your layout to fill the entire screen by setting the width and height to `"fill_parent"`.

Working with views

As stated previously, views in Android are the basic building blocks for user interface components. Anytime you implement a user interface component, such as a `Layout`, `TextView`, and so on, in the Android system, you are using a view. When you work with views in Java, you have to cast them to their appropriate type to work with them.

Setting layout_width and layout_height values

Before a view can be presented to the screen, a couple of settings must be configured on the view so that Android knows how to lay out the view on the screen. The attributes that are required are `layout_width` and `layout_height`. These are known as `LayoutParams` in the Android SDK.

The `layout_width` attribute specifies the given width a view should be, and the `layout_height` attribute specifies the given height a view should be.

Setting fill_parent and wrap_content values

The `layout_width` and `layout_height` attributes can take any pixel value or density-independent pixel value to specify their respective dimension. However, two of the most common values for `layout_width` and `layout_height` are `fill_parent` and `wrap_content` constants.

The `fill_parent` value informs the Android system to fill as much space as possible on the screen based on the available space of the parent layout. The `wrap_content` value informs the Android system to only take up as much space as needed to show the view. As the view's contents grow, as would happen with a `TextView`, the view's viewable space grows. This is similar to the `Autosize` property in Windows forms development.

If you're using a static layout, these two attributes must be set in the XML layout. If you're creating views dynamically through code, the layout parameters must be set through Java code. Either way, you cannot be without them. I do not cover dynamic creation of views in this book. If you'd like to find out more about dynamic creation of views, see the API samples that come with the Android SDK.

If you forget to provide values for `layout_width` or `layout_height`, your Android application will crash when rendering the view. Thankfully, you find this out real quickly when you test your application.

As of Android 2.2, `fill_parent` has been renamed to `match_parent`. However, to maintain backward compatibility, `fill_parent` is still supported, which is why I'm using it here. However, if you plan on developing for Android 2.2 and above, it would be best to use `match_parent`.

Adding an Image to Your Application

Now you need to put some stuff on the screen! Although looking at text is fun and all, the real interesting components are added through input mechanisms and images. In the following sections, I demonstrate how to include images in your application.

Why you should worry about density folders

Android supports various screen sizes and densities. Earlier, you placed an image in the `mdpi` folder, which is for medium-density devices. What about small- and large-density devices? If Android cannot find the requested resource in the desired density, it opts for a density of the resource that it can find. What does this mean? If you're running on a high-density screen, the image will be stretched out and most likely quite pixilated. If you're running on a low-density device, it means that the image will be compressed to fit within the screen dimensions. To avoid this, create multiple versions of your image to target each screen density. For more information, see the Supporting Multiple Screens best practice guide in the Android documentation located at `http://developer.android.com/guide/practices/screens_support.html`.

Placing an image on the screen

The first thing you add is the phone image to the screen. This is the phone image that you see in Figure 4-4, earlier in this chapter. First you need (uh, yeah) the phone image. You can download that from the book's source code that is available online, or you can use your own.

Adding images to your project is simple. We simply drag them over and then reference them in the project.

1. **Drag the phone image into the `res/drawable-mdpi` folder in the Eclipse project, as shown in Figure 4-8.**

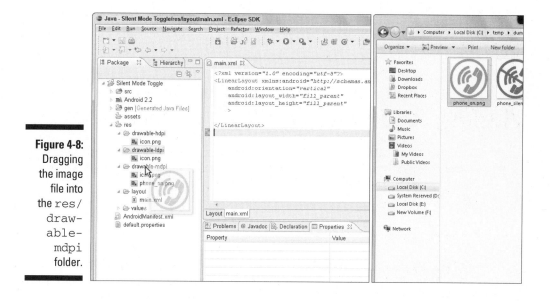

Figure 4-8:
Dragging the image file into the `res/drawable-mdpi` folder.

Notice that you see two states of the application: regular, as shown earlier in Figure 4-2, and silent, as shown earlier in Figure 4-3.

2. **Drag the other phone image — the silent one (or one of your own) — into the `res/drawable-mdpi` folder.**

To follow along with the rest of the chapter, the names of the images should be as follows:

- Regular mode image: `phone_on.png`

- Silent mode image: `phone_silent.png`

If your images are not named accordingly, you can rename them now. Your Eclipse project should now look like what is shown in Figure 4-9.

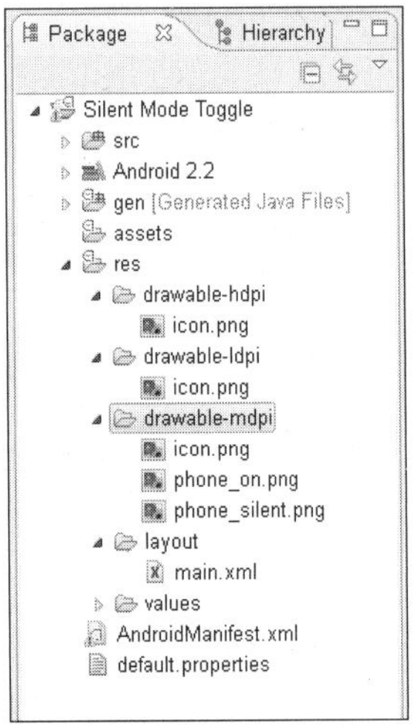

Figure 4-9:
The Silent
Mode
Toggle
project with
the phone
images.

When you dragged the images into Eclipse, the ADT recognized that the project file structure changed. At that time, the ADT rebuilt the project because the Build Automatically selection is enabled in the Project menu. This regenerated the `gen` folder, where the `R.java` file resides. The `R.java` file now includes a reference to the two new images that were recently added. You may now use these references to these resources to add images to your layout in code or in XML definition. You're going to declare them in XML layout in the following section.

Adding the image to the layout

Now it's time to add the image to the layout. To do that, you need to type the following into the `main.xml` file, overwriting the current contents of the file:

```xml
<?xml version="1.0" encoding="utf-8"?>
<LinearLayout xmlns:android="http://schemas.android.com/apk/res/android"
    android:orientation="vertical"
    android:layout_width="fill_parent"
    android:layout_height="fill_parent"
    >
    <ImageView
            android:id="@+id/phone_icon"
            android:layout_width="wrap_content"
            android:layout_height="wrap_content"
            android:layout_gravity="center_horizontal"
            android:src="@drawable/phone_on" />

</LinearLayout>
```

In this step, you added the `ImageView` inside the `LinearLayout`. An `ImageView` allows you to project an image to the device's screen.

Setting image properties

The `ImageView` contains a couple of extra parameters that you have not seen yet, so I cover those now:

- **The `android:id="@+id/phone_icon"` property:** The `id` attribute defines the unique identifier for the view in the Android system. I gave it a good college try to come up with a better explanation of the `android:id` value nomenclature, but nothing beats the actual Android documentation on the subject, which is located at `http://developer.android.com/guide/topics/ui/declaring-layout.html`.

- **The `layout_gravity` property:** This property defines how to place the view, both its x- and y-axis, with its parent. Here, I have defined the value as the `center_horizontal` constant. This value informs the Android system to place the object in the horizontal center of its container, not changing its size. You can use many other constants, such as `center_vertical`, `top`, `bottom`, `left`, `right`, and many more. See the `LinearLayout.LayoutParams` Android documentation for a full list.

- **The `android:src="@drawable/phone_on"` property:** This property is a direct child of the `ImageView` class. You use this property to set the image that you would like to show up on the screen.

Notice the value of the `src` property — `"@drawable/phone_on"`. What you're seeing now is the use of the `R.java` file. Here, you can reference drawable resources through XML. This is done by typing the at symbol (@) and the resource you're after.

Setting drawable resources

I did not type **@drawable-mdpi** for the drawable resource identifier; I typed **@drawable**. This is because it is Android's job to support multiple screen sizes, not yours (which makes life easy for you!). The Android layout system knows about drawables and that's all. It knows nothing of low-, medium-, or high-density drawables during design time. At run time, Android determines whether and when it can use low/medium/high-density drawables.

For example, if the app is running on a high-density device and the requested drawable resource is available in the `drawable-hdpi` folder, Android uses that resource. Otherwise, it uses the closest match it can find. Supporting various screen sizes and densities is a large topic (and complex in some aspects). Therefore, for an in-depth view into this subject, read the Managing Multiple Screen Sizes best practice article in the Android documentation.

The `phone_on` portion identifies the drawable that you want to use. The image filename is actually `phone_on.png`. However to stay within Java's member-naming guidelines, the file extension is removed, leaving `phone_on`. If you were to open the `R.java` file in the `gen` folder, you would see a member variable with the name of `phone_on`, not `phone_on.png`.

Thanks to the ADT, you can see your available options for this property through code completion. Place your cursor directly after `"@drawable/"` in the `src` property of the `ImageView` in the Eclipse editor. Then press Ctrl+spacebar. You should see the code completion dialog box, as shown in Figure 4-10. See the other resource names in there? These are other options that you could also choose for the `src` portion of the drawable definition.

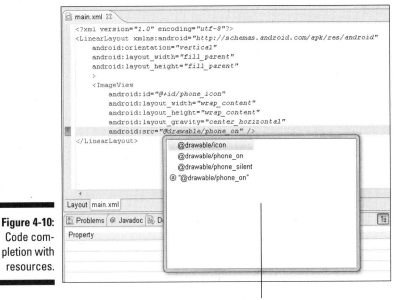

Figure 4-10: Code completion with resources.

Code completion

Creating a Launcher Icon for the Application

When your app gets installed, it has an icon that helps users identify its presence in the application launcher. When you created the Silent Mode Toggle application, the ADT automatically included a default launcher icon for you, as shown in Figure 4-11.

Figure 4-11:
The default
Android 2.2
launcher
icon.

Well, that's kind of bland, right? Exactly! You should change this icon to one of your own. I have a round phone icon that I created in an image-editing program, as shown in Figure 4-12. You can create your own (as shown in the following section) or use the one from the downloaded source code.

Figure 4-12:
The new
phone appli-
cation icon.

Designing a custom launcher icon

Creating your own launcher icons is fairly easy thanks to the Android project. The Android documentation contains a full article, entitled "Icon Design Guidelines, Android 2.0," that covers all aspects of icon design. This article contains a how-to manual for creating icons for the Android platform. The article also contains a style guide, dos and don'ts, materials and colors, size and positioning guidelines, and best of all, icon templates that you can use. You can find all of the design guidelines at `http://d.android.com/guide/ practices/ui_guidelines/icon_design.html`.

Working with templates

Because you've already downloaded the Android SDK, these icon templates and materials are available for you to use right now on your hard drive! Navigate to your Android SDK installation directory (from Chapter 2), and from there navigate to the `docs/shareables` directory. There you'll find various `.zip` files that contain templates and samples. Open the templates in the image-editing program of your choice and follow the design guidelines in the documentation to make your next rocking icon set.

Matching icon sizes with screen densities

Because each different screen density requires a different-size icon, how do you know how big the icon should be when designing it? Each density must have its own icon size to look appropriate (no pixilation, stretching, or compressing) on the screen.

Table 4-4 summarizes the finished icon sizes for each of the three generalized screen densities.

Table 4-4	Finished Icon Sizes
Screen Density	*Finished Icon Size*
Low-density screen (ldpi)	36 x 36 px
Medium-density screen (mdpi)	48 x 48 px
High-density screen (hdpi)	72 x 72 px

Adding a custom launcher icon

To place your custom launcher icon into the project, follow these steps:

1. **Rename your image icon to `icon.png`.**

2. **Drag your icon into the `mdpi` folder.**

    Eclipse asks whether you want to overwrite the existing `icon.png`, as shown in Figure 4-13. Click Yes.

Figure 4-13: Eclipse asks whether it's okay to overwrite the `icon.png` file.

You need to think about multiple densities when working with images. Icons are no different. You need to create three different versions of your icon (low-density, medium-density, and high-density) for it to show up correctly on the various devices. How to create your own launcher icons is discussed in the Android Design Guidelines, located at `http://d.android.com/guide/practices/ui_guidelines/icon_design.html`.

You're not done yet! What about the `ldpi` and `hdpi` folders? You need a low-density version of your icon as well as a high-density version. Copy those respective icons into the `ldpi` and `hdpi` folders.

If you don't copy the low- and high-density icons into their respective folders, users who have a low- or high-density device receive the default launcher icon, as shown in Figure 4-11, earlier in this chapter, whereas the medium-density devices receive the new icon that you dragged into the project.

How does this happen? You dragged the file into the `mdpi` folder; what gives? The `hdpi` and `ldpi` folders both contain their own version of the icon. Open the `drawable-hdpi` an `drawable-ldpi` folders in your Eclipse project and you can see that each density has its own `icon.png` file. Be sure to place the correct-size icon in each density-specific folder.

Adding a Toggle Button Widget

A widget is a `View` object that serves as an interface for interaction with the user. Android devices come fully equipped with various widgets that include buttons, check boxes, and text-entry fields so that you can quickly build your user interface. Some widgets are more complex, such as a date picker, a clock, and zoom controls.

Widgets also provide user interface events that inform you when a user has interacted with the particular widget, such as tapping a button.

The Android documentation can get a bit sticky at times and it is important to note that widgets and app widgets are regularly confused. They are two completely different topics. I am currently referring to widgets in the sense that you can find defined at `http://d.android.com/guide/practices/ui_guidelines/widget_design.html`.

You need to add a button widget to your application so that you can toggle the silent mode on the phone.

To add a button to your layout, type the following code after the `ImageView` that you added before:

```
<Button
        android:id="@+id/toggleButton"
        android:layout_width="wrap_content"
        android:layout_height="wrap_content"
        android:layout_gravity="center_horizontal"
        android:text="Toggle Silent Mode"
         />
```

You have now added a button to your view with an ID resource of toggleButton. This is how you will reference the button in the Java code (which I get to in the next chapter).

The height and width are set to wrap_content, which informs the Android layout system to place the widget on the screen and only take up as much usable space as it needs. The gravity property is the same as the ImageView above it, centered horizontally.

The final property that has been introduced in this view is the text property of the button. This sets the button's text to Toggle Silent Mode.

Your full code base should now look like this:

```
<?xml version="1.0" encoding="utf-8"?>
<LinearLayout xmlns:android="http://schemas.android.com/apk/res/android"
    android:orientation="vertical"
    android:layout_width="fill_parent"
    android:layout_height="fill_parent"
    >
    <ImageView
                android:id="@+id/phone_icon"
                android:layout_width="wrap_content"
                android:layout_height="wrap_content"
                android:layout_gravity="center_horizontal"
                android:src="@drawable/phone_on" />
    <Button
                android:id="@+id/toggleButton"
                android:layout_width="wrap_content"
                android:layout_height="wrap_content"
                android:layout_gravity="center_horizontal"
                android:text="Toggle Silent Mode"
                 />

</LinearLayout>
```

Previewing the Application in the Visual Designer

It's time to take a look at what the layout looks like in the visual designer. Click the Layouts tab to view the visual designer, as shown in Figure 4-14.

Figure 4-14: The visual designer view of the layout.

The ADT Visual Designer

The visual designer has many different configurations. By default, the designer is set to Android Development Phone 1 (ADP1). This was the first development phone that was offered by Google. As a developer, you could purchase an ADP1 device to test on. Future versions of the development phone have also been released. Selecting the Devices drop-down list in the visual designer shows you which ones you can work with. The configurations represent the various configurations that the device can be in. The ADP1 had three states that were valid at run time:

- **Landscape, closed:** Phone is in landscape mode, physical keyboard is hidden.
- **Portrait:** Phone is held in portrait mode.
- **Landscape, open:** Phone is in landscape mode, physical keyboard is extended.

Changing the orientation

Whoa! That doesn't look too good. You can't see the button. Thankfully that just requires a quick orientation change in the visual designer. To fix this, click the Config drop-down list and select Portrait.

Each device in the Devices drop-down list has its own set of configurations. You can create your own custom configurations by choosing Devices⇨Custom⇨Custom⇨New.

For purposes of this book, I use the ADP1 device.

Changing the background color

Yuck! The background is black and your image is white. That doesn't look right. You should make the background of your layout white to have the image blend into the background accordingly. Here's how to do that:

1. **Select the `main.xml` tab.**

2. **Add the `background` property to your `LinearLayout`:**

   ```
   android:background="#ffffff"
   ```

3. **Verify that the definition for `LinearLayout` looks like this:**

   ```
   <LinearLayout xmlns:android="http://schemas.android.
           com/apk/res/android"
       android:orientation="vertical"
       android:layout_width="fill_parent"
       android:layout_height="fill_parent"
       android:background="#ffffff">
   ```

4. **Save the file.**

5. **Select the Layout tab to view the visual designer.**

   Your screen should now look like what is shown in Figure 4-15.

   You set the background property to a hexadecimal value of #ffffff, which equates to an opaque white color. You can type any color in here, such as #ff0000, which equates to red. A background can also be set to an image through the use of a resource. However, you have no need for an image here; a color does just fine!

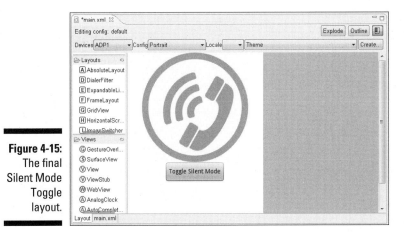

Figure 4-15:
The final
Silent Mode
Toggle
layout.

Congratulations! You just made the layout for the Slide Mode
Toggle application.

Chapter 5

Coding Your Application

I'm sure that you are champing at the bit to start coding your application; I know I would be if I were you! In this chapter, you're going to be coding your application, soup to nuts. But before you can start banging out some bits and bytes, you need a firm understanding of activities.

Understanding Activities

An activity is a single, focused thing a user can do. For example, an activity might present a list of menu items a use can choose from, or it might display photographs along with their caption. An application may consist of just one activity, or like most applications in the Android system, it can contain several. Though activities may work together to appear to be one cohesive application, they are actually independent of each other. An *activity* in Android is an important part of an application's overall life cycle, and the way the activities are launched and put together is a fundamental part of the Android's application model. Each activity is implemented as an implementation of the `Activity` base class.

Almost all activities interact with the user, so the `Activity` class takes care of creating the window for you in which you can place your user interface (UI). Activities are most often presented in full-screen mode, but in some instances, you can find an activity floating in a window or embedded inside another activity — this is known as an *activity group*.

Working with methods, stacks, and states

Almost all activities implement these two methods:

- ✔ onCreate: This is where you initialize your activity. Most importantly, this is where you tell the activity what layout to use using layout resource identifiers. This can be considered the entry point of your activity.

- ✔ onPause: This is where you deal with the user leaving your activity. Most importantly, any changes made by the user should be committed at this point (that is, if you need to save them).

Activities in the system are managed as an *activity stack*. When a new activity is created, it is placed on top of the stack and becomes the running activity. The previous running activity always remains below it in the stack and does not come to the foreground again until the new activity exits.

I cannot stress enough the importance of understanding how and why the activity works behind the scenes. Not only will you come away with a better understanding of the Android platform, but you will also be able to accurately troubleshoot why your application is doing very odd things at run time.

An activity has essentially four states, as shown in Table 5-1.

Table 5-1	Four Essential States of an Activity
Activity State	*Description*
Active/running	The activity is in the foreground of the screen (at the top of the stack).
Paused	The activity has lost focus but is still visible (that is, a new non-full-sized or transparent activity has focus on top of your activity). A paused activity is completely alive, meaning that it can completely maintain state and member information and remains attached to the window manager that controls the windows in Android. However, note that the activity can be killed by the Android system in extreme low-memory conditions.
Stopped	If an activity becomes completely obscured by another activity, it is stopped. It retains all state and member information, but it is not visible to the user. Therefore, the window is hidden and will often be killed by the Android system when memory is needed elsewhere.
Create and resuming	The system has either paused or stopped the activity. The system can either reclaim the memory by asking it to finish or it can kill the process. When it displays that activity to the user, it must resume by restarting and restoring to its previous state.

Tracking an activity's life cycle

Pictures are worth a thousand words, and flow diagrams are worth ten times that in my opinion. The following diagram (Figure 5-1) shows the important paths of an activity. This is the *activity life cycle.*

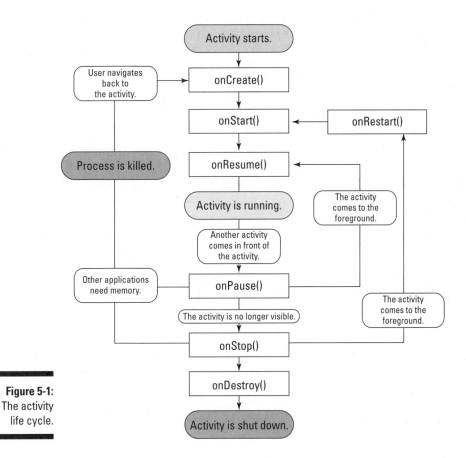

Figure 5-1:
The activity
life cycle.

The rectangles represent callback methods you can implement to respond to events in the activity. The shaded ovals are the major states that the activity can be in.

Monitoring key loops

You may be interested in monitoring these three loops in your activity:

✔ The **entire lifetime** takes place between the first call to `onCreate()` and the final call to `onDestroy()`. The activity performs all the global setup in `onCreate()` and releases all remaining resources in `onDestroy()`. For example, if you create a thread to download a file from the Internet in the background, that may be initialized in the `onCreate()` method. That thread could be stopped in the `onDestroy()` method.

✔ The **visible lifetime** of the activity takes place between the `onStart()` and `onStop()` methods. During this time, the user can see the activity on the screen (though it may not be in the foreground interacting with the user — this can happen when the user is interacting with a dialog box). Between these two methods, you can maintain the resources that are needed to show and run your activity. For example, you could create an event handler to monitor the state of the phone. The phone state could change, and this event handler could inform the activity that the phone is going into Airplane mode and react accordingly. You would set up the event handler in `onStart()` and tear down any resources you are accessing in `onStop()`. The `onStart()` and `onStop()` methods can be called multiple times as the activity becomes visible or hidden to the user.

✔ The **foreground lifetime** of the activity begins at the call to `onResume()` and ends at the call to `onPause()`. During this time, the activity is in front of all other activities and is interacting with the user. It is normal for an activity to go between `onResume()` and `onPause()` multiple times, for example, when the device goes to sleep or when a new activity handles a particular event; therefore, the code in these methods must be fairly lightweight.

Viewing activity methods

The entire activity life cycle boils down to the following methods. All methods can be overridden, and custom code can be placed in all of them. All activities implement `onCreate()` for initialization and may also implement `onPause()` for cleanup. You should always call the superclass (base class) when implementing these methods:

```
public class Activity extends ApplicationContext {
    protected void onCreate(Bundle savedInstanceState);
    protected void onStart();
    protected void onRestart();
    protected void onResume();
    protected void onPause();
    protected void onStop();
    protected void onDestroy();
}
```

Following an activity's path

In general, the movement an activity makes through its life cycle looks like this:

✔ onCreate(): Called when the activity is first created. This is where you would initialize most of your activity's class-wide variables. onStart() is always called next. Killable: No. Next: onStart().

✔ onRestart(): Called after your activity has been stopped prior to being started again. onStart() is always called next. Killable: No. Next: onStart().

✔ onStart(): Called when your activity is becoming visible to the user. Followed by onResume() if the activity is brought to the foreground or onStop() if it becomes hidden from the user. Killable: No. Next: onResume() or onStop().

✔ onResume(): Called when the activity will be available for interacting with the user. The activity is at the top of the activity stack at this point. Killable: No. Next: onPause().

✔ onPause(): Called when the system is about to resume a previous activity or if the user has navigated away to another portion of the system, such as pressing the home key. This stage is typically used to commit unsaved changes to data that needs to be persisted. If the activity is brought back to the foreground, onResume() is called; if the activity becomes invisible to the user, onStop() is called. Killable: Yes. Next: onResume() or onStop().

✔ onStop(): Called when the activity is no longer visible to the user because another activity has resumed and is covering this one. This may happen because another activity has started or a previous activity has resumed and is now in the foreground of the activity stack. Followed by onRestart() if this activity is coming back to interact with the user or onDestroy() if this activity is going away. Killable: Yes. Next: onRestart() or onDestroy().

✔ onDestroy(): The final call you receive before your activity is destroyed. This method gets called either because the activity is finishing (such as someone calling finish() on it or because the system is temporarily destroying the activity to reclaim space). You can distinguish between these two with the isFinishing() method, which helps identify whether the method is actually finishing or the system is killing it. The isFinishing() method is often used inside of onPause() to determine whether the activity is pausing or being destroyed. Killable: Yes. Next: Nothing.

Did you see the Killable notation at the end of each activity method description? Here's why you need to know about it. Methods that are marked as killable can be killed by the Android system at any time without notice. Because of this, you should use the onPause() method to do any last cleanup to write any persistent data (such as user edits to data) to your storage mechanism.

Recognizing configuration changes

One last item about the life cycle, and then you can start coding. The last tidbit you need to be aware of concerns configuration changes. *A configuration change* is defined as a change in screen orientation (the user moving the screen to the side and then back, portrait to landscape and vice versa), language, input devices, and so on. When a configuration change happens, this causes your activity to be destroyed, going through the normal activity life cycle of `onPause()`⇨`onStop()`⇨`onDestroy()`. After the `onDestroy()` method is called, the system creates a new instance of the activity to be created. This takes place because resources, layout files, and so on might need to change depending on the current system configuration. For example, an application may look completely different if it is interacting with the user in portrait mode as compared to being displayed in landscape mode (on its side).

The activity life cycle is a large and complex topic. I have introduced you to the basics so that you understand the applications you will be building in this book. I highly advise that you set aside some time after you get done reading this book to read through the Activity Life Cycle and Process Life Cycle documentation in the Android documentation. You can find out more about the process life cycle at `http://d.android.com/reference/android/app/Activity.html#ProcessLifecycle`.

You can find out more information about the activity life cycle at `http://d.android.com/reference/android/app/Activity.html#ActivityLifecycle`.

Creating Your First Activity

It's time to create your first activity! Well, you actually already created your first activity when you created a project through the New Android Project wizard. Therefore, you will not be creating a new activity in this project; you will be working with the `MainActivity.java` file in your project. Open this file now.

Starting with onCreate

As you read previously, the entry point into your application is the `onCreate()` method. The code for your `MainActivity.java` file already contains an implementation of the `onCreate()` method. This is where you're going to start writing some code. Right now, your code should look like this:

```
public class MainActivity extends Activity {
    /** Called when the activity is first created. */
    @Override
    public void onCreate(Bundle savedInstanceState) {
        super.onCreate(savedInstanceState);
        setContentView(R.layout.main);
    }
}
```

You will be writing initialization code directly below the setContentView() method shortly.

Pay attention to the following line:

```
super.onCreate(savedInstanceState);
```

This line of code is required for the application to run. This calls to the base Activity class to perform setup work for the MainActivity class. If you do not include this line of code, you will receive a run-time exception. Be sure that you always include this method call to your onCreate() method.

Handling the bundle

In the code snippet above, notice the following:

```
Bundle savedInstanceState
```

The *bundle* is a key value that maps between string keys and various parcelable types. A bundle gives you, the developer, a way to pass information back and forth between screens (different activities) in what's known as a bundle. You can place various types into a bundle and receive them on the target activity. I cover this later in Part III, when I walk you through building the Task Reminder application.

Telling Android to display the UI

By default, an activity has no idea what its UI is. It could be a simple form that allows the user to type information in to be saved, it could be a visual camera–based augmented virtual reality application (such as Layar in the Android Market), or it could be a drawn-on-the-fly UI such as a 2D or 3D game. As a developer, it is your job to tell the activity which layout the a ctivity should load.

To get the UI to show up on the screen, you have to set the content view for the activity. That is done with the following line of code:

```
setContentView(R.layout.main);
```

R.layout.main is the main.xml file that is located in the res/layouts directory. This is the layout you defined in the previous chapter.

Handling user input

The Silent Mode Toggle application does not have a lot of user interaction; actually it has very little. The only user interaction your application will have is a single button. The user taps the button to toggle the silent mode on the phone, and then the user can tap the button again to turn off the silent mode.

To respond to this tap event, you need to register what is known as an event listener. An *event listener* responds to an event in the Android system. You find various types of events in the Android system, but two of the most commonly used events are going to be touch events (also known as clicks) and keyboard events.

Keyboard events

Keyboard events occur when a particular keyboard key has been pressed. Why would you want to know about this? Take the example of providing *hot keys* for your application. If the user presses Alt+E, you may want your view to toggle into Edit mode. Responding to keyboard events allows you to do this. I will not be using keyboard events in this book, but if you need to in future applications, you need to override the onKeyDown method, as shown here:

```
@Override
public boolean onKeyDown(int keyCode, KeyEvent event) {
        // TODO Auto-generated method stub
        return super.onKeyDown(keyCode, event);
}
```

Touch events

Touch events occur when the user taps a widget on the screen. The Android platform recognizes each tap event as a click event. From here on, the terms *tap, click,* and *touch* are synonymous. Examples of widgets that can respond to touch events include (but are not limited to):

- Button
- ImageButton
- EditText

✔ Spinner

✔ List Item Row

✔ Menu Item

 All views in the Android system can react to a tap; however, some of the widgets have their *clickable* property set to false by default. You can override this in your layout file or in code to allow a view to be clickable by setting the `clickable` attribute on the view or the `setClickable()` method in code.

Writing your first event handler

In order for your application to respond to the click event of the user toggling the Silent Mode, you need to respond to the click event exposed by the button.

Entering the code

Type the code shown in Listing 5-1 into your editor. This code shows how to implement a click handler for the `toggleButton`. This is the entire `onCreate()` method with the new code. Feel free to either fill in the button code or overwrite your entire `onCreate` code.

Listing 5-1:   The Initial Class File with a Default Button OnClickListener

```
@Override
public void onCreate(Bundle savedInstanceState) {
    super.onCreate(savedInstanceState);
    setContentView(R.layout.main);

    Button toggleButton = (Button)findViewById(R.id.toggleButton);
    toggleButton.setOnClickListener(new View.OnClickListener() {

        public void onClick(View v) {

        }

    });

}
```

This code used the `findViewById()` method, which is available to all activities in Android. This method allows you to find any view inside the activity's layout and do some work with it. This method always returns a `View` class that you must cast to the appropriate type before you can work with it. In the following code (which is a snippet from the previous code), you are casting the returned `View` from `findViewById()` to a `Button` (which is a subclass of `View`).

```
Button toggleButton = (Button)findViewById(R.id.toggleButton);
```

Immediately following this line of code, you start setting up the event handler.

The event-handling code is placed inline after you retrieved the `Button` from the layout. Setting up the event handler is as simple as setting a new `View.OnClickListener`. This click listener contains a `Click()` method that will be called after the button is tapped. This is where I will be placing the code to handle the silent mode toggle.

If the type in your layout file is different than what you are casting it to (you have an `ImageView` in the layout file and you're trying to cast it to `ImageButton`), you will receive a run-time error. Be sure that you're casting to the appropriate type.

When you typed this code into your editor, you may have seen some red squiggly lines, as shown in Figure 5-2. These lines are Eclipse's way of telling you, "Hey! I don't know what this 'Button' thing is." If you place your cursor over the squiggly line and leave it there for a moment, you receive a small context window that gives you several options, as shown in Figure 5-2.

Figure 5-2:
Eclipse informing you that it cannot find the class with a red squiggly line. Hovering your cursor over the line provides a context menu of options.

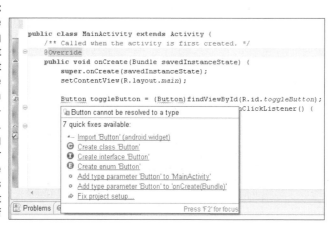

Choose the first option, Import 'Button'. This adds the following import statement to the top of the file:

```
import android.widget.Button;
```

This import statement informs Eclipse where the `Button` is located in the Android packages. You may also need to import the `android.view.package` as well.

As you start to develop more applications, you will include many other widgets as part of your application, and you will notice that you have to include quite a few imports to get your application to compile. While this is not a huge issue, you can provide a shorthand method of including everything in a particular package. You can do this by providing an asterisk at the end of the package name, as shown here:

```
import android.widget.*;
```

This informs Eclipse to include all widgets in the `android.widget` package.

Extracting the code to a method

The code is starting to get unwieldy and is becoming hard to read. At this point, the best thing you can do is extract your new button code to a method that you can call from within `onCreate()`. To do that, you need to create a private void method called `setButtonClickListener()` that contains the button code you just typed. This new method is placed in the `onCreate()` method. The new code is shown in Listing 5-2.

Listing 5-2   Button Listener Extracted to a Method

```
public class MainActivity extends Activity {
    /** Called when the activity is first created. */
    @Override
    public void onCreate(Bundle savedInstanceState) {
        super.onCreate(savedInstanceState);
        setContentView(R.layout.main);

        setButtonClickListener();                              → 16
    }

    private void setButtonClickListener() {                    → 19
        Button toggleButton = (Button)findViewById(R.id.toggleButton);
        toggleButton.setOnClickListener(new View.OnClickListener() {
            public void onClick(View v) {
                // TODO Auto-generated method stub
            }
        });
    }
}
```

→ 16   On this line, I call a method to set up the button click listener.

→ 19   The new method is getting called.

It's now time to respond to the click event by providing some code for the `onClick()` method of your button.

Working with the Android Framework Classes

You're now getting into the good stuff: the real nitty-gritty of Android development — the Android framework classes! Yes, activities, views, and widgets are integral parts of the system, but when it comes down to it, they're plumbing and they're required in any modern operating system (in one capacity or another). The real fun is just about to start.

You're now going to check the state of the phone ringer to determine whether it is in a normal mode (loud and proudly ringing) or in silent mode. At that point, you can begin to start toggling the phone ringer mode.

Getting good service

To access the Android ringer, you're going to need access to the `AudioManager` in Android, which is responsible for managing the ringer state. Because you're going to need to use the `AudioManager` a lot in this activity, its best to initialize it in `onCreate()`. Remember, all important initialization needs to happen in `onCreate()`!

You first need to create a private class-level `AudioManager` variable by the name of `mAudioManager`. Type this at the top of your class file, directly after the class declaration line, as shown in Listing 5-3.

Listing 5-3:   Adding the Class-Level `AudioManager` Variable

```
package com.dummies.android.silentmodetoggle;

import android.app.Activity;
import android.media.AudioManager;                                    → 4
import android.os.Bundle;
import android.view.View;
import android.widget.Button;

public class MainActivity extends Activity {

        private AudioManager mAudioManager;                           → 11

    @Override
    public void onCreate(Bundle savedInstanceState) {
        super.onCreate(savedInstanceState);
        setContentView(R.layout.main);

        setButtonClickListener();
```

```
      mAudioManager = (AudioManager)getSystemService(AUDIO_SERVICE);      → 20
    }

    private void setButtonClickListener() {
        Button toggleButton = (Button)findViewById(R.id.toggleButton);
        toggleButton.setOnClickListener(new View.OnClickListener() {
            public void onClick(View v) {
                // TODO Auto-generated method stub
            }
        });
    }
}
```

Here is a brief explanation of what the following lines do:

→ **4**   The `import` statement that brings in the necessary package so that you can use the `AudioManager`.

→ **11**   The `private` class-level `AudioManager` variable. This is class wide so that you can have access to it in other parts of the activity.

→ **20**   Initializing the `mAudioManager` variable by getting the service from the base `Activity getSystemService()` method call.

Whoa! What's this `getSystemService(...)` stuff? By inheriting from the base `Activity` class, you receive all the benefits of being an activity. In this case, you have access to the `getSystemService()` method call. This method returns the base Java `Object` class; therefore, you have to cast it to the type of service that you are requesting.

This call returns all available system services that you might need to work with. All the services that are returned can be found in the `Context` class in the Android documentation, located at `http://d.android.com/reference/android/content/Context.html`. Some popular system services include

✔ Audio service

✔ Location service

✔ Alarm service

Toggling silent mode with AudioManager

Now that you have a class-wide instance of `AudioManager`, you can start checking the state of the ringer as well as toggling the ringer. This is done in Listing 5-4; all new or modified code is presented in bold.

Listing 5-4: Adding the Application Toggle to the App

```
package com.dummies.android.silentmodetoggle;

import android.app.Activity;
import android.graphics.drawable.Drawable;
import android.media.AudioManager;
import android.os.Bundle;
import android.view.View;
import android.widget.Button;
import android.widget.ImageView;

public class MainActivity extends Activity {

        private AudioManager mAudioManager;
        private boolean mPhoneIsSilent;                                → 14

    @Override
    public void onCreate(Bundle savedInstanceState) {
        super.onCreate(savedInstanceState);
        setContentView(R.layout.main);

        mAudioManager = (AudioManager)getSystemService(AUDIO_SERVICE);

        checkIfPhoneIsSilent();                                        → 23

        setButtonClickListener();                                      → 25
    }

    private void setButtonClickListener() {
            Button toggleButton = (Button)findViewById(R.id.toggleButton);
            toggleButton.setOnClickListener(new View.OnClickListener() {
                public void onClick(View v) {

                    if (mPhoneIsSilent) {                              → 32
                        // Change back to normal mode
                        mAudioManager
                            .setRingerMode(AudioManager.RINGER_MODE_NORMAL);
                        mPhoneIsSilent = false;
                    } else {
                        // Change to silent mode
                        mAudioManager
                            .setRingerMode(AudioManager.RINGER_MODE_SILENT);
                        mPhoneIsSilent = true;
                    }

                    // Now toggle the UI again
                    toggleUi();                                        → 44
                }
        });
  }

    /**
     * Checks to see if the phone is currently in silent mode.
```

```
*/
        private void checkIfPhoneIsSilent() {                    → 53
            int ringerMode = mAudioManager.getRingerMode();
            if (ringerMode == AudioManager.RINGER_MODE_SILENT) {
                mPhoneIsSilent = true;
            } else {
                mPhoneIsSilent = false;
            }
        }


        /**
         * Toggles the UI images from silent to normal and vice versa.
         */
        private void toggleUi() {                                → 66

        ImageView imageView = (ImageView) findViewById(R.id.phone_icon);
        Drawable newPhoneImage;

        if (mPhoneIsSilent) {

            newPhoneImage =
                getResources().getDrawable(R.drawable.phone_silent);

        } else {
            newPhoneImage =
                getResources().getDrawable(R.drawable.phone_on);
        }

        imageView.setImageDrawable(newPhoneImage);
        }

    @Override                                                    → 84
    protected void onResume() {
        super.onResume();
        checkIfPhoneIsSilent();
        toggleUi();
    }
}
```

That's a lot of new stuff happening! Following is a brief explanation of what each new section of code does:

→ **14**   Sets up a new class-level `boolean mPhoneIsSilent` variable to keep track of what state the ringer is in.

→ **23**   Calls the `checkIfPhoneIsSilent()` method to initialize `mPhoneIsSilent`. The default value of a `boolean` is false — which could be wrong if the phone is currently in silent mode. This needs to be initialized to figure out what happens when the ringer mode gets toggled.

→ **25**   The button event-handling code was moved to the bottom of the `onCreate()` method because it depends on the setup of the `mPhoneIsSilent` variable. Even though most likely nothing will happen, it's best to keep the code organized. Clean code makes for manageable code.

→ 32 The code between lines 32 and 44 handles a user tap on the toggle button. This code checks to see whether the ringer is currently enabled through the class-level `mPhoneIsSilent` variable. If the ringer is silent, the code will fall into the first `if` block and change the ringer mode to `RINGER_MODE_NORMAL`, which turns the ringer back on. The `mPhoneIsSilent` variable also gets changed to `false` for the next time this code runs. If the ringer is not silent, the code falls into the `else` code block. This code block turns the ringer mode from its current state to `RINGER_MODE_SILENT`, which turns the ringer off. The `else` block also sets the `mPhoneIsSilent` variable to `true` for the next time around.

→ 44 The `toggleUi()` method changes the user interface to give the user a visual identifier that the mode has changed on the phone. Anytime the ringer mode is changed, the `toggleUi()` method needs to get called.

→ 53 The `checkIfPhoneIsSilent()` method initializes the `mPhoneIsSilent` class-level variable in the `onCreate()` method. Without doing this, your application would not know what state the `AudioManager`'s ringer was in. If the phone is silent, `mPhoneIsSilent` gets set to `true`; otherwise, it is `false`.

→ 66 This `toggleUi()` method changes the `ImageView` from the layout you created in the last chapter, depending on the state of the ringer. If the ringer is silent, the UI displays an image that shows the phone ringer is off, as shown in Figure 4-5. If the phone's ringer is in normal mode, the image is as shown in Figure 4-4. Both of these images were created in the resource directories in Chapter 4. The `ImageView` is found inside the layout, and after the mode is determined, the `View` is updated by pulling the correct image from `getResources().getDrawable(...)` and set with the `setImageDrawable(...)` call on the `ImageView`. This method updates the image that is displayed on the `ImageView` on the screen.

→ 84 Remember when I said that you need to know the activity life cycle? This is one of those instances where we're practicing such a claim! The `onResume()` method is overridden for your application to correctly identify what state it currently is in. Yes, the `mPhoneIsSilent` variable is used to keep track of the phone ringer state, but that's only for the class. The user of your application needs to know what state the phone is in as well! Therefore `onResume()` calls `ToggleUi()` to toggle the UI. Because `onResume()` takes place after `onCreate()`, `toggleUI()` can rely on the `mPhoneIsSilent` variable to be in the correct state to update the UI. The `toggleUi()` call is strategically placed in the `onResume()` method for one simple reason: to assume that the user opens the Silent Toggle Mode application and then returns to the home screen and turns the phone off with the phone controls. When the user returns to the activity, it resumes, bringing it to the foreground. At that time, `onResume()` is called to check the state of the ringer mode and update the UI accordingly. If the user changed the mode, the app will react as the user would expect!

Installing Your Application

You've done it! You wrote your first application. In the next couple of steps, you're going to install it on the emulator and get this baby into action!

Returning to the emulator

The application will run on an emulator (I know; I tried already), so that's the next step. You previously set up a run configuration to run the Hello Android application. You will be using the same launch configuration as you did previously. Because the ADT is smart enough to know about this launch configuration, it will use it by default. Therefore, it's time to install this app on the emulator! Follow these steps:

1. **In Eclipse, choose Run⇨Run or press Ctrl+F11 to run the application.**

   You are presented with the Run As window, as shown in Figure 5-3. Choose Android Application and click the OK button. This starts the emulator.

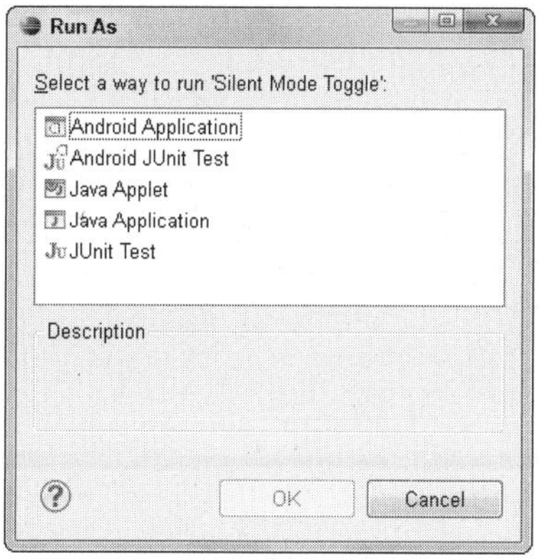

Figure 5-3: The Run As configuration dialog box.

2. **Wait for the emulator to load and then unlock the emulator.**

If you're not sure how to unlock the emulator, refer to Chapter 3. When the emulator is unlocked, your application should start. If it does not start, rerun the application by choosing Run➪Run or pressing Ctrl+F11. After the application starts, you should see the emulator running your program, as shown in Figure 5-4.

Figure 5-4:
The emulator running the application.

3. **Click the Toggle Silent Mode button to see the image change to the strikethrough red phone, as shown in Figure 5-5.**

Also, notice in the notification bar that a new icon is present — the Silent Notification icon.

Silent notification icon

Figure 5-5:
The app in silent mode with the Silent Notification icon present.

4. Return to the home screen by clicking the home button on the emulator.

Open the application (center button at the bottom of screen). You now see the application launcher icon present in the list of applications.

Installing on a physical Android device

Installing the application on a device is no different than installing an application on the emulator. You need to make a few small adjustments to get it to work. You installed the driver in Chapter 2, so the rest is fairly straightforward:

1. Enable the installation of non–Android Market applications.

2. From the home screen of your phone, access the Settings panel (choose Menu⇨Settings). Choose Applications.

3. Select the Unknown Sources check box, as shown in Figure 5-6.

You will most likely want to be able to debug on your device.

Figure 5-6: Setting to allow the installation of non–Android Market applications.

4. While in the Applications Settings screen (the same screen where you made the last change), choose Development and select the USB Debugging option, as shown in Figure 5-7.

This allows you to debug your application on your device (more on debugging in a moment).

Figure 5-7:
Enabling
your device
to perform
USB
debugging.

5. **Plug your phone into the computer using a USB cable.**

6. **When the phone is detected on your system, run the application by either choosing Run⇨Run or pressing Ctrl+F11.**

   At this point, the ADT has recognized another option for a launch configuration; therefore, it is going to ask you which device you want to run the application under with the Android Device Chooser dialog box. In Figure 5-8, I have plugged in my Nexus One phone, and it is showing up with a different icon than the emulator to help me identify which is a device and which is an emulator. Please note: The emulator won't show up in the list of available options unless the emulator is running.

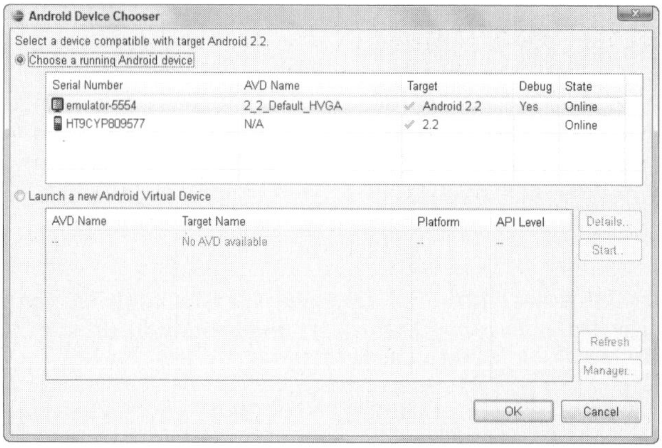

Figure 5-8:
The Android
Device
Chooser.

7. **Choose your phone from the list and click the OK button.**

   This sends the application to your phone, and it launches it just as it would with the emulator. In a few seconds, the app should show up on your phone.

   You've now deployed the application to your phone.

Reinstalling Your Application

You may have noticed that installing your application to a physical device was fairly simple. In fact, after the device is set up to allow non-Market applications to be installed, you take virtually the same steps.

Well, the same goes for reinstalling your application. You don't have to do anything special to reinstall your application. When would you reinstall your application? Simple — you change something in the app and you need to test it again.

Understanding the state of the emulator

After the emulator is running, it's running on its own. The emulator has no dependencies on Eclipse. In fact, you can close Eclipse and still interact with the emulator.

The emulator and Eclipse speak to each other through the Android Debugging Bridge (ADB). ADB is a tool that was installed with the Android Development Tools (ADT).

Doing the reinstallation

The application reinstall process is fairly simple. To reinstall an application, perform the same steps that you would when you initially installed the application: Choose Run⇨Run or press Ctrl+F11.

Now that was easy.

Uh-oh!: Responding to Errors

You wrote perfect code, right? I thought so! Well, I have a secret to tell: I don't always write perfect code. When things don't go as planned, I have to figure out what is going on. To help developers in these dire situations of random application crashes, the ADT provides some valuable tools to help debug your application.

Using the Dalvik Debug Monitor Server

The Dalvik Debug Monitor Server (DDMS) is a debugging tool that provides the following features (among others):

- Port forwarding
- Screen capture
- Thread and heap information on the device
- LogCat (provides dumps of system log messages)
- Process and radio state information
- Incoming call and SMS spoofing
- Location data spoofing

DDMS can work with an emulator and a connected device. DDMS is located in the Android SDK `tools` directory. In Chapter 1, you added the `tools` directory to your path; therefore, you should be able to access DDMS from the command line.

Why you should get to know DDMS

Debugging is rarely fun. Thankfully, DDMS provides the tools necessary to help you dig yourself out of a hole of bugs. One of the most commonly used features in DDMS is the LogCat viewer, which allows you to view the output of system log messages from your system, as shown in Figure 5-9. This system log reports everything from basic information messages, which include the state of the application and device, to warning and error information. When you receive an Application Not Responding or a Force Close error on the device, it's not clear what happened. Opening DDMS and reviewing the entries in LogCat can help identify, down to the line number, where the exception is occurring. DDMS won't solve the problem for you (darn it!), but it can make tracking down the root cause of the issue much easier.

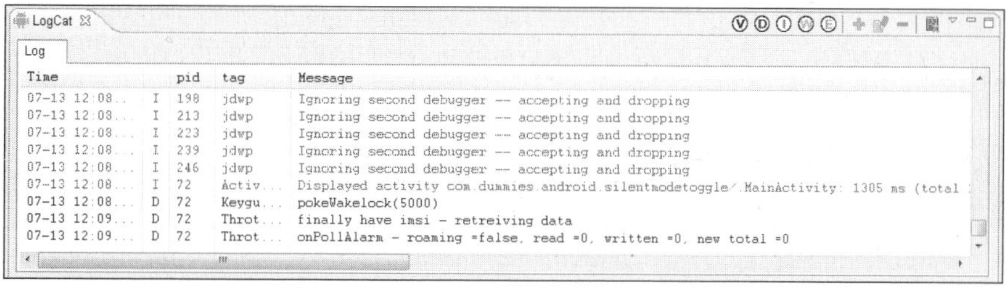

Figure 5-9:
A view of
LogCat.

DDMS is also very useful in scenarios where you do not have an actual device to test with. A key example of this is that you might be developing an application that uses GPS and a Google MapView to show a map on the screen. Your application is based on a user moving across a map. If you don't have a device that has GPS, or a device at all for that matter, this becomes a very nontrivial task! Thankfully, DDMS is here to help. DDMS provides tools through what's known as location control. As a developer, you can manually provide GPS coordinates, or you can provide a GPS eXchange Format (GPX) file or a Keyhole Markup Language (KML) file that represents points on a map that can be timed accordingly (for example, stay at this point for 5 seconds, go to this point, and then go to the next point, and so on).

I'm barely scratching the surface of DDMS and its feature set. I'm going to show you how to get messages into DDMS as well as how to view them from Eclipse.

How to get log messages into DDMS

Getting messages into DDMS is as simple as supplying one line of code. Open the `MainActivity.java` file, and at the bottom of the method, add a log entry, as shown in bold in Listing 5-5.

Listing 5-5:   The onCreate() Method

```
@Override
public void onCreate(Bundle savedInstanceState) {
    super.onCreate(savedInstanceState);
    setContentView(R.layout.main);

    mAudioManager = (AudioManager)getSystemService(AUDIO_SERVICE);

    checkIfPhoneIsSilent();

    setButtonClickListener();

    Log.d("SilentModeApp", "This is a test");           → 12
}
```

The code listed at → **12** demonstrates how to get a message into the system log. `SilentModeApp` is known as the `TAG` that you're giving this log entry; the second parameter to the log call is the message that you want to output. The tag helps filter messages while looking at them in DDMS.

A good convention to follow is to declare a `TAG` constant in your code and use that instead of repeatedly typing the `TAG`. An example would be

```
private static final String TAG = "SilentModeApp";
```

Notice the `d` in `Log.d` in Listing 5-5. The `d` means that this is a debug message. Other options are as follows:

- ✔ `e`: error.
- ✔ `I`: info.
- ✔ `wtf`: What a terrible error (yes, I'm serious, it's there!).
- ✔ `v`: verbose.

The various logging types exist for you to decide how various messages should be logged.

You have to import the `android.util.Log` package for logging to work.

How to view DDMS messages

You're probably wondering how you can view the DDMS messages. You can view DDMS by either opening DDMS manually or by opening the DDMS perspective in Eclipse:

- ✔ **Manual method:** Navigate to where you installed the Android SDK. Inside the tools directory, double-click the `ddms.bat` file. This starts the DDMS application outside of the Eclipse IDE, as shown in Figure 5-10.

- ✔ **In Eclipse:** The ADT has installed a DDMS perspective. To open the DDMS perspective, click the Open Perspective button, as shown in Figure 5-11, and choose DDMS. If DDMS is not visible in this view, select the Other option and then select DDMS. This adds a DDMS perspective to the list of perspectives that you can easily toggle between. You should have been automatically switched to the DDMS perspective. You can view LogCat (usually near the bottom of the screen). I prefer to move my LogCat window to the main area of the screen, as shown in Figure 5-12. To move your LogCat window to this location, simply drag the LogCat tab title and drop it to the location you want.

Figure 5-10:
An instance
of DDMS
running
separately
from
Eclipse.

Dalvik Debug Monitor

File Edit Actions Device Help

Name			
◢ 📱 emulator-5554	Online		2_2_Def...
?	72		8600
?	118		8601
?	113		8602
?	121		8603
?	140		8604
?	153		8605

Info | Threads | VM Heap | Allocation Tracker | Sysinfo | Emulator Control | Event Log

DDM-aware? -
App description: -
VM version: -
Process ID: -
Supports Profiling Control: -
Supports HPROF Control: -

Log

Time	pid	tag	Message
07-13 12:4...	I 113	jdwp	Ignoring second debugger -- accepting and dropping
07-13 12:4...	I 121	jdwp	Ignoring second debugger -- accepting and dropping
07-13 12:4...	I 140	jdwp	Ignoring second debugger -- accepting and dropping
07-13 12:4...	I 153	jdwp	Ignoring second debugger -- accepting and dropping
07-13 12:4...	I 184	jdwp	Ignoring second debugger -- accepting and dropping
07-13 12:4...	I 195	jdwp	Ignoring second debugger -- accepting and dropping
07-13 12:4...	I 198	jdwp	Ignoring second debugger -- accepting and dropping
07-13 12:4...	I 213	jdwp	Ignoring second debugger -- accepting and dropping
07-13 12:4...	I 223	jdwp	Ignoring second debugger -- accepting and dropping
07-13 12:4...	I 239	jdwp	Ignoring second debugger -- accepting and dropping
07-13 12:4...	I 246	jdwp	Ignoring second debugger -- accepting and dropping
07-13 12:4...	I 252	jdwp	Ignoring second debugger -- accepting and dropping
07-13 12:4...	I 270	jdwp	Ignoring second debugger -- accepting and dropping
07-13 12:4...	D 72	SntpClient	request time failed: java.net.SocketException: Address family not supported by protocol

Filter:

Open Perspective button

Figure 5-11:
The Open
Perspective
button.

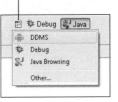

🖥 ⚙ Debug 🔵 Java

📱 DDMS
⚙ Debug
🔍 Java Browsing
Other...

Now, start your application by choosing Run⇨Run or by pressing
Ctrl+F11. When your application is running in the emulator, open the
DDMS perspective and look for your log message. It should look somewhat similar to what is shown in Figure 5-13. The other system log messages may be different on your machine, but the log you typed will be
the same as mine.

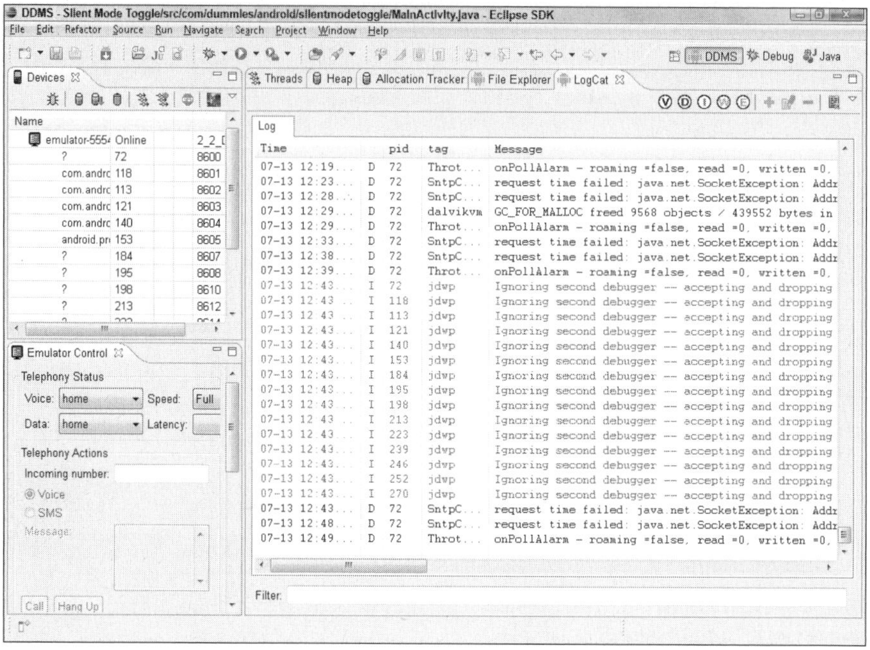

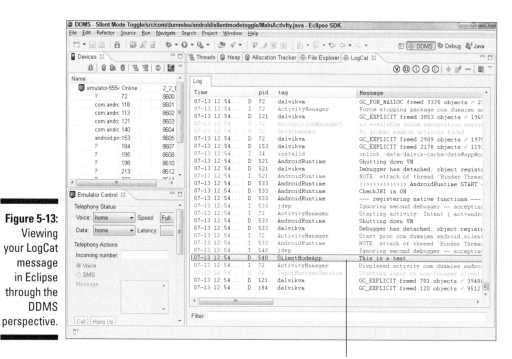

Figure 5-12:
The LogCat window in the main viewing area of Eclipse.

Figure 5-13:
Viewing your LogCat message in Eclipse through the DDMS perspective.

Your log message

You can now switch back to the Java perspective by clicking the Java Perspective button, as shown in Figure 5-14.

Choose to open the Java perspective.

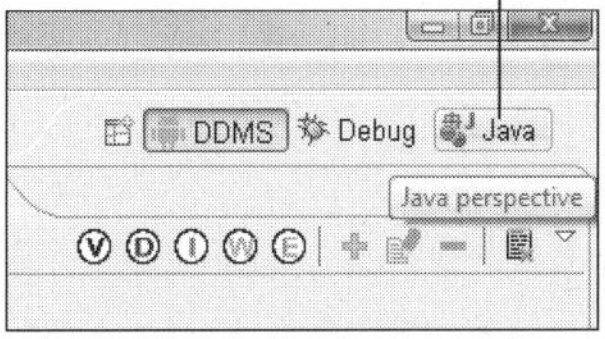

Figure 5-14:
Opening the
Java per-
spective.

Using the Eclipse debugger

Although DDMS might be one of your best allies, you number-one weapon in the battle against the army of bugs is Eclipse's debugger. The debugger that Eclipse provides allows you to set various breakpoints, inspect variables through the watch window, view LogCat, and much more.

You would use the debugger for either run-time errors or logic errors. Syntax errors will be caught by Eclipse. The application won't compile at this point, and Eclipse alerts you by placing a colored squiggly line underneath the problematic area to inform you that something is awry.

Checking run-time errors

Run-time errors are the nasty wicked witch of the east. They come out of nowhere and leave everything a mess. In Android, run-time errors occur while the application is running. For example, your application might be humming along just fine, and then all of a sudden, your application crashes when you perform an action, such as clicking a menu or a button. The reasons for this are unlimited. Perhaps you didn't initialize the `AudioManager` in the `onCreate()` method, and then you tried to access the variable later in the app. This would cause a run-time exception to occur.

The debugger would help in this situation because you could set a breakpoint at the start of `onCreate()` that would allow you to inspect the values of the variables through the debug perspective. You would then realize that you forgot to initialize the `AlarmManager`. Listing 5-6 demonstrates what would create this scenario. Here, commenting out the `AlarmManager` initialization causes an exception to be thrown at run time.

Listing 5-6: **Commenting Out the `AlarmManager` Initialization**

```
private AudioManager mAudioManager;                                    → 1
private boolean mPhoneIsSilent;

@Override
public void onCreate(Bundle savedInstanceState) {
    super.onCreate(savedInstanceState);
    setContentView(R.layout.main);

    //mAudioManager =                                                  → 9
    //    (AudioManager)getSystemService(AUDIO_SERVICE);

    checkIfPhoneIsSilent();

        setButtonClickListener();

        Log.d("SilentModeApp", "This is a test");
}
/**
 * Checks to see if the phone is currently in silent mode.
 */
private void checkIfPhoneIsSilent() {
        int ringerMode = mAudioManager.getRingerMode();              → 22
        if (ringerMode == AudioManager.RINGER_MODE_SILENT) {
            mPhoneIsSilent = true;
        } else {
            mPhoneIsSilent = false;
        }

}
```

→ **1**   The class-level `AudioManager` is introduced.

→ **9**   I accidentally commented out this code when doing some testing. This left the `mAudioManager` variable in a null state.

→ **22**   When `onCreate()` called `checkIfPhoneIsSilent()`, the application threw a run-time exception because `mAudioManager` was null and I was trying to reference a member on that object (that did not exist!).

Attaching a debugger to the `onCreate()` method would allow me to track down the root cause of the error.

Creating breakpoints

You have several ways to create a breakpoint:

- Choose the line where you'd like the breakpoint by clicking it with your mouse. Now, choose Run⇨Toggle Breakpoint, as shown in Figure 5-15.

- Choose the line where you'd like the breakpoint by clicking it with your mouse. Now press Ctrl+Shift+B. This key combination is shown in Figure 5-15.

- Double-click the left *gutter* of the Eclipse editor where you'd like a breakpoint to be created.

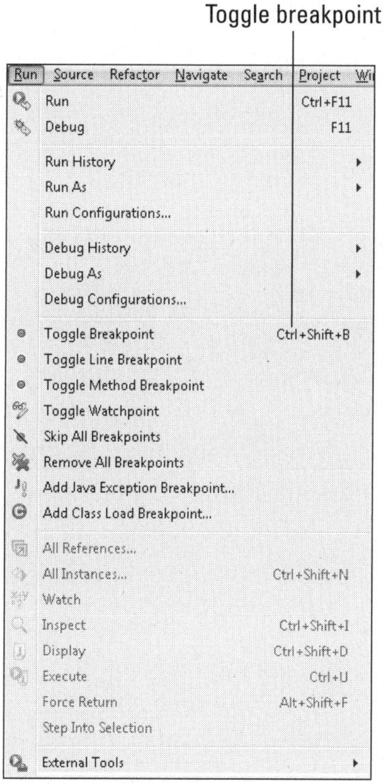

Toggle breakpoint

Figure 5-15: Setting a breakpoint through a menu or hot keys.

Any of the previous methods creates a small round icon in the left gutter of the Eclipse editor, as shown in Figure 5-16.

I want you to get your hands dirty with debugging, so comment out line → **3** of the onCreate() method, as I've done in Listing 5-7.

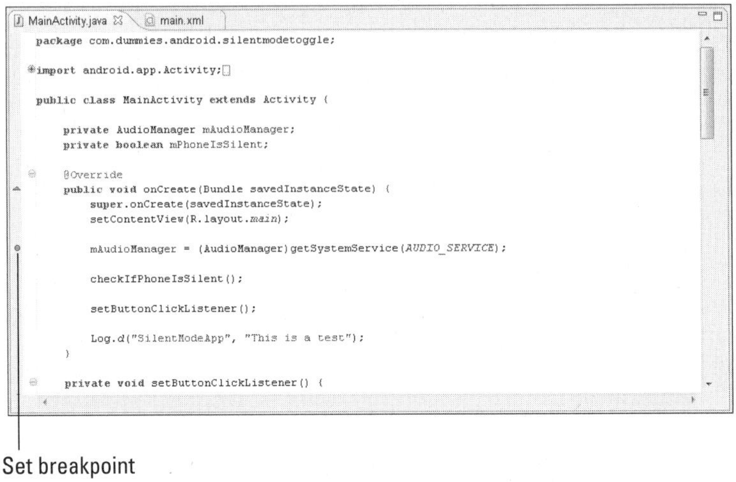

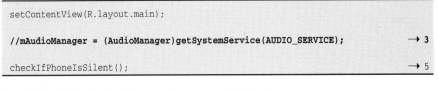

Figure 5-16:
A set break-
point in the
left gutter
of Eclipse's
editor
window.

Set breakpoint

Listing 5-7:   Commenting Out Code to Throw an Error

```
setContentView(R.layout.main);

//mAudioManager = (AudioManager)getSystemService(AUDIO_SERVICE);      → 3

checkIfPhoneIsSilent();                                                → 5
```

→ 3 The AudioManager is commented out.

→ 5 The method is called that will cause the application to fail.

Now set a breakpoint on line → **5** as shown previously.

Starting the debugger and the Debug perspective

You have one last thing to do before you get started with debugging. You have to tell the Android application that it is debuggable. To do that, open the `ApplicationManifest.xml` file, select the Application tab at the bottom as shown in Figure 5-17, and then choose the debuggable property and set it to `true`, as shown in Figure 5-17. Now save the file.

Failing to set the debuggable property to `true` ensures that you never get to debug your application. Your application will not even attempt to connect to the debugger. If I have problems with debugging, this is the first place I check because I often forget to set this property to `true`.

You've created buggy code, you're ready for it to fail, and you're ready to start debugging. I bet you never thought you'd say that out loud!

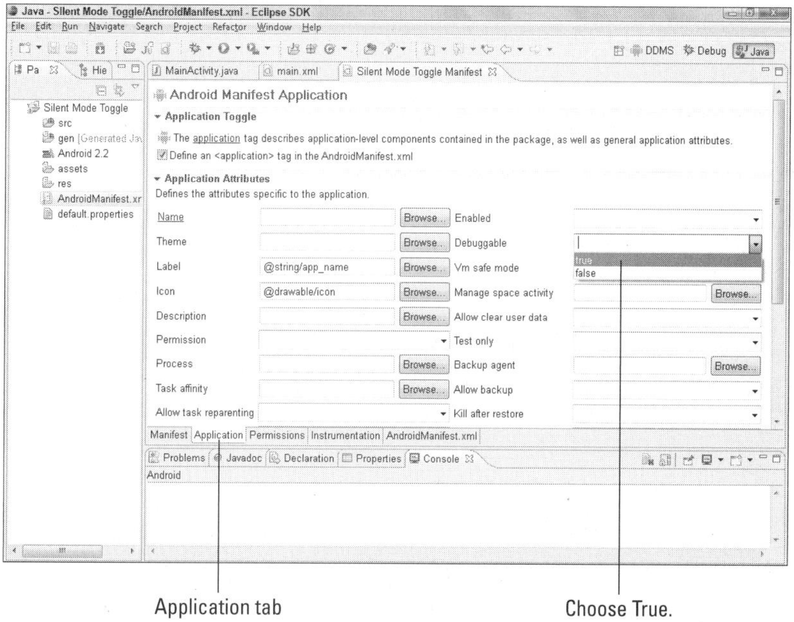

Figure 5-17:
Setting the
application
up as
debuggable.

Application tab   Choose True.

To start the debugger, choose Run➪Debug or press F11. This tells the ADT
and Eclipse to install the application onto the emulator (or device) and then
attach the debugger to it.

If your emulator is not already brought to the foreground, do that now. The
application installs, and now you see a screen that looks like what is shown
in Figure 5-18. This screen informs you that the ADT and the emulator are
trying to make a connection behind the scenes.

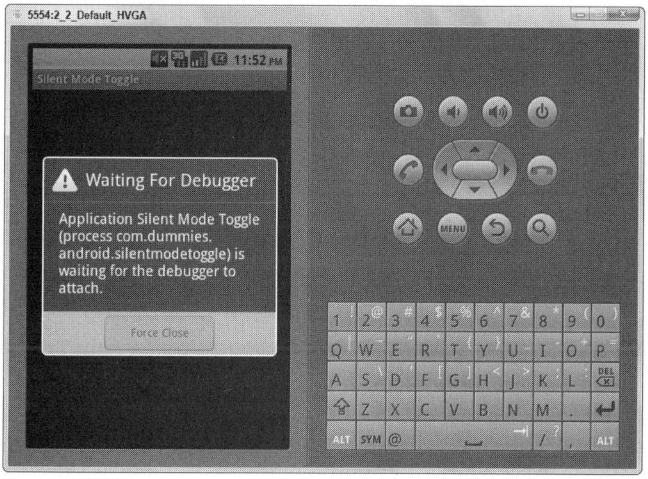

Figure 5-18:
The
emulator
waiting for
the debugger
to attach.

The emulator might sit for a moment while the debugger attaches. After the debugger attaches, it runs your application code and stops when it finds its first breakpoint. Upon doing so, you are presented with a dialog box asking whether it's okay to open the Debug perspective, as shown in Figure 5-19. Click Yes.

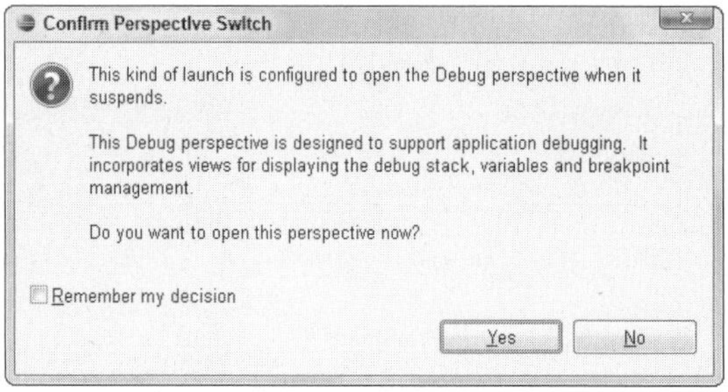

Figure 5-19:
Enabling the
Debug
perspective.

You should now be at a breakpoint, as shown in Figure 5-20. You can hover over variables and see their values.

Disconnect

Resume   Step execution navigation

Figure 5-20:
The Debug
perspective
explained.

Hovering over a variable while debugging

Code execution stopped at your breakpoint

Hover your cursor over the `mAudioManager` variable. You should see that it is currently null because you had commented out the code, as shown in Figure 5-20.

You can also step through the execution of the code by operating the debug navigation, as shown in Figure 5-20. If you click the Continue button (or press F8) three times, you can see the Debug perspective change and eventually say `source not found`. Open the emulator, and you can see that your application has crashed, as shown in Figure 5-21. In the Android Market, users have come to know of this screen as the Force Close, or FC, screen. A force close happens when a run-time exception occurs that is not handled inside your code.

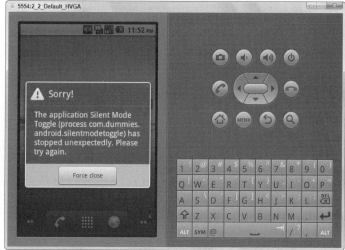

Figure 5-21:
A Force
Close
dialog box
presented
due to a
run-time
exception.

To disconnect the debugger, click the Disconnect button, as shown in Figure 5-20. Return to the Java perspective, and uncomment line → **3** from Listing 5-7 in the `MainActivity.java` file to ensure that the application builds successfully.

Checking logic errors

Computers do exactly what you tell them to do, and this little *smartphone* isn't smart enough to understand what's right or wrong when it comes to literal logic. An example of an error in literal logic is demonstrated in Listing 5-8.

Listing 5-8:   Code That Doesn't Check the Phone for Silent Mode

```
/**
 * Toggles the UI images from silent
 * to normal and vice versa.
 */
private void toggleUi() {

    ImageView imageView =
        (ImageView) findViewById(R.id.phone_icon);
            Drawable newPhoneImage;

        if (mPhoneIsSilent) {                                          → 11
                newPhoneImage =
                    getResources().getDrawable(R.drawable.phone_silent);

        } else {
            newPhoneImage =
                getResources().getDrawable(R.drawable.phone_on);
        }

        imageView.setImageDrawable(newPhoneImage);
}

@Override
protected void onResume() {
    super.onResume();
    //checkIfPhoneIsSilent();                                          → 26
    toggleUi();
};
```

→ 11   This line checks to see whether the phone is currently in the silent mode.

→ 26   For the `toggleUi()` method to properly display the correct user interface to the user, the application has to know what state the ringer is currently in. On this line, I accidentally commented out the `checkIfPhoneIsSilent()` method, which updates the class-level `mPhoneIsSilentVariable`. Because this occurs in the `onResume()` method, the user could leave the app, change the ringer state through the settings of the phone, and then return to the app, and the app would be in an incorrect state simply because of a logic error! Using a debugger, you could attach a breakpoint on the first line of the `toggleUi()` method to inspect the various variables that help make the logic calls. At that time, you would notice that `mPhoneIsSilent` is not being set.

Thinking Beyond Your Application Boundaries

At times, the device may be performing extraneous work that might affect your application, such as downloading a large file in the background while playing music from an online radio application. Will these heavy network-bound activities affect the application in any way? Well, it depends. If your app needs a connection to the Internet and for some reason your app cannot get to the Internet, will it crash? What will happen? Knowing the answers to these questions is what I refer to as *thinking beyond your application boundaries.*

Not all apps are created equal — and trust me, I've seen some good ones and some *really bad* ones. Before building or releasing your first Android application, you need to make sure that you know the ins and outs of your application and anything that could affect the application. You need to make sure that it doesn't crash when users perform routine tap events and screen navigation.

Building applications on embedded devices is much different than on a PC or Mac, and the reason is simple: Your resources (memory, processor, and so on) are very limited. If the Android device happens to be a phone, its main purpose is to perform phone-like duties such as recognizing an incoming call, keeping a signal, sending and receiving text messages, and so on.

If a phone call is in progress, the Android system is going to treat that process as vital, while a downloading file in the background would be considered nonvital. If the phone starts to run out of resources, Android will kill off all nonvital processes to keep the vital ones alive. A file can be redownloaded, but when a call is lost, it's lost forever — you have to make that call again. Sure, you can make the call again, but that only frustrates the user of the Android device if the main purpose for the purchase was a phone. Your app could be downloading a file in the background and the process gets killed — this is a scenario you need to test. This could also happen if your phone encounters an area where a wireless signal is poor or nil. The connection could get dropped, and your file would not be downloaded. You need to test for all possible solutions and have a safety guard for them. Otherwise, your app will be prone to run-time exceptions, which can lead to poor reviews on the Android Market.

Interacting with your application

To ensure that your app works, it's as simple as firing up the application and playing with the features. While your app is running, start another app, such as the browser. Surf around the Net for a moment, and then return to your app. Click some button(s) on your app and see what happens. Try all kinds of things to see whether you find outcomes that you may not have thought of. What happens if a user is interacting with your app when a phone call comes in? Are you saving the necessary state in onPause() and restoring it in onResume()? Android handles the hard task management for you, but its ultimately your responsibility to manage the state of your application.

Does it work?: Testing your application

In your emulator, open the Silent Mode Toggle application from the launcher. You've already performed the first step in your testing process — making sure that the app starts!

After the app is open, check to see whether the phone is in silent mode by looking for the small phone icon in the notification bar, as shown in Figure 5-22.

Silent phone icon

Figure 5-22:
The silent phone icon in the notification bar.

Click the Toggle Silent Mode button to toggle the ringer mode. Did the application's image change from the green phone to the silent phone (or vice versa)? Try various different things to ensure that your application works as expected. If you find a flaw, use the debugging tools featured in this chapter to help identify where the issue may be.

TECHNICAL STUFF

What about automated testing?

With the rise of agile methodologies over the last decade, it's only a matter of time before you start to wonder how to perform automated testing with Android. The SDK installs Android unit testing tools that you can use to test not only Java classes but also Android-based classes and user interface interactions. You can learn more about unit testing Android from the Android documentation at `http://d.android.com/guide/topics/testing/testing_android.html`.

An entire book could easily be written on unit testing with Android alone; therefore, I'm going to mention the tools that are at your disposal. You can look into them when you have time:

✔ **jUnit:** The SDK installs jUnit integration with the ADT. jUnit is a very popular unit testing framework that is used in Java. You can use jUnit to perform unit testing or interaction testing. More info about jUnit can be found at `www.junit.org`. To make life easier, Eclipse has built-in tools to help facilitate testing in jUnit through Eclipse.

✔ **Monkey:** Monkey is a UI/application exerciser. This program runs on your emulator or device and generates pseudorandom streams of user events. This would include taps, gestures, touches, clicks, as well as a number of system events. Monkey is a great way to stress-test your application. Monkey is installed with the Android SDK.

Chapter 6

Understanding Android Resources

- -

In This Chapter

▶ Knowing why resources are so important in Android

▶ Extracting resources

▶ Working with image resources

- -

I covered resources in pretty good detail throughout the book, so you might be wondering, why am I covering them again? The information about resources and their usage covered in Chapters 3–4 were necessary to help you understand the basics of the resource directory and to see how resources were used to build a simple application. You have many other compelling reasons to utilize resources in your application, one being globalization — which I cover in this chapter.

Understanding Resources

Resources are no fly-by-night type of Android idiom. They're first-class citizens in the Android platform.

Resources can be

- ✔ Layouts
- ✔ Strings
- ✔ Images
- ✔ Dimensions
- ✔ Styles
- ✔ Themes
- ✔ Values
- ✔ Menus
- ✔ Colors

You've already been introduced to layouts, strings, and images because they are the most common types of resources that you will utilize in everyday Android application development. The other resources may be a little muddy for you, so I take a moment to clear that up.

Dimensions

In an Android resource, a *dimension* is a number followed by a unit of measurement such as 10px, 2in, or 5sp. You would use dimensions when specifying any property in Android that would require a numeric unit of measure. For example, you may want the padding of a layout to be 10px. The following units of measure are supported by Android:

- ✔ **dp (density-independent pixels):** This is an abstract unit that is based on the physical density of the screen. These units are relative to a 160-dots-per-inch (dpi) screen; therefore, 1 dp is equivalent to one pixel on a 160-dpi screen. The ratio of dp to pixels changes with screen density, but not necessarily within proportion. This is the unit of measure that I use most when developing my layouts. The dp topic is quite in-depth and should be investigated if you plan to actively support multiple screen densities. You can read more information about this topic at Supporting Multiple Screen Sizes, located here: `http://developer.android.com/guide/practices/screens_support.html`.

- ✔ **sp (scale-independent pixels):** This is like the dp unit but is scaled according to the user's font-size preference. You should use sp dimensions when specifying font sizes in your application.

- ✔ **pt (points):** A point is ½ inch, based on the physical size of the screen.

- ✔ **px (pixels):** These correspond to actual pixels on the screen. This unit of measure is not recommended because your app may look great on a medium-density device but look very distorted and out of place on a high-density screen (and vice versa) because the dpi differs on both devices.

- ✔ **mm (millimeters):** Based on the size of the screen.

- ✔ **in (inches):** Based on the physical size of the screen.

Styles

Styles allow you to, well you guessed it, style your application! Styles in Android are very similar to Cascading Style Sheets (CSS) in the Web development realm. A style is a collection of properties that can be applied to any individual view (within the layout file), activity, or your entire application (from within the manifest file). Styles support inheritance, so you can provide a very basic style and then modify it for each particular use case you have in your application. Example style properties include font size, font color, and screen background.

Themes

A theme is a style applied to an entire activity or application, rather than just an individual view. When a style is applied as a theme, every view in the activity and/or application inherits the style settings. For example, you can set all `TextView` views to be a particular font, and all views in the themed activity or application now display their text in that font.

Values

The values resource can contain many different types of value type resources for your application. They include the following:

- **Bool:** A Boolean value defined in XML whose value is stored with an arbitrary filename in the `res/values/<filename>.xml` file, where *<filename>* is the name of the file. An example would be `bools.xml`.

- **Integer:** An integer value defined in XML whose value is stored with an arbitrary filename in the `res/values/<filename>.xml` file. An example would be `integers.xml`.

- **Integer array:** An array of integers defined in XML whose set of values is stored with an arbitrary name in the `res/values/<integers>.xml` file, where *<integers>* is the name of the file. An example would be `integers.xml`. You can reference and use these integers in your code to help define loops, lengths, and so on.

- **Typed array:** A typed array is used to create an array of resources, such as `drawables`. You can create arrays of mixed types. Therefore, the arrays are not required to be homogeneous — however, you must be aware of the data type so that you can appropriately cast it. As with the others, the filename is arbitrary in the `res/values/<filename>.xml` file. An example would be `types.xml`.

Menus

Menus can either be defined through code or through XML. The preferred way to define menus is through XML, therefore the various menus that you create should be placed into the `menus/` directory. Each menu has its own `.xml` file.

Colors

The colors file is located in the `values/colors.xml` file. This file allows you to give colors a name such as `login_screen_font_color`. This might depict the color of the font that you're using in the logon page. Each color is defined as a hexadecimal value.

Working with Resources

You've worked with resources a few times in this book already, and it's probably familiar to you at this point to use the R class to access resources from within your application. If you're still a bit rusty on resources and the generated R file, see the Chapter 3 section on resources.

Moving strings into resources

During development, I've been known to take shortcuts to get the project building and working. At times, I forgot to put strings into resources, and I've had to come back later and do this. I've actually done this on purpose in the Silent Mode Toggle application. I'm going to walk you through how to extract a string into a resource using the built-in tools.

The long way

What I'm about to show you can be done "the long way":

1. Create a new string resource.

2. Copy its name.

3. Replace the string value in your layout with the resource identifier.

This may not be a huge pain, but it takes time, possibly 30–45 seconds for the average developer.

The fast way

I'm going to show you how to cut that number to under 15 seconds. If you do this 30 times a day (which is feasible in an 8-hour day), you can save 15 minutes of just copying and pasting. That's five hours a month doing the copy-and-paste dance! Follow these steps:

1. **If Eclipse is not open, open it now and open the `main.xml` file in the `layouts` directory.**

2. Find the following chunk of code in the file:

```
<Button
        android:id="@+id/toggleButton"
        android:layout_width="wrap_content"
        android:layout_height="wrap_content"
        android:layout_gravity="center_horizontal"
        android:text="Toggle Silent Mode"
/>
```

3. Select the boldface line "Toggle Silent Mode".

4. Press Shift+Alt+A.

This opens a menu with three options.

5. Choose the Extract Android String option.

This opens the Extract Android String dialog box, as shown in Figure 6-1. This dialog box allows you to set various options for the resource.

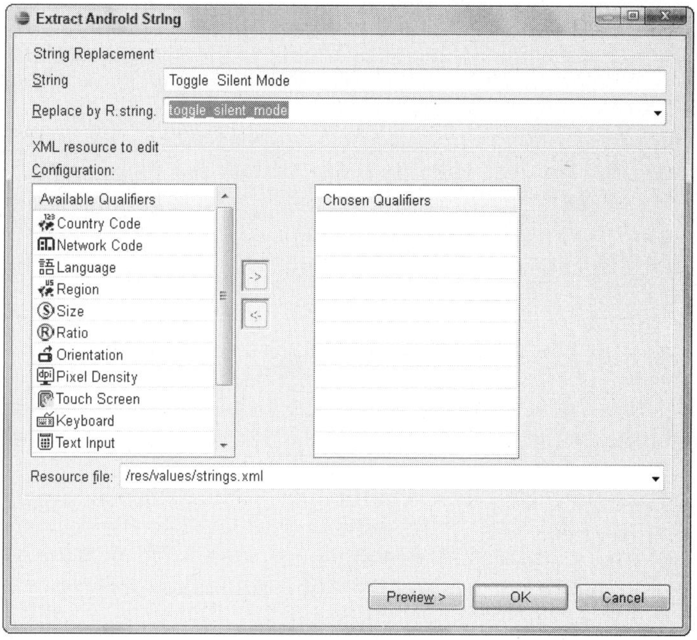

Figure 6-1:
The Extract
Android
String dialog
box.

I'm not going to use any of those features for this, so leave the defaults as they are and click the OK button.

You can now see that the layout file has been modified. The text `"Toggle Silent Mode"` has been replaced with `"@string/toggle_silent_mode"`. If you open the `strings.xml` file in the `res/values` folder, you can see a new string resource with that name, and the value of `"Toggle Silent Mode"`.

Now, that's pretty cool! You can see that doing this 20–30 times a day can add up and save you a lot of time.

Wrestling the image beast

One of the most difficult parts about resources can be the images. Images might look great on a medium-density device, but the same image might look like garbage on a high-density device. This is where the multiple-density folders come into play. These density-specific drawable folders are explained in Chapter 3.

Battling pixilation and compression

The issue that you'll most likely encounter is the one I just mentioned: pixilation and compression/expansion (going from higher- to lower-density devices and vice versa). To get around this issue, design your graphics at a very high resolution, such as 300dpi in large-size format. For example, if you're building your launcher icon, build it at 250px height and 250px width. Although the `hdpi` folder might only need a 72px-height-x-72px-width image (which is the largest used right now), it doesn't mean that in two to three months an Android tablet or Google TV won't come out.

This can be painful because working with large image files in image-editing programs can be difficult if you don't have a decent-performing computer. But this is one you have to trust me on: Having a large raw image file that is high density is much easier to mold and shape into the correct densities that you'll need.

Downsizing a high-density image does not distort the quality (other than losing the fine edges and detail of it), but upscaling does because it creates pixilation and distortion. Starting with a large file reduces the chances that you'll ever have to upscale, which means that your app graphics will always look crisp.

Using layers

If you're creating your graphics in an image-editing tool that supports layers, I highly advise you to place each item in your graphic on a different layer. The reasons for this are many, but here are the key factors:

 ✓ **Changes:** At some time, you will need to change something in your graphic — maybe the background, maybe the font, maybe the logo. If you have all these items in different layers, you can do that without affecting the rest of the graphic.

> ✔ **Localization:** Remember the example earlier in the chapter that talked about various strings in different languages? Graphics are no different. Many times in your application development career, you will encounter graphics with stylized text in the graphic itself. If your application is being translated into Japanese, and your graphics contain stylized English text, you'll want to create a Japanese version of those graphics and place them in a Japanese drawable region folder such as `res/drawable-ja`. The Android platform recognizes which region it is in (in this case, Japan). If the region's resource folders (`res/drawable-ja`, `res/values-ja`, and so on) are available, Android uses those in the application.

Making your apps global with resources

The Android platform surpassed Apple's iPhone in U.S. market share in the first quarter of 2010, trailing only Research In Motion's BlackBerry, according to ZDNet. Now carriers around the world are developing Android-based smartphones, which means one simple thing: more potential users for your apps.

So what does this mean to you as a developer? It means that Android is a huge market with tons of opportunity waiting to be tapped. This opportunity is very exciting, but to take the greatest advantage of it, you need to understand resources and how they affect the usability of your apps. For example, if a user in the United States uses your app and your app was written for an English audience (using resources or not), the user would be able to use it. However, if you hardcoded all of your string values into your views and activities and then needed to release a Chinese version, you would have to rewrite your application to use resources. When you use resources, you can have a linguist translate your strings and drawables into the region in which you're targeting — such as China.

Resources allow you to extract human-readable strings, images, and viewable layouts into resources that you can reference. Various resource folders can be created to handle various-size screens, different languages (think strings and drawables), and layout options such as landscape or portrait. Landscape and portrait views come into play when a user rotates the device 90 degrees in either direction.

If you want your apps to be viewable on as many Android devices as possible around the world, you want to use resources at all times. As an example, I advise that you always put all your strings into the `strings.xml` file because someday, someone from another country will want your application in another language. To get your application into another language, you simply need to have a linguist translate your `strings.xml` file into his or her language, and then you can create various `values` folders to hold the appropriate region's values. Android takes care of the hard work. For example, if the user is in China and his phone is set to the Chinese character set, Android looks for a values folder called `values-cn`, which is where Chinese values are stored — including the Chinese version of the `strings.xml` file. If Android cannot find such folder, the platform defaults to the default `values` folder, which contains the English version of the `strings.xml` file. (For more on strings, see the section "Moving strings into resources," earlier in this chapter.)

When it comes down to it, having a linguist update your strings and creating a new folder with the new `strings.xml` file located within are very simple things to do. Take this and expand it to other languages and devices and eventually Google TV . . . and you can see where I'm going. You're no longer looking at mobile users as your target audience. You're looking at Android users, and with the options coming out — this could be billions of users. Using resources correctly can make your expansion into foreign markets that much easier.

Designing your application for various regions is a big topic. You can find more in-depth information in the Localization article of the SDK documentation here: `http://developer.android.com/guide/topics/resources/localization.html`.

Although designing your application to be ready for various regions sounds compelling, it also helps to know that the Android Market allows you to specify which region your device is targeted for. You're not forced into releasing your application to all regions. Therefore, if you have written an application for the Berlin bus route system in Germany, it probably doesn't make sense to have a Chinese version, unless you want to cater to Chinese tourists as well as German residents. I cover the Android Market in depth in Chapter 8.

Chapter 7

Turning Your Application into a Home-Screen Widget

. . . .

In This Chapter

▶ Seeing how app widgets work in Android

▶ Understanding pending intents

▶ Building an App Widget Provider

▶ Putting your widget on the home screen

. . . .

*U*sability is the name of the game in regard to all disciples of application development. When it comes down to it, if your application is not usable, users will not use it. It's that simple.

You've built the Silent Mode Toggle application, and it works great and it's very usable. Unfortunately, if this application were published to the Android Market, the application would not be very popular. Why? In short, the user is required to open the app and then click a button to silence the phone. If the user has not created a home-screen shortcut to the application, and the app is buried in the application launcher with thirty other applications, that means taking a few extra steps: unlocking the phone, opening the launcher, finding the application, opening the app, and then clicking the Silent button. At this point, the user might as well use the up and down volume keys found on most phones to silence the phone. Pressing the down volume key numerous times results in the phone eventually being set into silent mode. Therefore, the application's usability is not very good. So how would you make this application more usable and feasible for the end user? Simple: Turn it into a home-screen widget.

In this chapter, I demonstrate how to build a home-screen widget for your application. App widgets normally resemble small icons or very small views that exist on your home screen. This widget allows users to interact with your application by simply tapping an icon (the home-screen widget). When you tap this icon, core functionality kicks in and toggles the silent mode for the user. In this chapter, you are introduced to the following classes:

✔ The `Intent`

✔ The `BroadcastReceiver`

✔ The `AppWidgetProvider`

✔ The `IntentService`

✔ The `AppWidgetProviderInfo`

Each of these classes plays a vital role in Android as well as in the app widget framework.

Working with App Widgets in Android

Home-screen widgets in Android are miniature applications that can be embedded within other applications such as the home screen. These are also known as *app widgets*. These app widgets can accept user input through click events and can update themselves on a regular schedule. App widgets are applied to the home screen by long-pressing (pressing on the screen for a couple of seconds) and then selecting widgets, as shown in Figure 7-1.

Figure 7-1: The dialog box that shows up after you long-press the home screen.

To make the Silent Mode Toggle application more usable, I'm going to show you how to build a home-screen widget for the application so that users can add it to their home screen. After adding the widget, the user can tap it — this will change the phone's ringer mode without having to open the application. The widget also updates its layout to inform the user what state the phone is in, as shown in Figure 7-2.

Figure 7-2: The two states of the app widget you're about to build.

Silent mode is enabled.　　Phone is in regular mode.

Working with remote views

When dealing with Android, you should remember that Android is based on the Linux 2.6 kernel. Linux comes with some of its very own idioms about security, and the Android platform inherits those idioms. For example, the Android security model is heavily based around the Linux user, file, and process security model.

Each application in Android is (usually) associated with a unique user ID. All processes run under a particular user. This prevents one application from modifying the files of another application — which could result in a malicious developer injecting code into another app.

Because the home screen is actually an application that is currently running on the Android device — hosted by the Android system, not you — it would not be feasible to allow you as a developer to modify actual running code on the home screen because a malicious developer could do some really evil things, such as shut down your home screen. How would you use your phone then? This is a big issue.

The Android engineers still wanted to give you a way to access the home screen and modify the contents of a particular area of the home screen from your application. Therefore, they decided to handle the problem by implementing what is known as the `RemoteView` architecture. This architecture allows you to run code inside your application, completely away from the home screen application, but still allowing you to update a view inside the home screen. The end result is that no arbitrary code can be run inside the home screen application — all your app widget code runs within your application.

This app widget stuff may sound confusing, but imagine it like this: The user taps the home-screen app widget (in this case, an icon on the home screen that he added). This action fires off a request to change the ringer mode. This request is addressed to *your* application. Android routes that request to your application, and it processes the request. During the processing of that request, your application instructs the Android platform to change the ringer mode as well as update the app widget on the home screen with a new image to indicate that the ringer mode has been changed. None of this code was run in the home-screen application — all of it was run remotely in your application with Android messaging performing the message routing to the appropriate application.

Remote views are a little bit of magic mixed with innovative engineering. Remote views (known as the RemoteView class in the Android platform) allow your application to programmatically supply a remote UI to the home screen in another process. The app widget code is not an actual activity as in previous chapters, but an implementation of an AppWidgetProvider. As stated in the previous example, Android routes messages to the appropriate application. When Android routes a message to your application from the home screen, your implementation of the AppWidgetProvider class is where you handle the message.

Using AppWidgetProviders

The AppWidgetProvider class provides the hooks that allow you to programmatically interface with the app widget on the home screen. When the user interacts with the app widget, messages are sent form the home screen app widget to your application through what is known as a broadcast event. Through these broadcast events, you can respond to when the app widget is updated, enabled, disabled, and deleted. You can also update the look and feel of the app widget on the home screen by providing a new view. Because this view is located on the home screen and not within your actual running application, you will use what is known as a RemoteView to update the layout on the home screen. All the logic that determines what should happen is initiated through an implementation of an AppWidgetProvider.

The app widget framework can be thought of as a translator for a conversation between two entities. Imagine that you need to speak to someone who knows Italian, but you don't know Italian. How would you do this? You'd find a translator. The translator would accept your input, translate it to Italian, and relay the message to the native Italian speaker. The same goes for the app widget framework. This framework is your translator.

Here's a great analogy: When the Italian native (the home screen, in this case) needs to let you know that something has happened (such as a button click), the translator (the app widget framework and the Android system) translates that into a message that you can understand (a tap occurred on a particular button). At that time, you can respond with what you'd like to do (such as changing the app widget background color to lime green), and the translator (the app widget framework) relays the message to the native Italian speaker (through the Android system to the home screen). The home screen updates the view to have a background color of green.

Updating the view is about the only thing you can do in regard to app widgets. App widgets can only accept input from tap-type events. You do not have access to other basic input widgets, such as an editable text box, drop-down lists, or any other input mechanism when working within an app widget.

Working with Pending Intents

When the user needs to interact with your application, she will communicate through the system using the Android messaging architecture as described previously. Because of this, you will not be immediately notified when the user taps the app widget. However, this does not mean you cannot be notified when a click event happens on your app widget — it's just done a little differently.

App widget click events contain instructions on what to do when a click event happens through the use of the `PendingIntent` class in the Android framework. Pending intents are an implementation of the `Intent` class in Android, as explained in the following section.

Understanding the Android intent system

Before you go any further, you should understand what an `Intent` object is and why they're used.

An `Intent` object in Android is, well, exactly that: an intent. The best way to think about intents is to envision yourself turning on a light with a light switch. The action of your intent is to turn on the light, and to do so, you flip the switch to the On position. In Android, this would correlate to creating an instance of the `Intent` class with an `Action` in it specifying that the light is to be turned on, as shown here:

```
Intent turnLightOn = new Intent("TURN_LIGHT_ON");
```

This intent would be fired off into the Android messaging system (as I describe in Chapter 1), and the appropriate activity (or various different `Activity` objects) would handle the `Intent` (if many activities respond, Android lets the user choose which one to do the work). However, in the physical world, an electrical connection is made by positioning the switch to the On position, resulting in the light illuminating. In Android, you have to provide code to make the same type of thing happen in the form of an activity. This would be an activity (that could be named `TurnLightOnActivity`) that responds to the `turnLightOn` intent. If you're working with an app widget, you must handle the intent in a `BroadcastReceiver`. An `AppWidgetProvider` is an instance of a `BroadcastReceiver` with a few extra bells and whistles that wire up a lot of the app widget framework for you. The `BroadcastReceiver` object is responsible for receiving broadcast messages.

The `AppWidgetProvider` is essentially a translator. Therefore, the `AppWidgetProvider` handles the intent from the home screen and responds with the appropriate result that you determined through your code inside of your custom `AppWidgetProvider`. The `AppWidgetProvider` does not work with any intent, though. If you want to receive input from your app widget, you need to use what's called a `PendingIntent`.

A `PendingIntent` contains a child `Intent` object. At a high level, a pending intent acts just like a regular intent. To understand what a `PendingIntent` is, you need to fully grasp the basic `Intent` class. As stated in Chapter 1, an intent is a message that can carry a wide variety of data that describes an operation that needs to be performed. Intents can be addressed to a specific activity or broadcast to generic category of receivers known as `BroadcastReceivers` (which, as you know, an `AppWidgetProvider` is). The `Intent`, `Activity`, and `BroadcastReceiver` system is reminiscent of the message bus architecture where a message is placed onto a message bus and one (or many) of the endpoints on the bus respond to the message if and only if they know how to. If each endpoint has no idea how to respond to the message, or if the message was not addressed to the endpoint, the message is ignored.

An intent can be launched into the message bus system a couple of ways:

✔ To start another activity, you would use the `startActivity()` call. The `startActivity()` accepts an `Intent` object as a parameter.

✔ To notify any interested `BroadcastReceiver` components, you would use the `sendBroadcast()` call, which also takes an intent as a parameter.

✔ To communicate with a background service (covered later in this chapter), you would use the `startService()` or `bindService()` call, which both take intents as parameters.

An activity can be thought of as the glue between various components of the application because it provides a late-binding mechanism that allows inter/intra-application communication.

Understanding intent data

An intent's primary data is as follows:

✔ **Action:** The general action to be performed. A few common actions include `ACTION_VIEW`, `ACTION_EDIT`, and `ACTION_MAIN`. You can also provide your own custom action if you choose to do so.

✔ **Data:** The data to operate on, such as a record in a database or a uniform resource identifier that should be opened, such as a Web site URL.

Table 7-1 demonstrates a few action and data parameters for Intent objects and their simple data structure.

Table 7-1   **Intent Data Examples**

Action	Data	Result
ACTION_VIEW	tel:123	Display the dialer with the given number (123) filled in to the dialer
ACTION_DIAL	content:// contacts/ people/1	Display the dialer with the phone number from the contact with the ID of 1 in the dialer
ACTION_EDIT	content:// contacts/ people/1	Edit the information about the person whose given identifier is 1
ACTION_VIEW	http://www. example.org	Display the Web page of the given intent
ACTION_VIEW	content:// contacts/ people	Display a list of all the people in the contacts system

Intents can also carry an array of other data that include the following:

✔ **category:** Gives additional information about the action to execute. As an example, if CATEGORY_LAUNCHER is present, it means that the application should show up in the application launcher as a top-level application. Another option is CATEGORY_ALTERNATIVE, which can provide alternative actions that the user can perform on a piece of data.

✔ **type:** Specifies a particular type (MIME type) of the intent data. An example would be setting the type to audio/mpeg — the Android system would recognize that you are working with an MP3 file. Normally the type is inferred by the data itself. By setting this, you override the inferred type inference by explicitly setting it in the intent.

✔ **component:** Specifies an explicit component name of the class to execute the intent upon. Normally, the component is inferred by inspection of other information in the intent (action, data/type, and categories), and the matching component(s) can handle it. If this attribute is set, none of that evaluation takes place, and this component is used exactly as specified. This is probably going to be the most common use case in your applications. You can provide another activity as the component — this addresses Android to interact with that specific class.

✔ **extras:** A bundle of additional information that is key based. This is used to provide extra information to the receiving component. For example, if you needed to send an e-mail address, you use the extras bundle to supply the body, subject, and other components of the e-mail.

Evaluating intents

Intents are evaluated in the Android system in one of two ways:

✔ **Explicitly:** The intent has specified an explicit component or the exact class that will execute the data in the intent (again, this will probably be the most common way you address intents). These types of intents often contain no other data because they are a means to start other activities within an application. I show you how to use an explicit intent in this application later in the chapter.

✔ **Implicitly:** The intent has not specified a component or class. Instead, the intent must provide enough information about the action that needs to be performed with the given data for the Android system to determine which available components can handle the intent. This is sometimes referred to as an *address* and *payload*.

An example of this would be setting up an e-mail intent that contains e-mail fields (To, CC, Subject, and Body) and an e-mail MIME type. Android interprets this as an e-mail and gives the user of the device the opportunity to choose which application should handle the intent. A couple of possibilities include Gmail, Exchange, or a POP e-mail account that are all enabled on the device. This allows the user to determine where the e-mail should originate from. Android's feature of identifying the possible matches for the given intent is known as *intent resolution*.

Using pending intents

A `PendingIntent` is an intent at the core, but with a slight paradigm shift in regard to functionality. A `PendingIntent` is created by your application and given to another completely different application. By giving another application a `PendingIntent`, you're granting the other application the right to perform the operation you have specified as if the application was your application. In laymen's terms, you are giving information on how to call your application to perform work on another application's behalf. When the other application deems that the given work needs to take place, it executes the `PendingIntent`, which instructs the Android messaging system to inform your application to perform the necessary work.

CPU-expensive

Working with RemoteViews is very expensive in terms of CPU cycles, memory, and battery life because of the work that the Android system has to do to transfer RemoteViews across process boundaries. Because of this, when working with RemoteViews, it's very important that you do all your work as quickly as possible. If your application takes too long to respond, the application will be subject to an Application Not Responding (ANR) error, which takes place after the Android system deems that the application is frozen and is not responding. An example of this is network communication to download status updates from a service such as Twitter. If downloading the statuses takes too long, Android raises an ANR error, letting the user know that the app widget is not responding; at that point, the user can Force Close the application.

One way to avoid the ANR error is to implement a service inside your AppWidgetProvider. You will be implementing an IntentService in the following sections that allows you to avoid the ANR errors and allows the widget to remain very fast.

For our purposes, to obtain a pending intent instance, I will use the PendingIntent.getBroadcast() call. This call returns a PendingIntent that is used for broadcasts throughout the system. The call takes four parameters:

- ✔ Context: The context in which this PendingIntent should perform the broadcast.
- ✔ RequestCode: The private request code for the sender. Not currently used; therefore, a zero is passed in.
- ✔ Intent: The intent to be broadcast.
- ✔ Flags: A set of controls used to control the intent when it is started. Not currently used; therefore, a zero is passed in.

Wait a second, this looks a bit funky. This code does use an Intent as well as a PendingIntent. Why? The Intent object is wrapped inside a PendingIntent because a PendingIntent is used for cross-process communication. When the PendingIntent is fired off, the real work that needs to be done is wrapped up in the child Intent object.

Whoa, that was a lot of information! Now that you understand the basics of the Android intent system, it's time to implement the guts of the application inside this app widget.

Creating the Home-Screen Widget

A lot is going on when it comes to interacting with an app widget. The process of sending messages between the home app widget and your application is handled through the Android messaging system, the `PendingIntent` class, and the `AppWidgetProvider`. In this section, I demonstrate how to build each component so that you can get your first app widget up and running on your home screen.

Implementing the AppWidgetProvider

Implementing the `AppWidgetProvider` is fairly straightforward. Open Eclipse and open the Silent Mode Toggle application.

Add a new class to the `com.dummies.android.silentmodetoggle` package and provide a name; I prefer to use `AppWidget.java`. To add a new class, right-click `com.dummies.android.silentmodetoggle` in the `src/` folder and choose New⇨Class. This opens the New Java Class dialog box. In this dialog box, provide the name of the class and set its superclass to `android.appwidget.AppWidgetProvider`, as shown in Figure 7-3. Click Finish when you are complete. A new class has been added to the selected package, and the code with the name you chose should now be visible.

The `AppWidgetProvider` does all the work of responding to events from the `RemoteView`, but how so? If you look at the `AppWidgetProvider` Android documentation, you can see that it is a direct subclass of a `BroadcastReceiver`. At a high level, a `BroadcastReceiver` is a component that can receive broadcast messages from the Android system. When a user taps a clickable view in the `RemoteView` on the home screen (such as a button), the Android system broadcasts a message informing the receiver that the view was clicked. The message is broadcast to a particular destination in the Android system. After the message is broadcast, the `AppWidgetProvider` can handle that message.

Note that these messages are broadcast, meaning that they are sent system-wide. If the payload of the message and the destination address information are vague enough, various `BroadcastReceiver` objects might handle the message. The `AppWidgetProvider` I am building in this section will be addressed to a single destination. This is similar to walking into a room full of building contractors and asking whether any contractors in the room could do some work for you. Everyone would respond. This would be an example of a vague message address and payload. However, if you asked the same group for a small electronics electrician contractor by the name of Bob Smith, only one might respond (if he were there, of course). This is an example of a specifically addressed message with detailed address and payload information.

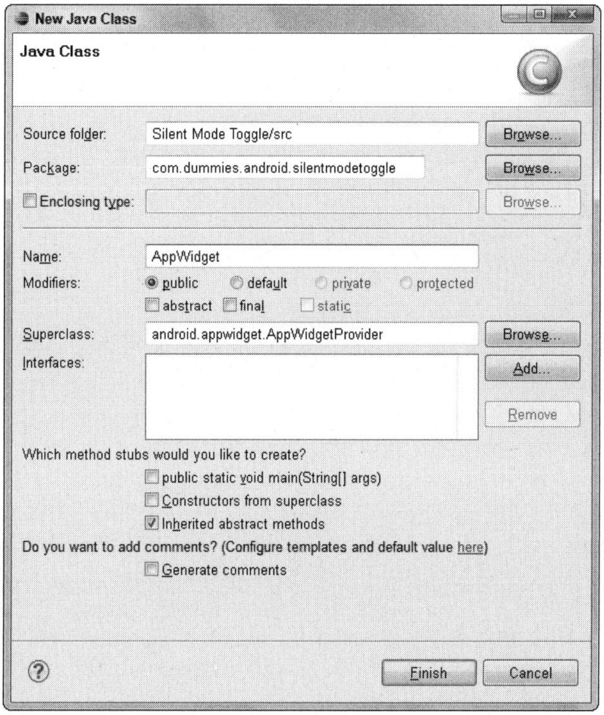

Figure 7-3:
The New
Java Class
dialog box.

Communicating with the app widget

Right now, your `AppWidgetProvider` class has no code in it — it's an empty shell. For your `AppWidgetProvider` to do anything, you need to add a bit of code to respond to the intent (the message) that was sent to your `AppWidgetProvider`. In the code file you just created, type the code shown in Listing 7-1 into the editor. (*Note:* My class is called `AppWidget.java`, so if yours is different, you need to change that line.)

Listing 7-1:   The Initial Setup of the App Widget

```
public class AppWidget extends AppWidgetProvider {          → 1
     @Override
     public void onReceive(Context ctxt, Intent intent) {   → 4
               if (intent.getAction()==null) {              → 5
                 // Do Something
               } else {                                     → 8
                  super.onReceive(ctxt, intent);            → 10
               }
          }
```

(continued)

Listing 7-1 *(continued)*

```
        @Override
        public void onUpdate(Context context, AppWidgetManager
         appWidgetManager, int[] appWidgetIds) {                    → 15
         // Do Something
        }
    }
```

Here is a brief explanation of what the various lines do:

→ **1**   This line of code informs Android that this class is an `AppWidgetProvider` because the class is inheriting from `AppWidgetProvider`.

→ **4**   This line overrides the `onReceive()` method to be able to detect when a new intent is received from the `RemoteView`. This intent could have been initiated by a user tapping a view to perform an action such as a button click. The `Intent` object is contained within the `PendingIntent`, which initiated the request.

→ **5**   As described previously, `Intent` objects can contain various pieces of data. One such slice of data is the action. On this line of code, I am checking to see whether the intent has an action. If it does not have an action, I know that I fired off the intent. This may sound a bit backward, but I explain why this is done in the upcoming sections.

→ **8**   An action was found in the `Intent` object; therefore, a different logical sequence of events needs to take place.

→ **10**   Delegating the work to the super class because I don't need to do anything with the intent because it is not what I was expecting (the intent had an action — I'm expecting an intent without an action). This would happen if the app widget automatically updated itself on a regular period that I define in widget metadata (explained in the "Working with app widget metadata" section later in this chapter). Doing so would call one of the many built-in methods for enabling, disabling, starting, stopping, or updating the app widget, as done on line 15.

→ **15**   The `onUpdate()` method is called by the Android framework on a timed basis that you can set in the widget metadata. This method is called because the Android framework realized that time has elapsed, and it would like you to have the opportunity to do some proactive view updating without interaction from the user. A great example for this would be if you had a news application widget that updated itself every 30 minutes with the latest headlines. This would require no user interaction as it would occur on a timed basis. In this method, I eventually perform work to check that our widget is set up correctly.

Building the app widget's layout

The app widget needs to have a particular layout for Android to determine how to display the widget on the home screen. The widget layout file defines what the widget will look like while on the home screen. Earlier in the chapter, in Figure 7-2, I showed two screen shots of the real app widget running in the emulator. These screen shots of the icon on the home screen were defined by the widget layout file. If I were to change the background color of the layout file to lime green, the background color of the widget on the home screen would be lime green instead of transparent, as shown in Figure 7-4.

Figure 7-4:
The result of changing the widget's background color to lime green.

By showing the lime green background, I've also illustrated the concept of widget screen space. The lime green box shown in Figure 7-4 identifies the available screen space for the app widget. Your app widget can take up one home screen cell or many cells. This app widget is only taking up one cell.

To create your widget layout, create an XML layout file in the res/layouts directory. Create one now — I'm going to name mine widget.xml.

The contents of widget.xml are shown in Listing 7-2.

Listing 7-2: The Contents of `widget.xml`

```xml
<?xml version="1.0" encoding="utf-8"?>
<RelativeLayout xmlns:android="http://schemas.android.com/apk/res/android"
    android:layout_width="fill_parent"
    android:layout_height="fill_parent">
    <ImageView android:id="@+id/phoneState"
        android:layout_height="wrap_content"
        android:layout_width="wrap_content"
        android:layout_centerInParent="true"
        android:src="@drawable/icon"
        android:clickable="true" />                                    → 9
</RelativeLayout>
```

This layout is nothing that you have not seen before. It's a `RelativeLayout` that has one child view: a clickable `ImageView`. You can click this `ImageView` by setting the clickable property to `true` on line 9 in Listing 7-2.

Note the `src` property of the `ImageView`. It is set to the icon of the application. I'm sure that seems a bit odd to you, but here is why I did that. When I built the layout, I had not yet created the phone-state buttons that represented silent and normal states. However, I did need to preview what the view would look like in the layout designer while designing the layout. Therefore, I used `@drawable/icon` as the value of the `ImageView` to glean some vision of how the view is going to look. The fact that I'm using the application icon does not concern me at this point because when the app widget loads, the `ToggleService` switches the icon value to either the silent or normal mode state icon, as shown later in this chapter.

These icons help the end user of the application identify the current state of the application. The `phone_state_normal` icon signifies when the phone is in a normal ringer mode. The `phone_state_silent` icon signifies when the phone is in the silent ringer mode. I created these icons in an image editing program.

Doing work inside an AppWidgetProvider

After the pending intent has started your `AppWidgetProvider`, you need to perform some work on behalf of the calling application (in this case, the home-screen application). In the following sections, I show you how to perform time-sensitive work on behalf of the caller.

Before I hop into the code, it's best to understand how the work will be done in the `AppWidgetProvider`. Due to the nature of remote processes and how resource-intensive they can be, it's best to do all work inside a background service. I will be performing the changing of the ringer mode via a background service.

Understanding the IntentService

You're probably wondering why I'm using a background service for such a trivial task as changing the phone ringer mode. I explain that in this section.

Any code that executes for too long without responding to the Android system is subject to the Application Not Responding (ANR) error. App widgets are especially venerable to ANR errors because they are executing code in a remote process. This is because app widgets execute across process boundaries that can take time to set up, execute, and tear down — the entire process is very CPU-, memory-, and battery-intensive. The Android system watches app widgets to ensure that they do not take too long to execute. If they do take an extended period of time to execute, the calling application (the home screen) locks up and the device is unusable. Therefore, the Android platform wants to make sure that you're never capable of making the device unresponsive for more than a couple of seconds.

Because app widgets are very expensive in regard to CPU and memory, it's really hard to judge whether an app widget will cause an ANR error. If the device is not doing any other expensive tasks, the app widget would probably work just fine. However, if the device is in the middle of one or many expensive CPU operations, the app widget could take too long to respond — causing an ANR error. This unknown CPU state is a dangerous variation to introduce to your app widget. Therefore, to get around it, it's best to move the work of the app widget into an `IntentService` that can take as long as it needs to complete — which in turn will not affect the home-screen application.

Unlike most background services, which are long-running, an `IntentService` uses the work queue processor pattern that handles each intent in turn using a worker thread, and it stops when it runs out of work. In laymen's terms, the `IntentService` simply takes the work given to it, runs it as a background service, and then stops the background service when no more work needs to be done.

Implementing the AppWidgetProvider and IntentService

In your `AppWidgetProvider` class, type the code in Listing 7-3 into your code editor.

Listing 7-3:   The Full `AppWidget` Implementation

```
public class AppWidget extends AppWidgetProvider {
        @Override
        public void onReceive(Context context, Intent intent) {
            if (intent.getAction()==null) {
                context.startService(new Intent(context,
                                    ToggleService.class));          → 6
            } else {
                super.onReceive(context, intent);
```

(continued)

Listing 7-3 *(continued)*

```
            }
        }

        @Override
        public void onUpdate(Context context, AppWidgetManager
            appWidgetManager, int[] appWidgetIds) {
        context.startService(new Intent(context,
                            ToggleService.class));            → 16
    }

    public static class ToggleService extends IntentService {   → 19

    public ToggleService() {
        super("AppWidget$ToggleService");                        → 22
    }

    @Override
    protected void onHandleIntent(Intent intent) {               → 26
        ComponentName me=new ComponentName(this, AppWidget.class); → 27
        AppWidgetManager mgr=AppWidgetManager.getInstance(this);  → 28
        mgr.updateAppWidget(me, buildUpdate(this));               → 29
    }
    private RemoteViews buildUpdate(Context context) {           → 30
        RemoteViews updateViews=new
        RemoteViews(context.getPackageName(),R.layout.widget);   → 32
        AudioManager audioManager =
(AudioManager)context.getSystemService(Activity.AUDIO_SERVICE);  → 34

        if(audioManager.getRingerMode() ==
            AudioManager.RINGER_MODE_SILENT) {

            updateViews.setImageViewResource(R.id.phoneState,
                R.drawable.phone_state_normal);                  → 40

        audioManager.setRingerMode(AudioManager.RINGER_MODE_NORMAL);
        } else {
          updateViews.setImageViewResource(R.id.phoneState,
            R.drawable.phone_state_silent);                      → 45

          audioManager.setRingerMode(AudioManager.RINGER_MODE_SILENT);
        }
        Intent i=new Intent(this, AppWidget.class);              → 49

        PendingIntent pi
            = PendingIntent.getBroadcast(context, 0, i,0);       → 52

        updateViews.setOnClickPendingIntent(R.id.phoneState,pi); → 54

        return updateViews;                                       → 56
    }
  }
}
```

The following list briefly explains what each major section of code does:

→ **6**   This line of code starts a new instance of the `ToggleService`. The `context` object in this line of code refers to the Android `Context object`, which is an interface to global information about the application. The context is passed into the `onReceive()` and `onUpdate()` method calls. A new intent is created to let the Android system know what should happen. This method is initiated by the user when the user taps the app widget on the home screen.

→ **16**   This line performs the same actions as are done in line 6.

→ **19**   This is an implementation of an `IntentService`. This `Intent-Service` handles the same logic as your `MainActivity` for handling the phone-mode switching but in regard to the app widget infrastructure. This is an implementation of a background service in the Android platform, as described previously. This class is a nested static class within the app widget.

→ **22**   This method calls the superclass with the name `AppWidget$-ToggleService`. This method call is taking place to help with debugging purposes for the thread name. If you leave this line of code out, you receive a compiler error informing you that you must explicitly invoke the super's constructor. If your app widget is named something else other than `AppWidget`, you should change this to the class name of your class.

→ **26**   The `HandleIntent()` method is responsible for handling the intent that was passed to the service. In this case, it would be the intent that was created on lines 6 and 16. Because the intent that you created was an explicit intent (you specified a class name to execute), no extra data was provided, and therefore by the time you get to line 26, you don't need to utilize the intent anymore. However, you could have provided extra information to the `Intent` object that could have been extracted from this method parameter. In this case, the `Intent` object was merely a courier to instruct the `ToggleService` to start its processing.

→ **27**   A `ComponentName` object is created. This object is used with the `AppWidgetManager` (explained next) as the provider of the new content that will be sent to the app widget via the RemoteViews instance.

→ **28**   An instance of `AppWidgetManager` is obtained from the static `AppWidgetManager.getInstance()` call. The `AppWidget-Manager` class is responsible for updating the state of the app widget and provides other information about the installed app widget. You will be using it to update the app widget state.

→ **29**   The app widget gets updated with a call to `updateAppWidget()` on this line. This call needs two things: the Android `ComponentName` that is doing the update and the `RemoteView` object used to update the app widget with. The `ComponentName` is created on line 27.

The RemoteView object that will be used to update the state of the app widget on the home screen is a little more complicated and is explained next.

→ **30** The method definition for the buildUpdate() method. This method returns a new RemoteView object that will be used on line 29. The logic for what should happen and the actions to proceed with are included in this method.

→ **32** Here I am building a RemoteView object with the current package name as well as the layout that will be returned from this method. The layout, R.layout.widget, is shown in Listing 7-3.

→ **34** I'm obtaining an instance of the AudioManager, and then, directly afterward, I'm checking the state of the ringer. If the ringer is currently silent, that means that the user wants the phone's ringer to now be normal (remember, the user tapped the app widget to change its state).

→ **40** After I have the RemoteView object, I need to update it. This is done with the same logic that was used in the MainActivity in the previous chapters. The RemoteView object is changing the R.id.phoneState ImageView drawable to the R.drawable. phone_state_normal drawable (right-side icon of Figure 7-2).

→ **45** The else statement located above this line flows through to update the image in the ImageView to R.drawable.phone_ state_silent because the ringer mode was not in silent mode previously (the user wants to now silence the phone).

→ **49** Creating an Intent object that will start the AppWidget class when initiated.

→ **52** Unfortunately, app widgets cannot communicate with vanilla intents; they require the use of a PendingIntent. Remember, app widgets are cross-process communication; therefore, PendingIntent objects are needed for communication. On this line, I build the PendingIntent that instructs the app widget of its next action via the child intent built on line 49.

→ **54** Because you're working with a RemoteView, you have to rebuild the entire event hierarchy in the view. This is because the app widget framework will be replacing the entire RemoteView with a brand new one that you supply via this method. Therefore, you have one thing left to do: tell the RemoteView what to do when it's tapped/ clicked from the home screen. The PendingIntent that you built on line 52 instructs the app widget what to do when someone clicks or taps the view. The setOnClickPendingIntent() sets this up. This method accepts two parameters: the ID of the view that was clicked (in this case an image), and the pi argument, which is the PendingIntent that you created on line 52. In other words, you're setting the click listener for the ImageView in the app widget.

→ **56** Return the newly created `RemoteView` object so that the `updateAppWidget()` call on line 29 can update the app widget.

Working with the app widget's metadata

Now that the code is written to handle the updating of the app widget, you might be wondering how to get the app widget to show up on the Widgets menu after a long press on the home screen. This is a fairly simple process and requires that you add a single XML file to your project. This XML file describes some basic metadata about the app widget so that the Android platform can determine how to lay out the app widget onto the home screen. Here's how you do this:

1. **In your project, right-click the `res` directory and choose New⇨ New Folder.**

2. **For the folder name, type `xml` and click Finish.**

3. **Right-click the new `res/xml` folder, choose New, and then choose Android XML File.**

4. **In the New Android XML File Wizard, type `widget_provider.xml` for the filename.**

5. **The file type will be of the type `AppWidgetProvider`. Select that radio button and then click Finish.**

6. **After the file opens, open the XML editor and type the following into the `widget_provider.xml` file:**

```xml
<?xml version="1.0" encoding="utf-8"?>
<appwidget-provider xmlns:android="http://schemas.android.com/apk/res/
            android"
        android:minWidth="79px"
        android:minHeight="79px"
        android:updatePeriodMillis="1800000"
        android:initialLayout="@layout/widget"
/>
```

The `minWidth` and `minHeight` properties are used for setting the very minimum space that the view will take on the home screen. These values could be larger if you want.

The `updatePeriodMillis` property defines how often the app widget should attempt to update itself. In the case of the Silent Mode Toggle application, you rarely, if ever, need this to happen. Therefore, this value is set to 180000 milliseconds — 30 minutes. Every 30 minutes, the app attempts to update itself through sending an intent that executes the `onUpdate()` method call in the `AppWidgetProvider`.

The `initialLayout` property identifies what the app widget will look like when the app widget is first added to the home screen before any work takes place. Note that it may take a couple of seconds (or longer) for the app widget to initialize and update your app widget's `RemoteView` object by calling the `onReceive()` method.

An example of a longer delay would be if you had an app widget that checked Twitter for status updates. If the network is slow, the `initialLayout` would be shown until updates were received from Twitter. Therefore, if you foresee this becoming an issue, you should inform the user in the `initialLayout` that information is loading. Therefore, the user is kept aware of what is happening when the app widget is initially loaded to the home screen. You could do this by providing a `TextView` with the contents of `"Loading . . ."` while the `AppWidgetProvider` does its work.

At this point, you can install the Silent Mode Toggle application, long-press the home screen, and choose the Widgets category; now you should see the Silent Mode Toggle present. The metadata that you just defined is what made this happen. The icon defaults to the application icon. However, the app widget would throw an exception if you attempted to add it to the home screen. This is a fairly common mistake: I forget to let the `ApplicationManifest.xml` file know about my new `IntentService` and `BroadcastReceiver`. If the `ApplicationManifest.xml` does not know about these new items, exceptions will be thrown because the application context has no idea where to find them.

Registering your new components with the manifest

Anytime you add an `Activity`, `Service`, or `BroadcastReceiver` (as well as other items) to your application, you need to register them with the application manifest file. The application manifest presents vital information to the Android platform, namely, the components of the application. The `Activity`, `Service`, and `BroadcastReceiver` objects that are not registered in the application manifest will not be recognized by the system and will not be able to be run. Therefore, if you added the app widget to your home screen, you would have it crash because your `AppWidgetProvider` is a `BroadcastReceiver`, and the code in the receiver is using a service that is also not registered in the manifest.

To add your `AppWidgetProvider` and `IntentService` to your application manifest file, open the `ApplicationManifest.xml` file and type the code shown in Listing 7-4 into the already-existing file. Bolded lines are the newly added lines for the new components.

**Listing 7-4: An Updated `AndroidManifest.xml`
File with New Components Registered**

```xml
<?xml version="1.0" encoding="utf-8"?>
<manifest xmlns:android="http://schemas.android.com/apk/res/android"
    package="com.dummies.android.silentmodetoggle"
    android:versionCode="1"
    android:versionName="1.0">
    <application android:icon="@drawable/icon"
        android:label="@string/app_name"
        android:debuggable="true">
        <activity android:name=".MainActivity"
                android:label="@string/app_name">
                <intent-filter>
                    <action android:name="android.intent.action.MAIN" />
                    <category android:name="android.intent.category.LAUNCHER" />
                </intent-filter>
        </activity>
        <receiver android:name=".AppWidget"
                android:label="@string/app_name"
                android:icon="@drawable/icon">                         → 18
                <intent-filter>
                    <action
                android:name="android.appwidget.action.APPWIDGET_UPDATE" />    → 21
                </intent-filter>
                <meta-data
                                        android:name="android.appwidget.provider"
                    android:resource="@xml/widget_provider" />          → 25
        </receiver>
        <service android:name=".AppWidget$ToggleService" />
    </application>
    <uses-sdk android:minSdkVersion="4" />
</manifest>
```

The following is a brief explanation of what each section does:

→ **18**   This line of code is the opening element that registers a
        `BroadcastReceiver` as part of this application. The `name`
        property identifies what the name of the receiver is. In this case,
        it is `.AppWidget`, which correlates to the `AppWidget.java`
        file in the application. The name and the label are there to
        help identify the receiver.

→ **21**   Identifies what kind of intent (based on the action of the intent
        in the intent filter) the app widget automatically responds to
        when the particular intent is broadcast. This is known as an
        `IntentFilter` and helps the Android system understand what
        kind of events your app should get notified of. In this case, your
        application is concerned about the `APPWIDGET_UPDATE` action

of the broadcast intent. This event fires after the `update-PeriodMillis` property has elapsed, which is defined in the `widget_provider.xml` file. Other actions include enabled, deleted, disabled, and more.

→ **25** Identifies the location of the metadata that you recently built into your application. Android uses the metadata to help determine defaults and lay out parameters for your app widget.

At this point, your application is ready to be installed and tested. To install the application, choose Run⇨Run or press Ctrl+F11. Your application should now show up on the emulator. Return to the home screen by pressing the Home key. You can now add the app widget you recently created to your home screen.

Placing Your Widget on the Home Screen

The usability experts on the Android team did a great job by allowing application widgets to be easily added to the home screen. Adding a widget to the home screen is super easy; follow these steps:

1. **Long-press the home screen on the emulator by clicking the left mouse button on the home screen and keeping the mouse button pressed.**

2. **When the Add to Home Screen dialog box is visible, select Widgets, as shown in Figure 7-5.**

3. **When the Choose Widget dialog box is visible, choose Silent Mode Toggle, as shown in Figure 7-6.**

Figure 7-5:
The Add to Home Screen dialog box.

You have now added the Silent Mode Toggle widget to your home screen, as shown in Figure 7-7. You can tap the icon to change the ringer mode, and the background will change accordingly, as shown in Figure 7-2.

Chapter 8

Publishing Your App to the Android Market

The Android Market is the official application distribution mechanism behind Android. Publishing your application to the market enables your application to be downloaded, installed, and utilized by millions of users across the world. Users can also rate and leave comments about your application, which helps you identify possible use trends as well as problematic areas that users might be encountering.

The Android Market also provides a set of valuable statistics that you can use to track the success of your application, as I show you in the last section of this chapter.

In this chapter, I show you how to publish your application to the Android Market. I also show you how to provide a couple of screen shots, a promo screen shot, and a short description of your application. To get your app into the Android Market, you have to package it up in a distributable format first.

Creating a Distributable File

You had a great idea and you developed the next best hit application and/ or game for the Android platform, and now you're ready to get the application into the hands of end users. The first thing you need to do is package your application so that it can be placed on end users' devices. To do so, you create an *Android package file,* also known as an *APK file.*

In the following sections, I guide you through the process of creating your first APK file.

Revisiting the manifest file

Before you jump in and create the distributable APK file, you should take great care to make sure that your application is available to as many users as possible. This is done by getting very familiar with the `uses-sdk` element in the `AndroidManifest.xml` file. Your `AndroidManifest.xml` file currently has a `uses-sdk` entry that was created in Chapter 4:

```
<uses-sdk android:minSdkVersion="4" />
```

The `minSdkVersion` property identifies which versions of the Android platform can install this application. In this instance, level 4 has been selected. The Silent Mode Toggle application was developed by setting the target software development kit (SDK) to version 8. Wait, I know, I'm using version 4 as the minimum SDK but I'm telling Eclipse and Android that I'm targeting the version 8 SDK. How can all this madness work?

The Android platform, for the most part, is backward compatible. Most all the features that are in version 3 are also in version 4. Yes, small changes and sometimes new large components are released in each new version, but for the most part, everything else in the platform remains backward compatible. Therefore, stating that this application needs a minimum of SDK version 4 signifies that any Android operating system that is of version 4 or greater can run the application.

Using the `minSdkVersion` information, the Android Market can determine which applications to show each user of each device. If you were to release the application right now with `minSdkVersion` set to the value of 4, and you opened the Android Market on an Android device running version 3 (Android 1.5) or lower, you would not be able to find your application. Why? The Android Market filters it out for you. You, the developer, told the Android Market, "Hey! This app can only run on devices that are of API Level 4 or greater!" If you were to open the Android Market on a device running API Level 4 or above, you would be able to find and install your application.

If you do not provide a `minSdkVersion` value in the `uses-sdk` element of the application's manifest, the Android Market defaults the `minSdkVersion` to 0, which means that this application is compatible with all versions of Android. If your application happens to use a component not available in older versions of the platform (such as the Bluetooth technology in Android 2.0) and a user installs your application, he or she receives a run-time error informing the user that the application could not continue because an exception occurred.

Choosing your tools

You can build an Android APK file in numerous ways:

- ✔ Through the Android Development Tools (ADT) inside Eclipse
- ✔ Via an automated build process, like a continuous integration server, such as Hudson Continuous Integration Server
- ✔ Via the command line with Ant
- ✔ Via the Maven build system

You use the ADT within Eclipse to create your APK file. The ADT provides an array of tools that compiles, digitally signs, and packages your Android application into an APK file. In that process, the digital signature process takes place; this is discussed in the next section.

The other options, such as Ant and continuous integration, are possible but are used in more advanced scenarios. You can find more information about setting up an Ant build process to use in these types of build mechanisms in the Android documentation at `http://d.android.com/guide/publishing/app-signing.html`.

Digitally signing your application

The Android system requires that all installed applications be digitally signed with a certification that contains a public/private key pair. The private key is held by the developer. The certification that is used to digitally sign the application is used to identify the application, and the developer is used for establishing the trust relationships between applications.

You need to know a few key things about signing Android applications:

- ✔ All Android applications *must be signed.* The system will not install an application that is not signed.
- ✔ You can use self-signed certificates to sign your applications; a certificate authority is not needed.
- ✔ When you are ready to release your application to the market, you must sign it with a private key. You cannot publish the application with the debug key that signs the APK file when debugging the application during development.
- ✔ The certificate has an expiration date, and that expiration date is only verified at install time. If the certificate expires after the application has been installed, the application will continue to operate normally.

✔ If you don't want to use the ADT tools to generate the certificate, you can use standard tools such as Keytool or Jarsigner to generate and sign your APK files.

You can create modular applications that can communicate with each other if the applications were signed with the same certificate. This allows the applications to run within the same process, and if requested, the system can treat them as a single application. With this methodology, you can create your application in modules, and users can update each module as they see fit. A great example of this would be to create a game and then release "update packs" to upgrade the game. Users can decide to purchase the updates that they want.

The certificate process is outlined in detail in the Android documentation. The documentation describes how to generate certificates with various tools and techniques. You can find more information about APK signing at `http://d.android.com/guide/publishing/app-signing.html`.

Creating a keystore

A *keystore* in Android (as well as Java) is a container in which your personal certificates reside. You can create a keystore file with a couple of tools in Android:

✔ **ADT Export Wizard:** This tool is installed with the ADT and allows you to export a self-signed APK file that can digitally sign the application as well as create the certificate and keystore (if needed) through a wizard-like process.

✔ **Keytool application:** The Keytool application allows you to create a self-signed keystore via the command line. This tool is located in the Android SDK `tools` directory and provides many options via the command line.

You will be using the ADT Export Wizard to create your keystore during the APK generation process that follows.

Safeguarding your keystore

The keystore file contains your private certificate that Android uses to identify your application in the Android Market. You should back up your keystore in a safe location because if you happen to lose your keystore, you cannot sign the application with the same private key. Therefore, you cannot upgrade your application because the Android Market platform recognizes that the application is not signed by the same key and restricts you from upgrading it; the Market sees the file as a new Android application. This also happens if you change the package name of the app; Android does not recognize it as a valid update because the package and/or certificate are the same.

Creating the APK file

To create your first APK file, follow these steps:

1. **Open Eclipse, if it is not already open.**

2. **Right-click the Silent Mode Toggle app, choose Android Tools, and then choose Export Application Package.**

   This displays the Export Android Application dialog box, as shown in Figure 8-1, with the current project name filled in for you.

Figure 8-1:
The Export
Android
Application
dialog box.

3. **Click the Next button.**

   The Keystore Selection dialog box opens, as shown in Figure 8-2.

4. **You have not created a keystore yet, so select the Create a New Keystore radio button.**

5. **Choose the location of your keystore.**

   I prefer to use `c:\android` and choose a name for the keystore. The file-name should have the `.keystore` extension. My full path looks like this:

   ```
   c:\android\dummies.keystore
   ```

6. **Choose and enter a password that you'll remember; reenter it in the Confirm field.**

   I am choosing the word *dummies* as my password.

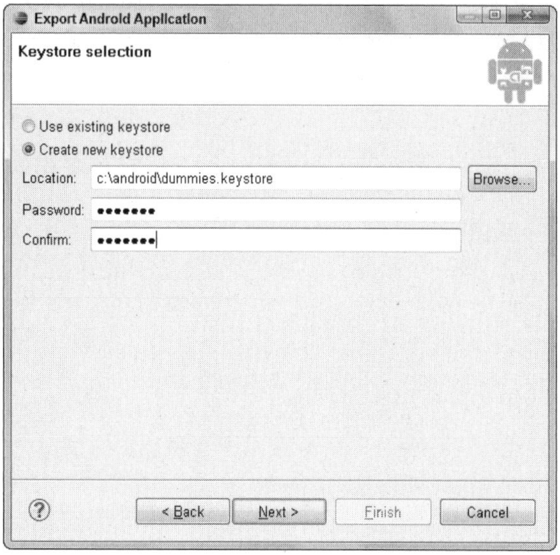

Figure 8-2:
The
Keystore
Selection
dialog box.

7. **Click the Next button.**

   This opens the Key Creation dialog box.

8. **Fill out the following fields:**

   • **Alias:** This is the alias that you will use to identify the key.

   • **Password and Confirm:** This is the password that will be used for the key.

   • **Validity:** This indicates how long this key will be valid for. Your key must expire after October 22, 2033. I normally insert a value of 30 years into this field to be safe.

9. **Complete the certificate issuer section of the dialog box, filling out at least one of these fields:**

   • First and Last Name

   • Organization Unit

   • Organization

   • City or Locality

   • State or Province

   • Country Code (XX)

   I have chosen to provide my name as the issuer field.

   When you finish, your dialog box should resemble Figure 8-3.

Figure 8-3:
The Key
Creation
dialog box.

10. **Click the Next button.**

    The final screen you encounter is the Destination and Key/Certificate
    Checks dialog box, as shown in Figure 8-4.

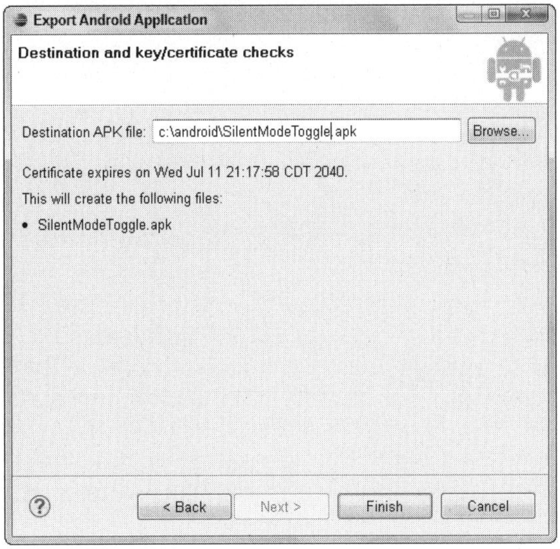

Figure 8-4:
Choosing a
name and
destination
for your first
APK file.

11. **Enter a name and location for a file with an extension of** `.apk`.

    I have chosen `c:\android\SilentModeToggle.apk`.

12. **Click the Finish button.**

This creates the `.apk` file in your chosen location as well as a keystore in the location you chose in Step 5. Open these locations, and you can see a `.keystore` file as well as an `.apk` file, as shown in Figure 8-5.

You have now created a distributable APK file and a reusable keystore for future updates.

Creating an Android Market Account

Now that you have your APK file created, you can now release the application on the Android Market. To do so, you need to create an Android Market account. To create such an account, you need a Google account. Any Google-based account such as a Gmail account is fine. If you do not have a Google account, you can obtain a free account by navigating to `www.google.com/accounts`. To create the Android Market account, follow the steps shown here. Note that to complete this step, you need to pay a $25 developer fee with a credit card. If you do not pay this developer fee, you cannot publish applications.

1. **Open your Web browser and navigate to** `http://market.android.com/publish`.

2. **On the right side of the screen, sign in with your Google account, as shown in Figure 8-6.**

3. **Fill out the following fields:**

   • **Developer Name:** The name that will show up as the developer of the applications you release. This could be your company name or your personal name. You can change this later after you've created your account.

   • **E-mail Address:** This is the e-mail address users can send e-mails to. They normally send questions and or comments about your application if they are interested in it.

Figure 8-6:
The
http://
market.
android.
com/
publish
page.

- **Web Site URL:** The URL of your Web site. If you do not have a Web site, you can get a free Blogger account that provides a free blog. This will suffice as a Web site. You can get a free Blogger account from www.blogger.com.

- **Phone Number:** A valid phone number at which to contact you in case problems arise with your published content.

When you finish, your form should resemble Figure 8-7.

Figure 8-7:
Developer
listing
details.

4. **Click the Continue button.**

   On the next page, you are required to pay the $25 developer fee (see Figure 8-8).

5. **Click the Continue button to pay the developer fee with Google Checkout.**

6. **On the secure checkout page (see Figure 8-9), fill in your credit card details and billing information; then click the Agree and Continue button.**

   If you already have a credit card on file with Google, you may not see this page. If you already have a card set up, select one and continue.

7. **On the resulting confirmation page (see Figure 8-10), type your password and click the Sign In and Continue button.**

8. **On the order confirmation page (see Figure 8-11), click the Place Your Order Now button.**

   Depending on how fast your Internet connection is and how fast your order is placed, you may or may not see a loading screen.

   When the process is complete, you see a message confirming that you're an Android developer (see Figure 8-12).

9. **Click the Android Market Developer Site link.**

   You arrive at the Android Developer Agreement page (see Figure 8-13).

10. **If you want to have a paid application in the Android Market, follow the directions in the "Google Checkout merchant accounts" sidebar.**

    I cover paid versus free applications in the next section of this chapter.

11. **Read the terms and then click the I Agree, Continue link.**

    You arrive at the Android developer home page (see Figure 8-14).

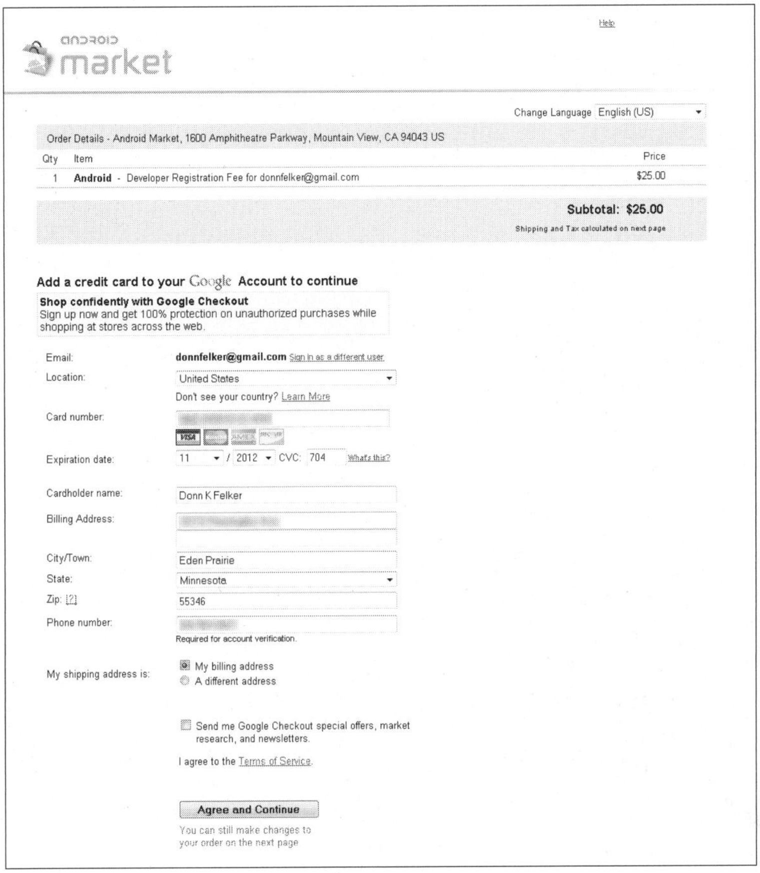

Figure 8-9:
Personal
and billing
information.

Figure 8-10:
The sign-in
confirmation
page for
registering
as a
developer.

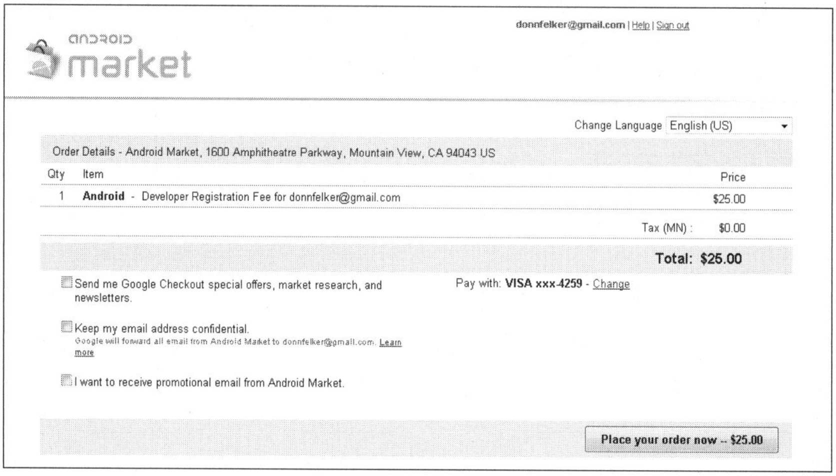

Figure 8-11:
Order
confirmation.

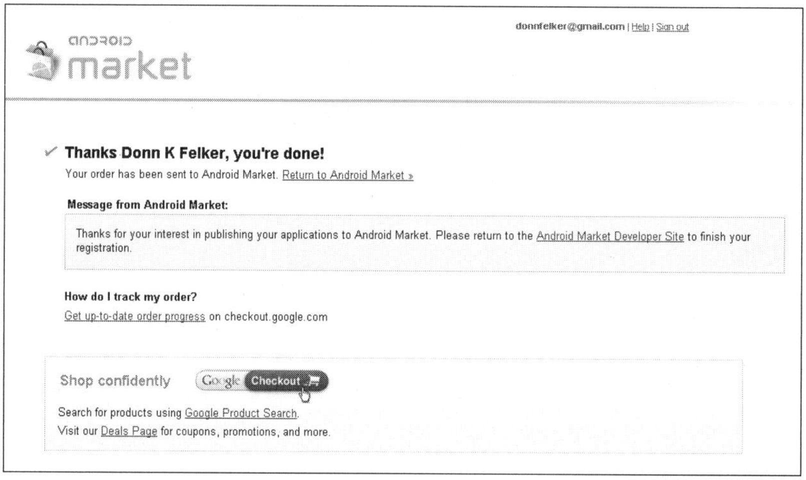

Figure 8-12:
Confirmation
of your
registration.

Figure 8-13:
The
agreement
terms.

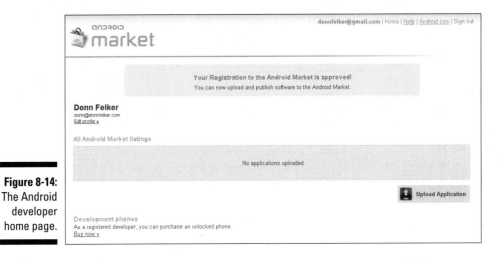

Figure 8-14:
The Android
developer
home page.

Google Checkout merchant accounts

To have a paid application on the Android Market, you must set up a Google Checkout merchant account. To set up this account, choose Setup Merchant Account. You need to provide

✔ Personal and business information

✔ Tax identity information (personal or corporation)

✔ Expected monthly revenue ($1 billion, right?)

After you have set up a Google Checkout merchant account, you can sell your applications. If you are still in the process of setting up your developer account, please return to Step 11 in the process.

Pricing Your Application

You have your APK file and you're a registered Android developer. Now you're ready to get your app into users' hands, finally. But you need to ask yourself one last important question — is my app a free app or a paid app?

This decision should be made before you release your app because it has psychological consequences with potential customers/users and monetary ones for you. If your application is a paid application, you have to decide what your price point is. While I cannot decide this for you, I would advise you to look at similar applications in the Market to help determine what their price point is so that you can determine a pricing strategy. Most apps seem to sell from the $0.99 value range up to the $9.99 range. I rarely see an app over the $10 threshold. Keeping your pricing competitive with your product is a game of economics that you have to play to determine what works for your application.

The paid-versus-free discussion is an evergreen debate, with both sides stating that either can be profitable. I've done both and I have found that both make decent income. You just have to figure out what works best for your application given your situation.

Why to choose the paid model

If you go with a paid model, that means you start getting money in your pocket within 24 hours of the first sale (barring holidays and weekends) — in that case, you'd then receive funds the following business day. However, from my experience, your application will not receive many active installs because it is a paid application. You are your own marketing team for your app, and if no one knows about your app, how is he or she going to know to buy it? This is a similar problem for free apps, but users can install them for free and the mental weight of the app remaining on their device is little to none. With paid apps, this works a little differently.

All Android Market users get a free 24-hour trial period of your paid application upon initial purchase. This means that they can purchase the app and install it, Google Checkout will authorize their credit card on file, and the charge will remain in an authorization state until 24 hours from the original purchase time. You can monitor this in your Google Checkout panel. During those 24 hours, the user can use the fully functional application, and if he decides that he does not like the application, he can uninstall it and get a full refund. This is very useful to an end user because he does not feel that he is getting penalized a fee for trying your app and not liking it (he has an out — a full refund). If he does not uninstall the app and get a refund within 24 hours, the credit card authorization turns into a charge and you receive the funds the following day.

Why to choose the free model

If you choose to go the free route, users can install the application free of charge. From my experience, 50–80 percent of the users who install your free app will keep the application on the device, while the others uninstall it. The elephant in the room at this point is, how do you make money with free apps?

As the age-old saying goes, nothing in life is free. The same goes for making money on free apps. When it comes down to it, it's fairly simple — advertising. Various mobile advertising agencies can provide you with a third-party library to display ads on your mobile application. The top mobile advertising companies at this time are Google AdSense, AdMob (which was recently acquired by Google), and Quattro Wireless (recently acquired by Apple). Obtaining a free account from one of these companies is fairly straightforward. They offer great SDKs and walk you through how to get ads running on your native Android application. Most of these companies pay on a net-60-day cycle, so it will be a few months before you receive your first check.

Getting Screen Shots for Your Application

Screen shots are a very important part of the Android Market ecosystem because they allow users to preview your application before installing it. Allowing users to view a couple running shots of your application can be the determining factor of whether a user will install your application. Imagine if you created a game and wanted users to play it. If you spent weeks (or months for that matter) creating detailed graphics, you'd want the potential users/buyers of the game to see them so that they can see how great your app looks.

To grab real-time shots of your application, you need an emulator or physical Android device. To grab the screen shots, perform the following:

1. **Open the emulator and place the widget onto the home screen.**

2. **In Eclipse, open the DDMS Perspective.**

3. **Choose the emulator in the Devices panel, as shown in Figure 8-15.**

4. **Click the Screen Shot button to capture a screen shot.**

You can make changes on the emulator or device and refresh the screen shot dialog box, as shown in Figure 8-15. After this screen shot is taken, you can publish it to the Android Market.

Choose the emulator.

Click for screen shot.   Screen shot

Figure 8-15:
The DDMS perspective with the emulator screen shot taken.

Uploading Your Application to the Android Market

You've finally reached the apex of the Android application development — the point when you publish the application. Publishing an application is easy; follow these steps:

1. **On the Android developer home page (refer to Figure 8-14), click the Upload Application button.**

   The Upload an Application page opens, as shown in Figure 8-16.

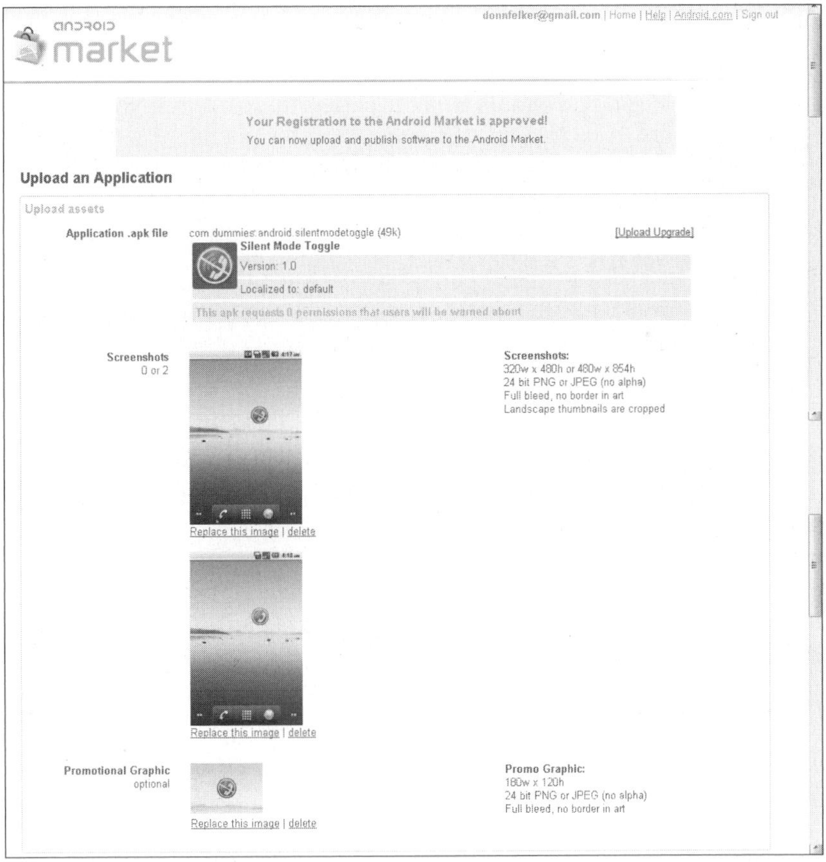

Figure 8-16: The upload page.

2. **For the Application .apk file, choose the** `.apk` **file that you created earlier in the chapter and then click Upload.**

The Android Market uses the Java package name as the identifier inside of the market. No two applications can have the same package name. Therefore, if you try to upload the application at this point, you receive an error that states the following: `The package name of your apk (com.dummies.android.silentmodetoggle) is the same as the package name of another developer's application. Choose a new package name.` I can't give you a unique package name. However, I would like to advise that you either use your name or your company's name when you develop your own application for the Android Market.

3. **In the Screenshots section, add two screen shots of your application.**

The sizes of these screen shots need to be 320px wide by 480px high or 480px wide by 854px high. These screen shots allow users to preview your application in a running state without having to install your application. You should provide screen shots of your app because apps with screen shots have higher install rates than apps without screen shots. Screen shots are not required to publish the app.

4. **Add a promo shot.**

This promo shot needs to be created in the dimensions of 180px wide by 120px high and should be created in an image-editing program. The promo shot is used for random promotions that Android chooses to showcase when browsing the market. A promo shot is not required to publish the app.

5. **Set the title of your application.**

I chose Silent Mode Toggle Widget. This text is indexed for the Android Market search.

6. **Set the description for your application.**

This is the description that the user sees when she inspects your application to determine whether she wants to install it. All of this text is indexed for the Android Market search.

7. **Set the promo text of your application.**

Promo text is used when your application is featured or promoted on the market. The process of getting your application featured is fairly muddy at this point and, from what I can tell, is based upon the popularity of your application. If your application gets chosen to be featured in the promo area of the market (usually the top part of the screen of each category in the Android Market), the promo text is what shows up as the promotional component for it.

8. **Set the application type.**

For this app, I set the type to Applications.

9. **Set the category for the app.**

   I chose Productivity for the Silent Mode Toggle application because the app is a productivity enhancer.

10. **Select your copy protection.**

    I always choose Off. When you choose On, the file footprint on the device is usually doubled. If your app is 2MB in size and you turn on copy protection, your new file footprint when installed on the device is around 4MB. I keep my files at the lowest possible setting. The reason for this is simple — if a user runs out of space on their phone, they are most likely to uninstall the largest applications in order to free up more space.

    Older devices, prior to Android 2.2, could not install applications to the SD card. Therefore, internal space was limited, and when users ran out of space, they would uninstall the heavyweight apps first to free the most space. If your app is very heavyweight, it will probably be removed to save space. Keeping the file size small and leaving copy protection set to Off keeps you out of the crosshairs in this issue.

11. **Select the list of locations that the application should be visible in.**

    For example, if your application is an Italian application, deselect All Locations and select Italy as the destination location. This ensures that only devices in the Italy region can see this in the Market. If you leave All Locations enabled, you guessed it — all locations can see your app in the Market.

12. **Fill out the Web Site and E-mail fields (and Phone, if you'd like).**

    I never fill out the Phone field because, well, users will call you! Yes, they will call at midnight asking you questions, giving feedback, and so on. I prefer to communicate with customers via e-mail. If you are writing an app for a different company yet publishing it under your developer account, you can change the Web Site, E-mail, and Phone fields so that the users do not contact you. Users use these fields to contact you for various reasons. The most common correspondence that I receive is app feature requests and bug reports.

13. **Verify that your application meets the Android content guidelines and that you complied with applicable laws by selecting the pertinent check boxes.**

14. **Choose one of the following options:**

    • *Publish:* Saves and publishes the app to the Market in real time.

    • *Save:* Saves the changes made, but does not publish the app.

    • *Delete:* Deletes all the work up until now. Don't do this.

    For this exercise, click the Save button. This saves your application and returns you to the Android developer home page, where an icon states that the app is in a saved state (see Figure 8-17). You can use this as a staging area until you're ready to release your app.

Figure 8-17:
The saved
app on your
Android
developer
home
screen.

15. **When you're ready to release the app, select the title of the app on the Android developer home page.**

    The Upload an Application page opens (refer to Figure 8-16).

16. **Scroll to the bottom of the page, and click the Publish button.**

    This publishes your application to the Android Market.

Figure 8-18 shows the application I just built running in the Android Market on my Nexus One device. I opened the Android Market, navigated to Apps — Productivity — and went to the Just In tab, which identifies the apps that have just been released.

You probably noticed one bonus of this process: no app-approval process like other mobile carriers! You can create an app, right now, and publish it, and then users can install it right away. This means that you can perform a quick release cycle and get new features out the door as quickly as you can get them done, which is very cool.

If you search for this app on the Android Market on your device, you will not find it because after this was written, I removed the app from the Market. This is because the app was an example that demonstrated the app-publishing process. I chose the app title from the Android developer home screen, scrolled to the bottom, and clicked the Unpublish button to remove it from the Android Market.

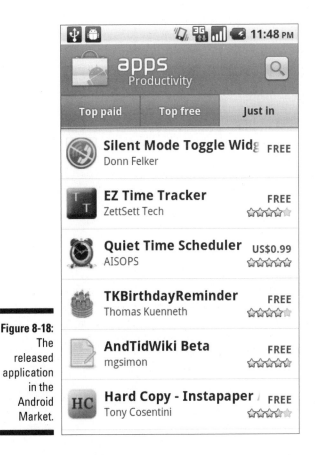

Figure 8-18:
The
released
application
in the
Android
Market.

Watching the Installs Soar

You've finally published your first application. Now it's time to watch the millions start rolling in, right? Well, kind of. You might be an independent developer who's releasing the next best first-person shooter game, or you might be a corporate developer who's pushing out your company's Android application. Regardless, you need to be aware of the end-user experience on various devices. You have various ways of identifying how your application is doing:

✔ **Five-star rating system:** The higher average rating you have, the better.

✔ **Comments:** Read them! People take the time to leave them, so provide them the courtesy of reading them. You'd be surprised at the great ideas that people provide to you for free. Most of the time, I've found if I implement the most commonly requested feature, users get excited about it and come back and update their comments with a much more positive boost in rating.

✔ **Error reports:** Users that were gracious enough to submit error reports want to let you know that the app experienced a run-time exception for an unknown reason. Open these reports, look at the error, review the stack trace, and try to fix the error. An app that gets a lot of force close errors receives a lot of really bad reviews, really quick. Stack traces are available only for devices that are running Android 2.2 and above.

✔ **Installs versus active installs:** While this isn't the best metric for identifying user satisfaction, it is an unscientific way to determine whether users who install your app tend to keep it on their phone. If users are keeping your app, they must like it!

✔ **Direct e-mails:** Users will return to the Android Market to find your e-mail address and/or Web site address. They will e-mail you to ask questions about features and send comments to you about their user experience. They may also send you ideas about how to improve your app, or they may ask you to create another app that does something they cannot find on the Market. People love to be part of something. I've found if I personally reply within 24 hours (less than 4 hours is really what I aim for), users become real happy with the response time. While this is difficult to sustain if your app has a million active users, it does make users very happy to know that they can get a hold of you if they run into an issue with your app that they love so much.

Keeping in touch with your user base is a large task itself, but doing so can reap rewards of dedicated, happy customers who will refer their friends and family to use your application.

Amazon announced the first third-party App Store for Android devices in 2011. Like the Google Android Market, the Amazon App Store offers applications for users to buy and install. Developers can sell their applications and receive a competitive rate for their apps from Amazon, or post free apps to the Amazon App Store. Amazon also provides great sales metrics for developers and marketers. Find out more at `http://developer.amazon.com`.

Part III

Creating a Feature-Rich Application

The 5th Wave
By Rich Tennant

Well, heck — that's just darn impressive! And you say it's programmed to sew up and dress the incision afterward as well?

In this part . . .

In Part III, I expand on the knowledge that you acquire in Part II by demonstrating how you can build a feature-rich application. I don't trudge through every detail as I do in Part II, but I expand on the details that you need to know to become a master Android application developer. I also mention a few advanced topics that can help bridge the gap between beginner and advanced Android developer.

In this part, I showcase how and why you would create certain features to enhance users' experiences with your application. At the end of Part III, you will have a fully-functioning advanced application that interacts with a local database and custom preferences.

Chapter 9

Designing the Task Reminder Application

*B*uilding Android applications is fun, but building truly in-depth applications is exciting because you dive into the real guts of the Android platform. In this chapter, I introduce you to the Task Reminder application, which will be built from end to end over the next couple of chapters.

The Task Reminder application allows users to create a list of items that have a reminder time associated with each individual item.

Reviewing the Basic Requirements

The Task Reminder application has a few basic requirements to fulfill what is expected of it:

✔ It must be able to accept user input — having a personalized task application that does not allow user input would be silly!

✔ The tasks must be easy to manage.

✔ Each task must have a reminder date and time in which the user will be reminded of the task.

✔ The user must be notified of the task when the reminder time has arrived.

✔ Users must be able to delete tasks.

✔ Users must be able to not only add tasks but to edit them.

You see a lot of interaction happening with the user and the Android system in this application. Throughout the development of this application, you are introduced to various facets of Android development that can help you in your career. I wish I would have known some of these things when I started; it would have saved me a lot of time!

That's alarming!: Scheduling a reminder script

For the Task Reminder application to truly work, you need to implement some sort of reminder-based system. As a fellow developer, the first thing that comes to mind is a scheduled task or `cron` job. In the Windows operating system, developers can create a scheduled task to handle the execution of code/scripts at a given time. In the UNIX/Linux world, developers can use `cron` (short for *chronos* — Greek for *time*) to schedule scripts or applications.

Because Android is running the Linux 2.6 kernel, it would be normal to assume that Android has a `crontab` you could edit. `Cron` is driven by `crontab`, which is a configuration file that specifies the commands to run at a given time. Unfortunately Android does not have `cron`; however, Android has the `AlarmManager` class, which achieves the same thing. The `AlarmManager` class allows you to specify when your application should start in the future. Alarms can be set as a single-use alarm or as a repeating alarm. The Task Reminder application utilizes the `AlarmManager` to remind users of their tasks.

Storing data

You will be exposed to many new features and tools in this application, and a big question that may be lingering in your head is, where am I going to put the activities, the task data, the alarms, and so on. These items will be stored in the following locations:

- ✔ **Activities and broadcast receivers:** In one Java package
- ✔ **Task data:** SQLite database
- ✔ **Alarm info:** Pulled from the SQLite database and placed in the `AlarmManager` via the intent system

Distracting the user (nicely)

After an alarm fires, you need to notify the user of the alarm. The Android platform provides mechanisms to bring your activity to the foreground when the alarm fires, but that is not an optimal notification method because it steals focus from what the user was doing. Imagine if the user was typing a phone number or answering a phone call and an alarm fired that brought an activity to the foreground. Not only would the user be irritated, he most likely would be confused because an activity started that he did not initiate manually. Therefore, you have various ways in which you can grab the user's attention without stealing the main focus away from his current activity. These mechanisms include the following:

- ✔ **Toasts:** A *toast* is a small view that contains a quick message for the user. This message does not persist because it is usually available for only a few seconds at most. A toast never receives focus. I won't use a toast for reminding the user, but instead I use a toast to notify the user when her activity has been saved so that she knows something happened.

- ✔ **Notification Manager:** The `NotificationManager` class is used to notify a user that an event or events have taken place. These events can be placed in the status bar, which is located at the top of the screen. The notification items can contain various views and are identified by icons that you provide. The user can slide the screen down to view the notification.

- ✔ **Dialog boxes:** A final, not-so-popular method to grab a user's attention is to open a dialog window that can immediately steal focus from the user's currently running app and direct it to a dialog window. While this may indeed work as a method for grabbing the attention of the user, the user may get irritated because your app is stealing focus (possibly on a constant basis if the user has a lot of reminders) from his current actions in another application.

I will be using the `NotificationManager` class to handle the alarms for the Task Reminder application.

Creating the Application's Screens

The Task Reminder application will have two different screens that perform all the basic CRUD (Create, Read, Update, and Delete) functions. The first view is a list view that lists all the current tasks in the application, by name.

This view also allows you to delete a task by long-pressing the item. The second view allows you to view (Read), add (Create), or edit (Update) a task. Each screen eventually interacts with a database for changes to be persisted over the long-term use of the application.

Starting the new project

To get started, Open Eclipse and create a new Android project with a `Build Target` of Android 2.2 and a `MinSDKVersion` of 4. Provide it with a valid name, package, and activity. The settings I have chosen are shown in Table 9-1. You may also choose to open the example Android project for Chapter 9 provided by the online source code download. This provides you with a starting point that has the same settings as my project.

Table 9-1	New Project Settings
Property	*Value*
Project Name	`Task Reminder`
Build Target	Android 2.2 (API Level 8)
Application Name	`Task Reminder`
Package Name	`com.dummies.android.` `taskreminder`
Create Activity	`ReminderListActivity`
Min SDK Version	`4`

Note the Create Activity property value — `ReminderListActivity`. Normally I give the first activity in an application the name of `MainActivity`; however, the first screen that the user will see is a list of current tasks. Therefore, this activity is actually an instance of a `ListActivity`; hence the name — `ReminderListActivity`.

Creating the task list

When working with `ListActivity` classes, I like to have my layout file contain the word *list*. This makes it easy to find when I open the `res/layout` directory. I'm going to rename the `main.xml` file located in the `res/layout` directory to `reminder_list.xml`. To rename the file in Eclipse, you can either right-click the file and choose Refactor⇨Rename or select the file and press Shift+Alt+R.

After you change the filename, you need to update the name of the file in the `setContentView()` call inside the `ReminderListActivity.java` file. Open the file and change the reference to the new filename you chose.

The `ReminderListActivity` class also needs to inherit from the `ListActivity` class instead of the regular base activity. Make that change as well. My new `ReminderListActivity` class looks like Listing 9-1.

Listing 9-1:   The `ReminderListActivity` Class

```
public class ReminderListActivity extends ListActivity {
    /** Called when the activity is first created. */
    @Override
    public void onCreate(Bundle savedInstanceState) {
        super.onCreate(savedInstanceState);
        setContentView(R.layout.reminder_list);
    }
}
```

Your `ReminderListActivity` references the `reminder_list` layout resource that currently contains the default code that was generated when you created the project. To work with a `ListActivity`, you need to update this layout with new code, as shown in Listing 9-2.

Listing 9-2:   The `reminder_list.xml` Contents

```
<?xml version="1.0" encoding="utf-8"?>
<LinearLayout xmlns:android="http://schemas.android.com/apk/res/android"
    android:layout_width="wrap_content"
    android:layout_height="wrap_content">
    <ListView android:id="@+id/android:list"                          → 5
        android:layout_width="fill_parent"
        android:layout_height="fill_parent"/>
        <TextView android:id="@+id/android:empty"                     → 8
        android:layout_width="wrap_content"
        android:layout_height="wrap_content"
        android:text="@string/no_reminders"/>                         → 11
</LinearLayout>
```

This code is briefly explained as follows:

→ **5**   Defines a `ListView`, which is an Android view that is used to show a list of vertically scrolling items. The ID of the `ListView` *must* be `@id/android:list` or `@+id/android:list`.

→ **8**   Defines the empty state of the list. If the list is empty, this is the view that will be shown. When this view is present, the `ListView` will automatically be hidden because there is no data to display. This view must have an ID of `@id/android:empty` or `@+id/android:empty`.

→ **11** This line uses a string resource called `no_reminders` to inform the user that no reminders are currently in the system. You need to add a new string resource to the `res/values/strings.xml` file with the name of `no_reminders`. The value I'm choosing is "No Reminders Yet."

Creating and editing task activities

The Task Reminder application needs one more screen that allows the user to edit a task and its information. This screen will be all-inclusive, meaning that one single activity can allow users to create, read, and update tasks.

In Eclipse, create a new activity that can handle these roles. I'm choosing to call mine `ReminderEditActivity` by right-clicking the package name in the `src` folder and choosing New⇨Class or by pressing Shift+Alt+N and then choosing Class. In the new Java class window, set the superclass to `android.app.Activity` and choose Finish.

A blank activity class now opens, and inside this class, type the following lines that are boldface:

```
public class ReminderEditActivity extends Activity {
    @Override
    protected void onCreate(Bundle savedInstanceState) {
        super.onCreate(savedInstanceState);
        setContentView(R.layout.reminder_edit);
    }
}
```

In line 5 of the preceding code, I am setting the layout of the activity to the `reminder_edit` resource, which is defined in the next section. This layout contains the various fields of the task in which the user can edit or create.

You also need to inform the Android platform about the existence of this activity by adding it to the Android Manifest. You can do so by adding it to the `Application` element of the `ApplicationManifest.xml` file, as shown here in boldface:

```
<application android:icon="@drawable/icon" android:label="@string/app_name">
    <activity android:name=".ReminderListActivity"
            android:label="@string/app_name">
        <intent-filter>
            <action android:name="android.intent.action.MAIN" />
            <category android:name="android.intent.category.LAUNCHER" />
        </intent-filter>
    </activity>
    <activity android:name=".ReminderEditActivity"
            android:label="@string/app_name" />
</application>
```

WARNING!

If you do not add the activity to the `ApplicationManifest.xml` file, you receive a run-time exception informing you that Android cannot find the class (the activity).

Creating the adding/editing layout

The layout for adding and editing is fairly simple because the form contains very few fields. These fields are as follows:

- ✔ **Title:** The title of the task as it will show in the list view.
- ✔ **Body:** The body of the task. This is where the user would type in the details.
- ✔ **Reminder Date:** The date on which the user should be reminded of the task.
- ✔ **Reminder Time:** The time at which the user should be reminded on the reminder date.

When complete and running on a device or emulator, the screen looks like Figure 9-1.

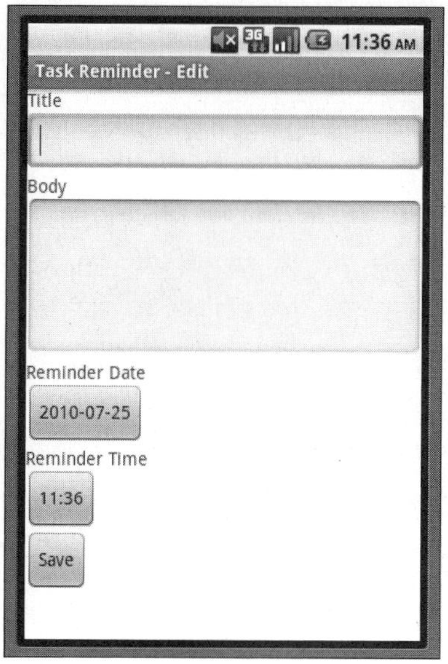

Figure 9-1:
The Add/
Edit Task
Reminder
screen.

To create this layout, create a layout file in the `res/layout` directory with an appropriate name — I'm using `reminder_edit.xml`. To create this file, perform the following steps:

1. **Right-click the `res/layout` directory and choose New⇨Android XML File.**

2. **Provide the name in the File field.**

3. **Leave the default type of resource selected — Layout.**

4. **Leave the folder set to `res/layout`.**

5. **Set the root element to `ScrollView`.**

6. **Click the Finish button.**

You now need to provide all the view definitions to build the screen that you see in Figure 9-1. To do this, type the code shown in Listing 9-3.

Listing 9-3:   The `reminder_edit.xml` File

```
<?xml version="1.0" encoding="utf-8"?>
<ScrollView
        xmlns:android="http://schemas.android.com/apk/res/android"
        android:layout_width="fill_parent"
        android:layout_height="fill_parent">                            → 5
<LinearLayout                                                           → 6
    android:orientation="vertical"                                     → 7
    android:layout_width="fill_parent"
    android:layout_height="fill_parent">
    <TextView android:layout_width="wrap_content"
            android:layout_height="wrap_content"
            android:text="@string/title" />                            → 12
    <EditText android:id="@+id/title"
            android:layout_width="fill_parent"
              android:layout_height="wrap_content" />                  → 15
    <TextView android:layout_width="wrap_content"
            android:layout_height="wrap_content"
            android:text="@string/body" />                             → 18
    <EditText android:id="@+id/body"
            android:layout_width="fill_parent"
            android:layout_height="wrap_content"
            android:minLines="5"
            android:scrollbars="vertical"
            android:gravity="top" />                                   → 24
    <TextView android:layout_width="wrap_content"
            android:layout_height="wrap_content"
            android:text="@string/date" />                             → 27
    <Button
            android:id="@+id/reminder_date"
            android:layout_height="wrap_content"
            android:layout_width="wrap_content"/>                      → 31
    <TextView android:layout_width="wrap_content"
            android:layout_height="wrap_content"
            android:text="@string/time" />                             → 34
    <Button
            android:id="@+id/reminder_time"
```

```
              android:layout_height="wrap_content"
              android:layout_width="wrap_content" />                    → 38
    <Button   android:id="@+id/confirm"
              android:text="@string/confirm"
              android:layout_width="wrap_content"
              android:layout_height="wrap_content" />                   → 42
</LinearLayout>
</ScrollView>
```

A brief explanation of the code in Listing 9-3 is as follows:

→ **5**   The parent view is a ScrollView, which creates a scroll bar and allows the view to be scrolled when the contents of the view are too big for the screen. The screen shown in Figure 9-1 is shown in portrait mode. However, if the device is rotated 90 degrees, the view flips and over half of the view is cut off. The parent ScrollView allows the remaining contents of the screen to be scrollable. Therefore, the user can fling his finger upward on the screen to scroll the contents up and see the remainder of the view.

→ **6**   A ScrollView can only have one child — in this case, it's the main LinearLayout that houses the rest of the layout.

→ **7**   The orientation of the linear layout is set to vertical to signify that the views inside this layout should be stacked on top of one another.

→ **12**   The label for the Title field.

→ **15**   The EditText that allows the user to provide a title for the task.

→ **18**   The label for the Body field.

→ **24**   The EditText that defines the Body field. The EditText view has set the minLines property to 5 and the gravity property to top. This informs the Android platform that the EditText is at least five lines tall, and when the user starts typing, the text should be bound to the top of the view (the gravity).

→ **27**   The reminder date label. This label also uses a string resource. You will need to add a string resource with the name of "date" and a value of "Reminder Date".

→ **31**   The reminder date button. When this button is clicked, a DatePickerDialog is launched — this allows the user to choose a date with a built-in Android date picker. When the date is set via the DatePicker, the value of the date is set as the button text.

→ **34**   The reminder time label. This label uses a string resource. You will need to add a string resource with the name of "time" and a value of "Time".

→ **38**   The time reminder button. When this button is clicked, a TimePicker is launched — this allows the user to choose a time with a built-in Android time picker. When the time is set via the TimePickerDialog, the value of the time is set as the button text.

→ **42** The confirmation button that will save the values of the form when clicked.

Creating Your First List Activity

The ListActivity class displays a list of items by binding to a data source such as an array or cursor, and exposes callback methods when the user selects an item. However, to build a list of items to display in a list, you need to add a layout that defines what each row will look like.

A cursor provides random read and write access to the result set that is returned by a database query.

Add a new layout to the res/layout directory with a root element of TextView and give it a proper name for a row type of item — I'm choosing to use reminder_row.xml as the name. Inside this view, type the code as shown in Listing 9-4.

Listing 9-4: The reminder_row.xml File

```xml
<?xml version="1.0" encoding="utf-8"?>
<TextView
    xmlns:android="http://schemas.android.com/apk/res/android"
    android:id="@+id/text1"
    android:layout_width="fill_parent"
    android:layout_height="fill_parent"
    android:padding="10dip"/>
```

This code simply defines a row in which text values can be placed with a padding of ten density-independent pixels. Line 4 defines the ID of the view that I will reference when loading the list with data.

The view you just added is actually provided out of the box in the Android system. If you look at the Android documentation under Android.R.layout under simple_list_item_1 and inspect it via the Android source control repository, you can see virtually the same XML definition. That source can be found here:

```
http://android.git.kernel.org/?p=platform/frameworks/base.git;a=blob;f=core/res/
        res/layout/simple_list_item_1.xml;h=c9c77a5f9c113a9d331d5e11a6016a
        aa815ec771;hb=HEAD
```

A shortened version can be found at http://bit.ly/9GzZzm.

The ListActivity requires that an adapter fill the contents of the list view. Various adapters are available, but because I have not built a data store yet (built with an SQLite database in Chapter 12), I create fake data so that I can see the list in action. After I have the fake data, I set the ListActivity's adapter with a call to setListAdapater(). But before I can do that, I need some fake/stub data to work with.

Getting stubby with fake data

Inside the onCreate() method of the ReminderListActivity.java file, after the call to setContentView(), add the following code:

```
String[] items = new String[] { "Foo", "Bar", "Fizz", "Bin" };                    → 1

ArrayAdapter<String> adapter =
    new ArrayAdapter<String>(this, R.layout.reminder_row, R.id.text1, items);     → 4
setListAdapter(adapter);                                            d              → 5
```

A brief explanation of the code is as follows:

→ **1**   An array of string items are being created. These are the items that will eventually be displayed in the list.

→ **4**   The creation of a new ArrayAdapter of string types. An ArrayAdapter manages a ListView backed by an arbitrary number of arbitrary objects — in this case, a simple string array. This code is using Java generics, which allow the developer to specify the type of object that the ArrayAdapter will be working with. The constructor of the ArrayAdapter contains the following:

   • this: The current context (Because the activity is an implementation of the Context class, I can use the current instance as the context.)

   • R.layout.reminder_row: The row layout that should be used for each row in the ListView

   • R.id.text1: The ID of the TextView inside R.layout. reminder_row in which to place the values from the array

   • items: The array of strings to load into the ListView

→ **5**   The call to setListAdapter() that informs the ListActivity how to fill the ListView. In this case, I am using the ArrayAdapter created on line 4 to load the ListView.

Start the Android application by choosing Run⇨Run or by pressing Ctrl+F11. The screen you should see should look similar to Figure 9-2.

The previous code and example illustrate how to use a static data source for the ListActivity. In Chapter 12, I remove this code loading the ListActivity from an SQLite database.

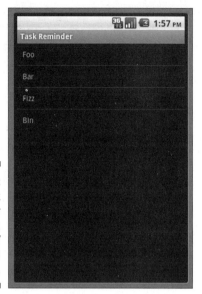

Figure 9-2:
The Task
Reminder
running
with fake/
stubbed
data.

Handling user click events

The items in the list expose click events that allow the user to interact with each item. Android `View` objects have two main types of click events:

- ✔ **Click:** The user taps a view such as a button.

- ✔ **Long click:** The user taps and holds his finger on a button for a few moments.

Each view and/or activity can intercept these events via various methods. In the following section, I show you how to respond to each type of event in a `ListActivity`. In Chapter 11, I demonstrate responding to `Button` click events.

Short clicks

The `ListActivity` in Android does a lot of the event-handling heavy lifting for you — which is good because programming shouldn't be a physical exercise!

After the `onCreate()` method, type this method:

```
@Override
protected void onListItemClick(ListView l, View v, int position, long id) {
    super.onListItemClick(l, v, position, id);
}
```

This code overrides the default implementation of onListItemClick() that is provided by the ListActivity. When a list item is clicked, this method is called and the following parameters are passed into the call:

- ✔ l: The ListView where the click happened
- ✔ v: The item that was clicked with the ListView
- ✔ position: The position of the clicked item in the list
- ✔ id: The row ID of the item that was clicked

Using these variables, you can determine which item was clicked and then perform an action based on that information. When an item is clicked in this list, I will be starting an intent that opens the ReminderEditActivity to allow me to edit the item, as shown in the section "Starting new activities with intents," later in this chapter.

Long clicks

Long clicks, also known as *long presses,* occur when a user presses a view for an extended period of time. To handle the list item's long-click event in a ListActivity, add the following line of code at the end of the onCreate() method:

```
registerForContextMenu(getListView());
```

The outer method, registerForContextMenu(), is responsible for registering a context menu to be shown for a given view — multiple views can show a context menu; it's not just limited to a single view. This means that each list item is eligible to create a context menu. The registerForContextMenu() accepts a View object as a parameter that the ListActivity should register as eligible for the context menu creation. The inner method, getListView(), returns a ListView object that is used for the registration. The call, getListView(), is a member of the ListActivity class.

Now that you've registered the ListView to be eligible to create a context menu, you need to respond to the long-click event on any given item. When an item is long-clicked in the ListView, the registerForContextMenu() recognizes this and calls the onCreateContextMenu() method when the context menu is ready to be created. In this method, you set up your context menu.

At the end of the class file, type the following method:

```
@Override
public void onCreateContextMenu(ContextMenu menu, View v, ContextMenuInfo
                menuInfo) {
    super.onCreateContextMenu(menu, v, menuInfo);
}
```

This method is called with the following parameters:

- ✔ `menu`: The context menu that is being built.
- ✔ `v`: The view for which the context is being built (the view you long-clicked on).
- ✔ `menuInfo`: Extra information about the item for which the context menu should be shown. This can vary depending on the type of view in the `v` parameter.

Inside this method, you can modify the menu that will be presented to the user. For example, when a user long-presses an item in the task list, I want to allow her to delete it. Therefore, I need to present her with a Delete context menu option. I add the Delete item to the context menu in Chapter 10.

Identifying Your Intent

Most applications are no run-of-the-mill introduction applications! Though some applications have only two screens (such as the Task Reminder application), a lot is happening behind the scenes. One such notable interaction that happens between the application and the user is the introduction of new screens as the user utilizes various features of the application. As with any application with a rich feature set, the user can interact with each screen independently. Therefore the big question arises: "How do I open another screen?"

Screen interaction is handled through Android's intent system. I have covered the intent system in detail in Chapter 7, but I have not covered an example of how to navigate from one screen to the next using an intent. Thankfully, it's a simple process — and I bet you're happy about that!

Starting new activities with intents

Activities are initiated through the Android intent framework. An `Intent` is a class that represents a message that is placed on the Android intent system (similar to a message-bus type of architecture), and whoever can respond to the intent lets the Android platform know, resulting in either an activity starting or a list of applications to choose from (this is known as a chooser, explained shortly). One of the best ways to think of an intent is to think of it as an abstract description of an operation.

Starting a particular activity is easy. In your `ReminderListActivity`, type the following code into the `onListItemClick()` method:

```
@Override
protected void onListItemClick(ListView l, View v, int position, long id) {
    super.onListItemClick(l, v, position, id);
    Intent i = new Intent(this, ReminderEditActivity.class);        → 4
    i.putExtra("RowId", id);                                        → 5
    startActivity(i);                                               → 6
}
```

A brief explanation of each line is as follows:

→ **4**   This line is creating a new intent using the `Intent` constructor that accepts the current context, which is `this` (the current running activity), as well as a class that the Intent system should attempt to start — the Reminder Edit activity.

→ **5**   This line places some extra data into the `Intent` object. In this instance, I'm placing a key/value pair into the intent. The key is `RowId`, and the value is the ID of the view that was clicked. This value is placed into the intent so that the receiving activity (the `ReminderEditActivity`) can pull this data from the `Intent` object and use it to load the information about the intent. Right now, I'm providing fake/stub data; therefore, nothing displays. However, after Chapter 12, you see data flowing into the `ReminderEditActivity`.

→ **6**   This line starts the activity from within the current activity. This call places the intent message onto the Android intent system and allows Android to decide how to open that screen for the user.

Retrieving values from previous activities

Sometimes, activities are simply started, and that's the end of it. No extra data is passed among various activities. However, in some instances, you need to be able to pull data out of the incoming intent to figure out what to do. As demonstrated in the section "Starting new activities with intents," earlier in this chapter, you provided some extra data with the intent. This is the `RowId`. In Chapter 12, you use this `RowId` on the `ReminderEditActivity` to pull the data from the SQLite database and display it to the user.

To pull the data out of an incoming intent, type the following at the end of the destination activity's `onCreate()` method — which would be the `ReminderEditActivity`:

```
if(getIntent() != null) {                                          → 1
    Bundle extras = getIntent().getExtras();                       → 2
    int rowId = extras != null ? extras.getInt("RowId") : -1;      → 3
    // Do stuff with the row id here
}
```

A brief explanation of each line of code is as follows:

→ **1**   The `getIntent()` method is provided by the `Activity` base class. This method retrieves any incoming intent to the activity. On this line, I am making sure that it is not null so that I know it's safe to work with.

→ **2**   The bundle is retrieved from the intent via the `getExtras()` call. A *bundle* is a simple key/value pair data structure.

→ **3**   On this line, I am using the ternary operator to identify whether the bundle is null. If the bundle is not null, I retrieve the `RowId` that is contained in the intent that was sent from the previous activity through the `getInt()` method. Although I am not doing anything with it in this instance, in Chapter 12, I use this row ID to query the SQLite database to retrieve the `Task` record to edit.

When the SQLite database is in place (which is done in Chapter 12), the record will be retrieved from the database and the various values of the task will be presented to the user on the screen via an editable form so that the user can edit the task.

Creating a chooser

At some point in your Android development career, you will run into a particular instance where you need to provide the user with a list of applications that can handle a particular intent. A common example of this would be to share some data with a friend via a common networking tool such as e-mail, SMS, Twitter, Facebook, Google Latitude, or any other similar tool.

The Android Intent system was built to handle these types of situations. Though not used in the Task Reminder application, this is something that can come in very handy — which is why I'm including it here. The code to display various available options to the user is shown in Listing 9-5.

Listing 9-5:   Creating an Intent Chooser

```
Intent i = new Intent(Intent.ACTION_SEND);                                    → 1
i.setType("text/plain");                                                      → 2
i.putExtra(Intent.EXTRA_TEXT, "Hey Everybody!");                              → 3
i.putExtra(Intent.EXTRA_SUBJECT, "My Subject");                              → 4
Intent chooser = Intent.createChooser(i, "Who Should Handle this?");         → 5
startActivity(chooser);                                                       → 6
```

A brief explanation of each line in Listing 9-5 is as follows:

→ **1**   The creation of a new intent that informs the Intent system that you would like to send something — think of this as something you want to mail to another person. You are intending to send something to someone else.

→ **2**   The content type of the message — this can be set to any explicit MIME type. MIME types are case-sensitive, unlike RFC MIME types, and should always be typed in lowercase letters. This specifies the type of the intent; therefore, only applications that can respond to this type of intent will show up in the chooser.

→ **3**   Placing extra data into the intent. This will be the body of the message that the application will use. If an e-mail client is chosen, this will end up as the e-mail body. If Twitter is chosen, it will be the message of the tweet. Each application that responds to the intent can handle the extra data in its own special manner. Do not expect the data to be handled as you might think it should in the destination application. The developer of such an application determines how the application should handle the extra data.

→ **4**   Similar to line 3, but this time the subject extra is provided. If an e-mail client responds, this normally ends up as the subject of the e-mail.

→ **5**   Creating the chooser. The `Intent` object has a static helper method that helps you create a chooser. The chooser is an intent itself. You simply provide the target intent (what you'd like to happen) as well as a title for the pop-up chooser that is shown.

→ **6**   Starting the intent. This creates the chooser for you to choose an application from.

The chooser that is created from Listing 9-5 is shown in Figure 9-3.

If the Intent system cannot find any valid applications to handle the intent, the chooser is created with a message informing the user that no applications could perform the action, as shown in Figure 9-4.

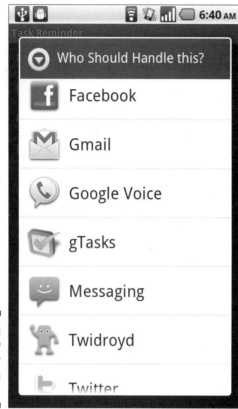

Choosers are a great way to increase the interoperability of your application. However, if you simply called startActivity() without creating a chooser, your application might crash. Starting an activity without the chooser in Listing 9-5 would be as such — startActivity(i) instead of startActivity (chooser). The application would crash because Android is giving you full reign on what you can do. This means that Android assumes you know what you're doing. Therefore, by not including a chooser, you're assuming that the destination device actually has at least one application to handle the intent. If this is not the case, Android will throw an exception (which is visible through DDMS) informing you that no class can handle the intent. To the end user, this means your app has crashed.

To provide a great user experience, always provide an intent chooser when firing off intents that are meant for interoperability with other applications. It provides a smooth and consistent usability model that the rest of Android already provides.

Chapter 10

Going a la Carte with Your Menu

Sure, I wish I were down at my favorite Mexican restaurant, ordering some excellent chips and salsa; alas, I'm not. I'm not talking about menus with regard to food; I'm talking about menus inside an Android application!

Android provides a simple mechanism for you to add menus to your applications. You find the following types of menus:

✔ **Options menu:** The options menu is the most common type of menu that you will most likely be working with because it is the primary menu for an activity. This is the menu that is presented when a user presses the Menu key on the device. Within the options menu are two groups:

  • *Icon:* These are the menu options that are available at the bottom of the screen. The device supports up to six menu items, and they are the only menu items that support the use of icons. They do not support check boxes or radio buttons.

  • *Expanded:* The expanded menu is a list of menu items that goes beyond the original six menu items that are present in the Icon menu. This menu is presented by the More menu icon that is automatically placed on-screen when the user places more than six items on the Icon menu. This menu is comprised of the sixth and higher menu items.

✔ **Context menu:** A floating list of menu items that is presented when a user long-presses a view.

✔ **Submenu:** A floating list of menu items that the user opens by clicking a menu item on the Options menu or on a context menu. A submenu item cannot support nested submenus.

You will be a creating an options menu as well as a context menu in this chapter. Feel free to grab the full application source code from the companion site if you happen to get lost.

Seeing What Makes a Menu Great

If you have an Android device and you've downloaded a few applications from the Android Market, I'm sure that you've encountered a few bad menu implementations. What does a bad menu implementation look like?

A bad menu is a menu that provides very little (if any) helpful text in the menu description and provides no icon. A few common menu faux pas include

- A poor menu title
- A menu without an icon
- No menu
- A menu that does not do what it states it will

While all these issues above indicate a bad menu, the biggest faux pas of the list is the lack of a menu icon. This may sound a bit odd, but think about it for a second. If a menu does not have an icon, that means the developer has not taken the time to provide a good user interface and a good user experience to the user. A good menu should have a visual as well as a textual appeal to the end user. The appearance of a menu icon shows that the developer actually thought through the process of creating the menu and deciding which icon best suits the application. This mental process provides some insight into how the menu was designed. Please note: Just because an application has menu icons does not mean that the menu is great.

I use the menu icon paradigm as a way to initially judge the usefulness of the menu. A menu without an icon is less useful to me than one with an icon.

Creating Your First Menu

You can create a menu through code or you can create it through an XML file that is provided in the res/menu directory. The preferred method of creating menus is to define menus through XML and then inflate them into a programmable object that you can interact with. This helps separate the menu definition from the actual application code.

Defining the XML file

To define an XML menu, follow these steps:

1. Create a `menu` folder in the `res` directory.

2. Add a file by the name of `list_menu.xml` to the menu directory.

3. Type the code from Listing 10-1 into the `list_menu.xml` file.

Listing 10-1: Menu for the `ReminderListActivity`

```xml
<?xml version="1.0" encoding="utf-8"?>
<menu
    xmlns:android="http://schemas.android.com/apk/res/android">
    <item android:id="@+id/menu_insert"
            android:icon="@android:drawable/ic_menu_add"
            android:title="@string/menu_insert" />
</menu>
```

Notice that a new string resource is included. You need to create that (which you do in Step 4). The `android:icon` value is a built-in Android icon. You do not have to provide this bitmap in your drawable resources. The ldpi, mdpi, and hdpi versions of this icon are all built into the Android platform. To view other resources available to you, view the `android.R.drawable` documentation here: `http://developer.android.com/reference/android/R.drawable.html`.

All resources in the `android.R` class are available for you to use in your application and are recommended because they give your application a common and consistent user interface and user experience with the Android platform.

4. Create a new string resource with the name `menu_insert` with the value of "Add Reminder" in the `strings.xml` resource file.

5. Open the `ReminderListActivity` class and type the following code into the file:

```java
@Override
public boolean onCreateOptionsMenu(Menu menu) {
    super.onCreateOptionsMenu(menu);
    MenuInflater mi = getMenuInflater();
    mi.inflate(R.menu.list_menu, menu);
    return true;
}
```

On line 4, I obtain a `MenuInflater` that is capable of inflating menus from XML resources. After the inflater is obtained, the menu is inflated into an actual menu object on line 5. The existing menu is the menu object that is passed into the `onCreateOptionsMenu()` method.

6. Install the application in the emulator, and click the Menu button.

You should see what's shown in Figure 10-1.

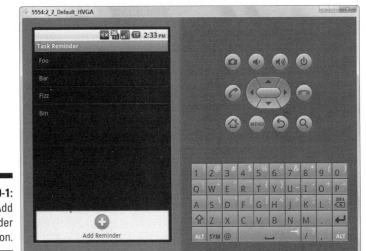

Figure 10-1:
The Add
Reminder
menu icon.

Handling user actions

The menu has been created, and now you'd like to perform some type of action when it is clicked. To do this, type the following code at the end of the class file:

```
@Override
public boolean onMenuItemSelected(int featureId, MenuItem item) {      → 2
    switch(item.getItemId()) {                                         → 3
        case R.id.menu_insert:                                         → 4
            createReminder();                                          → 5
            return true;                                               → 6
    }

    return super.onMenuItemSelected(featureId, item);
}
```

The lines of code are explained in detail here:

→ 2   This is the method that is called when a menu item is selected. The `featureId` parameter identifies the panel that the menu is located on. The `item` parameter identifies which menu item was clicked on.

→ 3   To determine which item you're working with, compare the ID of the menu items with the known menu items you have. Therefore, a `switch` statement is used to check each possible valid case. You obtain the menu's ID through the `MenuItem` method `getItemId()`.

→ 4   I'm using the ID of the menu item that was defined in Listing 10-1 to see whether that menu item was clicked.

→ **5** If the Add Reminder menu item was clicked, the application is instructed to create a reminder through the `createReminder()` method (defined in the next section).

→ **6** This line returns true to inform the `onMenuItemSelected()` method that a menu selection was handled.

You may be receiving compilation errors at this time, but don't worry! I resolve those in the "Creating a reminder task" section that follows.

Creating a reminder task

The `createReminder()` method is used to allow the user to navigate to the `ReminderEditActivity` to create a new task with a reminder. Type the following method at the bottom of your `ReminderListActivity` class file:

```
private static final int ACTIVITY_CREATE=0;
private void createReminder() {
    Intent i = new Intent(this, ReminderEditActivity.class);
    startActivityForResult(i, ACTIVITY_CREATE);
}
```

This code creates a new intent that starts the `ReminderEditActivity`. The `startActivityForResult()` call on line 4 is used when you would like a result for when the called activity is completed. You may want to know when an activity has been returned so that you can perform some type of action. In the case of the Task Reminder application, you would want to know when the `ReminderEditActivity` has returned to repopulate the task list with the newly added reminder. This call contains the following two parameters:

✔ `Intent i`: This is the intent that starts the `ReminderEditActivity`.

✔ `ACTIVITY_CREATE`: This is the request code that is returned to your activity through a call to `onActivityResult()` (shown as follows). The request code in this is a classwide constant.

The `ACTIVITY_CREATE` constant is defined at the top of the `Reminder-ListActivity` as such:

```
private static final int ACTIVITY_CREATE=0;
```

Completing the activity

The final call that takes place is after the `ReminderEditActivity` completes — the `onActivityResult()` call. When the `ReminderEditActivity` completes, the `onActivityResult()` method is called with a request code, a result code, and an intent that can contain data back to the original calling activity. Type the following code into the bottom of the `ReminderList-Activity` class file:

```
@Override
protected void onActivityResult(int requestCode, int resultCode, Intent intent)
{
    super.onActivityResult(requestCode, resultCode, intent);
    // Reload the list here
}
```

This call does nothing at this point, but I'm going to leave it here because it will be used in Chapter 12 when I need to reload the tasks from the SQLite database. These parameters are explained as follows:

- ✔ **requestCode:** The integer request code that was provided in the original `startActivityForResult()` call. If your activity starts various other child activities with various request codes, this allows you to differentiate each returning call through a switch statement — very similar to the `onMenuItemSelected()` item `switch` statement mechanism.

- ✔ **resultCode:** The integer result code returned by the child activity through its `setResult()` call. The result code allows you to determine whether your requested action was completed, canceled, or terminated for any other reason. These codes are provided by you to determine what happened between activity calls.

- ✔ **intent:** An intent that the child activity can create to return result data to the caller (various data can be attached to intent "extras"). In the example shown, this intent instance is the same one that is passed into the `onActivityResult()` method.

The superclass is called to take care of any extra processing that may need to take place.

Creating a Context Menu

A context menu is created when a user long-presses a view. The context menu is a floating menu that hovers above the current activity and allows users to choose from various options.

Thankfully, creating a context menu is quite similar to creating an option menu. The menu can be defined in XML and can be inflated using the same mechanism that is used in the creation of an options menu. Therefore, I'm going to jump right into it. To create a context menu, you need to call `registerForContextMenu()` with a view as the target. I create one of these in Chapter 9. After it is created, you need to override the `onCreateContextMenu()` call — also demonstrated in Chapter 9.

The Task Reminder application needs a mechanism in which to delete a task when it is no longer needed in the app. I am going to implement the feature as a context menu. Users long-press the task in the list, and they receive a context menu that allows them to delete the task when the context menu is clicked.

Creating the menu XML file

To create this menu, create a new XML file in the res/menu directory. I'm going to name mine list_menu_item_longpress.xml. Type the following into the XML file:

```
<?xml version="1.0" encoding="utf-8"?>
<menu
  xmlns:android="http://schemas.android.com/apk/res/android">
    <item android:id="@+id/menu_delete"
          android:title="@string/menu_delete" />
</menu>
```

Notice that the title property uses a new string resource menu_delete. You need to create a new string resource with the name of menu_delete and the value of "Delete Reminder." Also note that I do not have an icon associated with this menu. This is because a context menu does not support icons because they are simply a list of menu options that floats above the current activity.

Loading the menu

To load the menu, type the following code into the onCreateContextMenu() method:

```
@Override
public void onCreateContextMenu(ContextMenu menu, View v,
                                ContextMenuInfo menuInfo) {
    super.onCreateContextMenu(menu, v, menuInfo);
    MenuInflater mi = getMenuInflater();
    mi.inflate(R.menu.list_menu_item_longpress, menu);
}
```

This code performs the same function as the onCreateOptionsMenu() call, but this time you are inflating the menu for the context menu and you are loading the context menu. Now, if you long-press a list item in the list view, you receive a context menu, as shown in Figure 10-2.

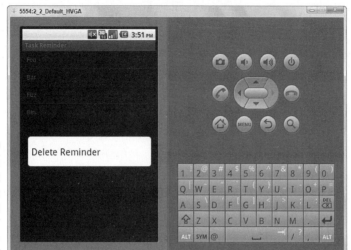

Figure 10-2:
The context
menu in
the Task
Reminder
application.

Handling user selections

Handling the selection of these menu items is very similar to an option menu
as well. To handle the selection of the context menu, type the following code
into the bottom of your class file:

```
@Override
public boolean onContextItemSelected(MenuItem item) {          → 2
    switch(item.getItemId()) {                                 → 3
        case R.id.menu_delete:                                 → 4
            // Delete the task
            return true;
    }
    return super.onContextItemSelected(item);
}
```

The code lines are explained here:

→ **2**   This is the method that is called when a context menu item is
           selected. The item parameter is the item that was selected in
           the context menu.

→ **3**   A switch statement is used to determine which item was
           clicked based upon the ID as defined in the list_menu_
           item_longpress.xml file.

→ **4** This is the ID for the menu_delete button in the list_menu_ item_longpress.xml file. If this menu option is selected, the following code would perform some action based on that determination. Nothing is happening in this code block in this chapter, but in Chapter 12, I delete the task from the SQLite database.

You can add many different context menu items to the list_menu_item_ longpress.xml file and switch between them in the onContextMenu- ItemSelected() method call — each performing a different action.

Chapter 11

Handling User Input

• •

In This Chapter

▶ Working with `EditText` widgets

▶ Creating date and time pickers

▶ Setting up alert dialog boxes

▶ Validating user input

• •

*I*t's rare that you find an application that does not allow you to interact with the user interface via input. Be it text, date pickers, time pickers, or any other input mechanism such as radio buttons or check boxes, users need to interact with your application in one way or another. Although the input mechanism may provide a way for users to interact with your application, unfortunately they won't be chit-chatting and spurring up small talk with you. The generalization of input also refers to buttons, screen dragging, menus, long pressing, and various other options. In this chapter, I focus solely on user input in the form of free-form text, date/times, and alerts.

Creating the User Input Interface

The most common input type is free-form text — known as an `EditText` widget. In other programming platforms, this is known as a text box. With an `EditText` widget, you can provide an on-screen keyboard or the user can elect to use the physical keyboard (if the device provides one) to enter input.

Creating an EditText widget

In Chapter 9, I create a view layout XML file with the name of `reminder_edit.xml` that contains the following code:

```
<EditText android:id="@+id/title"
    android:layout_width="fill_parent"
    android:layout_height="wrap_content" />
```

This snippet of code defines the text input for the title of the task. The snippet creates an input on the screen so that the user can type into it. The `EditText` widget spans the entire width of the screen and only takes up as much room as it needs in regard to height. When selected, Android automatically opens the on-screen keyboard to allow the user to enter some input on the screen. The previous example is a very minimalistic approach as compared to the following `EditText` example, which is also created in the `reminder_edit.xml` layout file:

```
<EditText android:id="@+id/body" android:layout_width="fill_parent"
    android:layout_height="wrap_content"
    android:minLines="5"
    android:scrollbars="vertical"
    android:gravity="top" />
```

Here, I am creating the body description text for the task. The layout width and height are the same as the previous EditText widget — the `EditText` view spanning the width of the screen. The difference in this `EditText` definition is outlined in the following three properties:

- `minLines`: This property specifies how tall the `EditText` view should be. The `EditText` view is a subclass of the `TextView` object; therefore, they share the same property. Here I am specifying that the `EditText` object on the screen be at least five lines tall. This is so that the view resembles a text input that is for long messages. Juxtapose this against the body portion of any e-mail client, and you can see that they're very much the same — the body is much larger than the subject. In this case, the body is much larger than the title.

- `scrollbars`: This property defines which scroll bars should be present when the text overflows the available input real estate. In this instance, I am specifying vertical to show scroll bars on the side of the `EditText` view.

- `gravity`: By default, when the user places focus into an `EditText` field, the text aligns to the middle of the view, as shown in Figure 11-1. However, this is not what users would expect when they work with a multiline input mechanism. The user normally expects the input to have the cursor placed at the top of the `EditText` view. To do this, you must set the gravity of the `EditText` view to "top." This forces the text to gravitate to the top of the `EditText` input.

Figure 11-1:
An `Edit-Text` view without the gravity set.

Displaying an on-screen keyboard

The `EditText` view is very versatile and can be configured many ways. The `EditText` view is responsible for how the on-screen keyboard is displayed. Because some devices do not have a physical keyboard, an on-screen keyboard must be present to interact with the input mechanisms. One of the properties that the `EditText` view provides is a way to manipulate the visual aspect of the on-screen keyboard.

Why would you need to adjust the on-screen keyboard? It's simple: Different `EditText` input types might need different keys. For example, if the `EditText` is a phone number, the on-screen keyboard should display numbers only. If the `EditText` value is an e-mail address, the on-screen keyboard should display common e-mail style attributes — such as an at symbol (@). Remember that you have various ways to configure the on-screen keyboard that, if done properly, can increase the usability of your application.

You can configure the way the on-screen keyboard is configured through the `inputType` property on the `EditText` view. Far too many options exist for me to cover in this book, but you can review the various options at this URL: `http://developer.android.com/reference/android/widget/TextView.html#attr_android:inputType`.

Getting Choosy with Dates and Times

The application I've been building is a Task Reminder application — and what would a reminder application be without a way to set the date and time that the reminder should notify the user that something needs to be reviewed? Well, it wouldn't be a Task Reminder application at all! It would simply be a task list application — and that's kind of boring if you ask me.

If you've done any programming with dates and times in another programming language, you know that building a mechanism for a user to enter a date and a time can be a painstaking process all in itself. I'm happy to let you know that the Android platform has relieved all Android programmers of this issue. The Android platform provides two classes that assist you in this process: the `DatePicker` and `TimePicker`. That's not the end of the rainbow either — these pickers also provide built-in classes that allow you to pop up a dialog box to allow the user to select a date and a time. Therefore, you can either embed the `DatePicker` and/or `TimePicker` into your application's views or you can use the `Dialog` classes, which can save you the process of creating a view in which to contain the `DatePicker` and `TimePicker` views.

Enough jibber-jabber about what the picker widgets can do. I'm sure you're ready to start using them, and so am I!

Creating picker buttons

I have not added the `DatePicker` or `TimePicker` to the Task Reminder application yet, but I do so in this section. Part of the `reminder_edit.xml` file contains mechanisms to help show the `DatePicker` and `TimePicker`. These mechanisms are below the `EditText` definitions that were explained previously — I have two buttons with two labels above them, as shown in Listing 11-1.

Listing 11-1: The Date and Time Buttons with Their Corresponding `TextView` Labels

```
<TextView android:layout_width="wrap_content"                    → 1
    android:layout_height="wrap_content"
    android:text="@string/date" />
<Button                                                          → 4
```

```
      android:id="@+id/reminder_date"
      android:layout_height="wrap_content"
      android:layout_width="wrap_content"
      />
<TextView android:layout_width="wrap_content"                        → 9
      android:layout_height="wrap_content"
      android:text="@string/time" />
<Button                                                              → 12
      android:id="@+id/reminder_time"
      android:layout_height="wrap_content"
      android:layout_width="wrap_content"
      />
```

The code lines are explained here:

→ **1**   This is the `TextView` label for the Date button. This displays the value of "ReminderDate" according to the string resource.

→ **4**   This line defines a button that the user clicks to open the `DatePickerDialog`, as explained in the next section, "Wiring up the date picker."

→ **9**   This is the `TextView` label for the Time button. This displays the value of "ReminderTime" according to the string resource.

→ **12**   This line defines a button that the user clicks to open the `TimePickerDialog`, as explained in the next section, "Wiring up the date picker."

Wiring up the date picker

When the user clicks the Date button, he should be able to edit the date, as I show you in the following sections.

Setting up the Date button click listener

To implement this functionality, open the activity where your code is to be placed — for the Task Reminder application, open the `ReminderEdit-Activity.java` file.

In the `onCreate()` method, type the following code:

```
registerButtonListenersAndSetDefaultText();
```

Eclipse informs you that you need to create the method, so do that now. The easiest way to do this is by hovering over the method call squiggly, and choosing the "Create method `registerButtonListenersAndSetDefaultText()`" option. In the `registerButtonListenersAndSetDefaultText()` method, type the code shown in Listing 11-2.

Listing 11-2: Implementing the Date Button Click Listener

```
mDateButton.setOnClickListener(new View.OnClickListener() {      → 1

    @Override
    public void onClick(View v) {                                → 4
        showDialog(DATE_PICKER_DIALOG);                          → 5
    }
});
updateDateButtonText();                                          → 8
updateTimeButtonText();                                          → 9
```

This code is explained as follows:

→ **1**   This line uses the `mDateButton` variable. As you have probably noticed, you have not defined this variable anywhere. You need to define this variable at the top of the class file. After this variable is defined, you can set the `onClickListener()` for the button. The `onClickListener()` is what executes when the button is clicked. The action that takes place on the button click is shown on line 5.

```
private Button mDateButton;
```

After this variable is created, you need to initialize it in the `onCreate()` method (right after the call to `setContentView()`):

```
mDateButton = (Button) findViewById(R.id.reminder_date);
```

→ **4**   This line overrides the default click behavior of the button so that you can provide your own set of actions to perform. The `View v` parameter is the view that was clicked.

→ **5**   This line defines what I want to happen when the button is clicked. In this instance, I am calling a method on the base activity class — `showDialog()`. The `showDialog()` method I am using accepts one parameter — the ID of the dialog box that I would like to show. This ID is a value that I provide. I am providing a constant called `DATE_PICKER_DIALOG`. You need to define these constants at the top of the class file by typing the following code. The second constant is utilized in the section titled "Wiring up the time picker" elsewhere in this chapter.

```
private static final int DATE_PICKER_DIALOG = 0;
private static final int TIME_PICKER_DIALOG = 1;
```

This constant provides the `showDialog()` method with the ID that I use to show the `DatePickerDialog`.

→ **8**   This method is called to update the button text of the date and time buttons. This method is created in Listing 11-5.

→ **9**   This method is called to update the time button text. This method is created in Listing 11-6.

Creating the showDialog () method

The showDialog() method performs some work for you in the base activity class, and at the end of the day, the only thing you need to know is that by calling showDialog() with an ID, the activity's onCreateDialog() method is called. At the bottom of your class file, type the code from Listing 11-3 to respond to the showDialog() method call.

Listing 11-3:   Responding to showDialog() with onCreateDialog()

```
@Override
protected Dialog onCreateDialog(int id) {                                → 2
    switch(id) {
        case DATE_PICKER_DIALOG:                                         → 4
            return showDatePicker();
    }
    return super.onCreateDialog(id);
}

private DatePickerDialog showDatePicker() {                              → 10
    DatePickerDialog datePicker = new DatePickerDialog(ReminderEditActivity.this,
                new DatePickerDialog.OnDateSetListener() {               → 13

            @Override
            public void onDateSet(DatePicker view, int year, int monthOfYear,
                    int dayOfMonth) {                                    → 17

                mCalendar.set(Calendar.YEAR, year);                     → 19
                mCalendar.set(Calendar.MONTH, monthOfYear);
                mCalendar.set(Calendar.DAY_OF_MONTH, dayOfMonth);       → 21
                updateDateButtonText();                                 → 22
            }
    }, mCalendar.get(Calendar.YEAR), mCalendar.get(Calendar.MONTH),
            mCalendar.get(Calendar.DAY_OF_MONTH));                      → 25
    return datePicker;                                                  → 26
}

private void updateDateButtonText() {                                    → 29
    SimpleDateFormat dateFormat = new SimpleDateFormat(DATE_FORMAT);     → 30
    String dateForButton = dateFormat.format(mCalendar.getTime());      → 31
    mDateButton.setText(dateForButton);                                 → 32
}
```

Each important line of code is explained as follows:

→ **2**   The onCreateDialog() method is overridden and called when the showDialog() method is called with a parameter. The int id parameter is the ID that was passed into the showDialog() method previously.

→ **4**   This line of code determines whether the ID passed into the `onCreateDialog()` is the same one that was passed in as a parameter to the `showDialog()` method. If it matches the `DATE_PICKER_DIALOG` value, it returns the value of the `show-DatePicker()` method. The `showDatePicker()` call must return a `Dialog` type for `onCreateDialog()` to show a dialog box.

→ **10**   The `showDatePicker()` method definition that returns a `DatePickerDialog`.

→ **13**   On this line, I am creating a new `DatePickerDialog` that accepts the current context as the first parameter. I have provided the current instance `ReminderEditActivity.this` as the `Context`. The full class name is included because it's inside a nested statement, therefore fully qualified names are required. The next parameter is the `onDateSetListener()`, which provides a callback that is defined from line 13 through line 22. This callback provides the value of the date that was chosen through the date picker. The other parameters for the `DatePickerDialog` are listed on line 25.

→ **17**   The implementation of the `onDateSet()` method that is called when the user sets the date through the `DatePickerDialog` and clicks the Set button. This method provides the following parameters:

- `DatePicker view`: The date picker used in the date selection dialog box

- `int year`: The year that was set

- `int monthOfYear`: The month that was set in format 0–11 for compatibility with the `Calendar` object

- `int dayOfMonth`: The day of the month

→ **19 through** → **21**   This code block uses a variable by the name of `mCalendar`. This is a classwide `Calendar` variable that allows me to keep track of the date and time that the user set while inside the `ReminderEditActivity` through the `DatePickerDialog` and `TimePickerDialog`. You also need this variable — define a classwide `Calendar` variable at the top of the class file with the name of `mCalendar`. In this code block, I am using the setter and `Calendar` constants to change the date values of the `Calendar` object to that of the values the user set through the `DatePickerDialog`.

```
private Calendar mCalendar;
mCalendar = Calendar.getInstance();
```

Inside the `onCreate()` method, provide the `mCalendar` object with a value using the `getInstance()` method. This method returns a new instance of the `Calendar` object.

→ **22**   After the `mCalendar` object has been updated, I make a call to `updateDateButtonText()` that updates the text of the button that the user clicked to open the `DatePickerDialog`. This method is explained on lines 29 through 31.

→ **25**   These are the remaining parameters to set up the `DatePicker-Dialog`. These calendar values are what shows when `DatePicker-Dialog` opens. I am using the `mCalendar` get accessor to retrieve the year, month, and day value of `mCalendar`. If `mCalendar` has not been previously set, these values are from today's date. If `mCalendar` has previously been set and the user decides to open the `DatePickerDialog` again to change the date, the `mCalendar` object returns the values that were set from the previous date selection as the default of the new `DatePickerDialog`.

→ **26**   At the end of this method, I return an instance of the `Dialog` class because `onCreateDialog()` requires it. Because the `DatePickerDialog` class is a subclass of `Dialog`, I can return the `DatePickerDialog`. This allows `onCreateDialog()` to create the dialog box for the user to see on-screen.

→ **29**   As shown on line 22, the `updateDateButtonText()` method is called after the `mCalendar` object is set up with new date values. This method is used to update the text of the Date button that the user selects when he wants to change the date. In this method, I set the button text to the value of the date that was selected so that the user can easily see what the reminder date is without having to open the `DatePickerDialog`.

→ **30**   This line sets up a `SimpleDateFormat` object. This object is used to format and parse dates using a concrete class in a local-sensitive manner, such as either Gregorian or Hebrew calendars. Using the date formatting options listed in the Java documentation (http://download-llnw.oracle.com/javase/1.4.2/docs/api/java/text/SimpleDateFormat.html), you can provide various output. On this line, I'm using a local constant called DATE_FORMAT as a parameter to set up the `SimpleDateFormat`. This constant defines the format in which I'd like the date information to be visible to the end user. You need to define this constant at the top of the class file as follows:

```
private static final String DATE_FORMAT = "yyyy-MM-dd";
```

This date format is defined as "yyyy-MM-dd," meaning a four-digit year, a two-digit month, and a two-digit day. Each is separated by a hyphen. An example of this would be 2010-09-10.

→ **31**   On this line, I use the `SimpleDateFormat` object to format the `mCalendar` date by calling the `getTime()` method on the `mCalendar` object. This method returns a date object that the `SimpleDateFormat` object parses into the DATE_FORMAT that I specified on line 30. I then set the result — a string result — into a local variable.

→ **32**   Using the local variable I set up on line 31, I set the text of the Date button using the `Button` class's `setText()` method.

The `DatePickerDialog` widget is now wired up to accept input from the user.

Wiring up the time picker

The `TimePickerDialog` allows users to select a time during the day in which they would like to be reminded of the task at hand.

Setting up the Time button click listener

Setting up a `TimePickerDialog` is almost identical to setting up a `Date-PickerDialog`. The first thing you need to do is declare the `onClick-Listener()` for the time button. To do so, create a local `mTimeButton` variable at the top of the class file with the following code:

```
private Button mTimeButton;
```

You then need to initialize the variable in the `onCreate()` method as follows:

```
mTimeButton = (Button) findViewById(R.id.reminder_time);
```

Now that you have a Time button to work with, you can set up the click listener for it. In the `registerButtonListenersAndSetDefaultText()` method, type the code shown in Listing 11-4.

Listing 11-4:   Implementing the Time Button's `OnClickListener`

```
mTimeButton.setOnClickListener(new View.OnClickListener() {
    @Override
    public void onClick(View v) {
        showDialog(TIME_PICKER_DIALOG);
    }
});
```

This entire method is the same as the Date button's `onClickListener()`, except that on line 4, I am using a different constant as a parameter to the `showDialog()` method. I am doing this because when `showDialog()` is called, it in turn calls `onCreateDialog()` with that ID. At that time, I can logically figure out how to create the `TimePickerDialog`. You need to create the `TIME_PICKER_DIALOG` constant at the top of the class file.

Now you need to go back to the `onCreateDialog()` method and add the following code after the `return showDatePicker()` code:

```
case TIME_PICKER_DIALOG:
    return showTimePicker();
```

Creating the showTimePicker() method

The `showTimePicker()` method has not been created. Create that method now. The full method definition with code is shown in Listing 11-5.

Listing 11-5: The `showTimePicker()` Method

```
private TimePickerDialog showTimePicker() {
    TimePickerDialog timePicker = new TimePickerDialog(this, new
        TimePickerDialog.OnTimeSetListener() {                      → 3
        @Override
        public void onTimeSet(TimePicker view, int hourOfDay, int minute){  → 5
            mCalendar.set(Calendar.HOUR_OF_DAY, hourOfDay);         → 6
            mCalendar.set(Calendar.MINUTE, minute);                → 7
            updateTimeButtonText();                                → 8
        }
    }, mCalendar.get(Calendar.HOUR_OF_DAY),                        → 10
            mCalendar.get(Calendar.MINUTE), true);                 → 11

    return timePicker;
}
```

The code in Listing 11-5 is fairly straightforward because it's almost identical to that of the `showDatePicker()` method. However, you can see differences on the following lines:

→ **3**   Here a `TimePickerDialog` is being set up with a new `OnTime-SetListener()` that is called when the user sets the time with the `TimePickerDialog`.

→ **5**   When the time is set, the hour and minute are passed into the `onTimeSet()` method, allowing you to perform necessary actions with the values.

→ **6**   Here I am setting the classwide `Calendar` object's hour of the day.

→ **7**   Here I am setting the classwide `Calendar` object's minute of the hour.

→ **8**   This line delegates the updating of the Time button's text to a method called `updateTimeButtonText()`. This method is explained in Listing 11-6.

→ **10** This line specifies the default hour for the `TimePickerDialog`. This value is retrieved from the classwide `Calendar` object.

→ **11** This line specifies the default minute for the `TimePickerDialog`. This value is retrieved from the classwide `Calendar` object. The last parameter is set to the value of `true`, which informs the `TimePickerDialog` to show the time in 24-hour format as opposed to a 12-hour time format with a.m. and p.m. distinctions.

At the end of the method, the instance of the `TimePickerDialog` is returned to the `onCreateDialog()` method to allow it to show the dialog box to the end user.

On line 8, I made a call to `updateTimeButtonText()`. This method is very similar to the `updateDateButtonText()`, as shown previously in this chapter. Type the code from Listing 11-6 into the editor to create the `updateTimeButtonText()` method.

Listing 11-6: The `updateTimeButtonText()` Method

```
private void updateTimeButtonText() {
    SimpleDateFormat timeFormat = new SimpleDateFormat(TIME_FORMAT);          → 2
    String timeForButton = timeFormat.format(mCalendar.getTime());           → 3
    mTimeButton.setText(timeForButton);                                      → 4
}
```

This code is explained as follows:

→ 2   This line of code creates a new `SimpleDateFormat`, but this time with a different constant. You need to create the `TIME_FORMAT` constant at the top of the class file as follows:

```
private static final String TIME_FORMAT = "kk:mm";
```

This constant informs the `SimpleDateFormat` class that you would like the calendar to output the minutes and seconds separated by a colon. An example would be 12:45 to represent 12:45 p.m.

→ 3   This line formats the current calendar's time to that of the prescribed format on line 2.

→ 4   This line updates the button text to the time that was retrieved on line 3.

At this point, you've set up the date and time picker dialog widgets to accept values from the user. The best part is, you did not have to write the date and time logic; you simply had to respond to the click listeners.

Creating Your First Alert Dialog Box

While creating date and time pickers may be what I need to do for the Task Reminder application, you might need to inform the user that something has happened in the form of a dialog box. The Android system has a framework built around dialog boxes that allows you to provide any implementation that you may need.

Various types of dialog boxes are available. Following are the most common:

✔ **Alert:** Alerts the user of something important. Also allows the user to set the text value of the buttons as well as the actions performed when they are clicked. As a developer, you can provide the `AlertDialog` with a list of items to display — allowing the user to select from a list of items.

✔ **Progress:** Used to display a progress wheel or bar. This dialog box is created through the `ProgressDialog` class.

✔ **Custom:** A custom dialog box created and programmed by you, the master Android developer. You create a custom dialog class by extending the `Dialog` base class or through custom layout XML files.

Seeing why you should work with dialog boxes

Have you ever worked with an application that did not inform you of a warning or alert you of something? If not, take the following example into consideration. Imagine an e-mail client that does not inform you that you have new e-mail. How annoying would that be? Alerting users of important issues or choices that need to be made is an integral part of any user experience. A few examples of where you might want to use a dialog box to inform the user of a message and/or to have the user perform an action are as follows:

✔ Something is happening in the background (this is what a `Progress-Dialog` does).

✔ The values in an `EditText` view are invalid.

✔ The network has become unavailable.

✔ The user needs to select a date or time (as I just demonstrated).

✔ The state of the phone is not compatible with the application. Maybe the app needs to be GPS enabled or needs an SD card, and you've detected these issues upon the application starting.

✔ The user needs to choose from a list of items.

While this is not a comprehensive list, it does give you an inkling into what is possible or feasible with dialog boxes.

If you ever work with any type of blocking process (network communication, long-running tasks, and so on), you should always provide the user with some type of dialog box or progress indicator letting the user know what is happening. If the user does not know something is happening, she is likely to think that the application has stopped responding and might stop using the app. The Android framework provides various progress indicators. A couple of common progress classes are `ProgressDialog` and `ProgressBar`.

While not covered in this book due to its advanced nature, the `AsyncTask` class is the class that you would use to help manage long-running tasks while updating the user interface. A great tutorial exists in the Android documentation under Painless Threading, located here: `http://d.android.com/ resources/articles/painless-threading.html`. You can also create a new thread in code, but the `AsyncTask` class helps simplify this process.

Choosing the right dialog box for a task

It's up to you to determine which dialog box you should use for each given scenario, but I follow a logical series of steps to determine which dialog box to use:

1. **Is this a long-running task?**

   - *Yes:* Use a `ProgressDialog` to let the user know something is happening in the background and that the app is not frozen. A great resource that explains how to do this is located here: `http://d.android.com/guide/topics/ui/dialogs. html#ProgressDialog`.

   - *No:* Continue to Step 2.

2. **Does the user need to be able to perform an advanced action in the dialog box?**

   (By *advanced action,* I mean something that is not supported by the `AlertDialog` class.)

   - *Yes:* Create a custom `Dialog` class by extending the `Dialog` base class or creating from a custom layout XML file. More info on custom dialog boxes can be found here: `http://d.android. com/guide/topics/ui/dialogs.html#CustomDialog`.

   - *No:* Continue to Step 3.

3. **Does the user need to answer a question such as "Are you sure?" with a value of Yes or No?**

   - *Yes:* Create an `AlertDialog` and react to the buttons on the `AlertDialog` through `onClickListener()` calls.

   - *No:* Continue to Step 4.

4. **Does the user need to make a selection from a simple list of items?**

   - *Yes:* Create an `AlertDialog`.

   - *No:* Continue to Step 5.

5. **Does the user simply need to be alerted?**

   - *Yes:* Create a simple `AlertDialog`.

   - *No:* You may not need a dialog box. Ask yourself whether you can notify the user in some other way.

Creating your own alert dialog box

At times, you need to notify the user of something important, and to do so, you need to present them with a dialog box. Android has made this very simple with the introduction of the `AlertDialog.Builder` class. This class allows you to easily create an `AlertDialog` with various options and buttons. You can react to these button clicks through the `onClickListener()` of each button.

The `AlertDialog.Builder` class is not used in the Task Reminder application. However, I demonstrate how to create one in Listing 11-7.

Assume that the user clicked the Save button on the Task Reminder application and that you wanted to pop up a confirmation window that resembles Figure 11-2, asking the user whether he is sure that he wants to save.

Figure 11-2:
The confirmation Alert-Dialog window.

To present an `AlertDialog` in this manner, you would need to set a click listener for the Save button. Inside that click listener, you create the dialog box as shown in Listing 11-7.

It's always best to show dialog boxes through the `showDialog()` and `onCreateDialog()` mechanisms. However, for brevity, I am going to create the dialog box inside the Save button click listener.

Listing 11-7:   Creating an `AlertDialog` with the `AlertDialog.Builder` Class

```
AlertDialog.Builder builder
    = new AlertDialog.Builder(ReminderEditActivity.this);          → 2
builder.setMessage("Are you sure you want to save the task?")      → 3
    .setTitle("Are you sure?")                                     → 4
    .setCancelable(false)                                          → 5
    .setPositiveButton("Yes",                                      → 6
    new DialogInterface.OnClickListener() {                        → 7
        public void onClick(DialogInterface dialog, int id) {
                // Perform some action such as saving the item     → 9
        }
    })
    .setNegativeButton("No", new DialogInterface.OnClickListener() {  → 12
        public void onClick(DialogInterface dialog, int id) {
                        dialog.cancel();                           → 14
        }
});
builder.create().show();                                           → 17
```

This code is explained as follows:

→ **2**   This line sets up the `AlertDialog.Builder` class with the context of the `AlertDialog.Builder` as the current running activity. In this case, it's `ReminderEditActivity`.

→ **3**   This line sets the message that will show in the middle of the `AlertDialog` (as shown in Figure 11-2). This value can be a string or a string resource.

→ **4**   This sets the title of the `AlertDialog`. This value can be a string or a string resource.

→ **5**   This sets the cancelable attribute to false. This means that the user is required to make a selection using the buttons on the `AlertDialog`. The user cannot click the Back button on the device to exit the `AlertDialog` if this flag is set to false.

→ **6**   This sets the positive button text. The positive button is the button that the user clicks when she would like to perform the action as indicated in the `AlertDialog`. In this case it is set to Yes, indicating that the user would like to perform the action. This value can be a string or a string resource.

→ **7**   This block of code that starts on line 7 and ends on line 11 is the definition of the `onClickListener()` for the positive (Yes) button. When the button is clicked, this code executes. A comment is included on line 9 indicating where your code would go.

→ **12**   This sets the negative button text. The negative button is the button that indicates that the user does not want to perform the action that is being requested through the `AlertDialog`. I have set the text value of this button to No. This value can be a string or a string resource.

→ **14** This is the `onClickListener()` for the negative button. The listener provides a reference to the dialog box that is currently shown. I am calling the `cancel()` method on the `Dialog` object to close the dialog box when the user clicks No on the `AlertDialog`.

→ **17** This line informs Android to create the `Dialog` through the `create()` method and then informs Android to show the dialog box to the end user with the `show()` method. This projects the `AlertDialog` onto the screen.

Creating a dialog box with the `AlertDialog.Builder` class makes life a lot easier than having to derive your own `Dialog` class. If at all possible, create your dialog box with the `AlertDialog.Builder` class because it gives your application a consistent user experience that is familiar to Android users.

When the user clicks the Save button (or whatever button you've attached this code to), he receives an `AlertDialog` confirming that he would like to save the task. I am not saving the task in this instance, but code could be provided to save the task as demonstrated in Chapter 12, when I save the task to an SQLite database.

Other options also exist on the `Dialog` class and can be found with great examples here: `http://d.android.com/guide/topics/ui/dialogs.html`.

Validating Input

You've created your form so that users can enter information, and perhaps you've already created the mechanism to save the content to a database or remote server. But what happens when the user enters invalid text or no text? This is where input validation enters the picture.

Input validation validates the input before the save takes place. Assume that the user does not enter text for the title or the message and attempts to save; should she be allowed to save? Of course not!

Unfortunately, a built-in Android validation framework does not exist. Hopefully in future versions of the Android platform this will be introduced. However, you have ways to validate input with the current framework.

The method in which you provide validation to the user is up to you. Here are some common methods in which I've seen developers implement validation:

✔ `TextWatcher`: Implement a `TextWatcher` on the `EditText` widget. This class provides callbacks to you each time the text changes in the `EditText` widget. Therefore, you can inspect the text on each keystroke.

✔ On Save: When the user attempts to save the form that he is working with, inspect all the form fields at that time and inform the user of any issues found.

✔ onFocusChanged(): Inspect the values of the form when the onFocus-Changed() event is called — which is called when the view has focus and when it loses focus. This is usually a good place to set up validation.

The Task Reminder application does not provide input validation; however, you can add validation via one of the methods described previously.

Toasting the user

The most common way to inform the user that something is incorrect is to provide a Toast message to her. A Toast message pops onto the screen for a short period of time informing the user of some type of information — in this case, an error with input values.

Providing a Toast is as simple as implementing the following code, where you'd like to inform the user of the input error:

```
Toast.makeText(ReminderEditActivity.this, "Title must be filled in", Toast.
              LENGTH_SHORT).show();
```

You might show this Toast message when the user does not enter a title into the title field, and the user clicks the Save button.

The only issue with Toast messages is that they are short-lived by default, yet they can be configured to display longer. If the user happens to glance away for a moment, he can miss the message because the Toast message only shows up for a few moments and then fades out.

Using other validation techniques

A Toast message is not the only way to inform users of a problem with their input. A couple of other popular validation techniques are as follows:

✔ **AlertDialog**: Create an instance of an AlertDialog that informs the user of the errors. This method ensures that the user will see the error message because the alert must either be canceled or accepted.

✔ **Input-field highlighting:** If the field is invalid, the input field (the EditText widget) could have its background color changed to red (or any color you choose) to indicate that the value is incorrect.

✔ **Custom validation:** If you're feeling adventurous, you could create a custom validation library that would handle validations of all sorts. This validation could highlight the field and draw small views with arrows pointing to the error with highlighting. This is similar to the validation that Google does for its sign-in window when you log on to a device (such as the G1) for the first time.

I've shown the most common methods of displaying input validation information. But as long as you can dream up new ways to inform users of an error, you can use those new methods. For example, in Chapter 14, I introduce you to the notification bar. I have used the notification bar in my own projects to inform users of a problem with a background service. While this is a special case, it is a valid one, and it provides the user with feedback that he needs to make adjustments to the application or the workflow.

Chapter 12

Getting Persistent with Data Storage

Most applications these days require you to save information for later use. The Task Reminder application would not be that useful if it did not save the tasks, now would it? Thankfully the Android platform — in combination with Java — provides a robust set of tools that you can use to store your data.

This chapter delves deeply into creating and updating an SQLite database. While I'm going to explain everything I do, I am not going to provide a lot of database theory in this chapter.

If you're not familiar with the SQL language or the SQL database, I advise you to review the SQLite Web site for more information: www.sqlite.org.

This chapter is also very code-intensive, and if you find yourself getting lost, feel free to reference the completed application source code — available online.

Finding Places to Put Data

Depending on the requirements of your application, you may need to store your data in a variety of places. For example, some applications may interact with music files. Users may want to play those files with other music programs — therefore you'd want to store the files in a location where all applications can access them. Other applications may need to store sensitive data such as encrypted username and password details. These types of applications would not want their data shared — placing data in a secure local storage environment would be best in that situation. Regardless of your situation, Android provides various options for you when it comes to storing data.

Viewing your storage options

The Android ecosystem provides various locations where you can persist your data. The most common are as follows:

- ✔ **Shared preferences:** Shared preferences are private data stored in key-value pairs. I cover how to use preferences in Chapter 15.

- ✔ **Internal storage:** Internal storage is a location where you can save files on the device's internal storage. By default, files stored in internal storage are private to your application, and other applications cannot access them (neither can the user of the device). When the user uninstalls the application, the private files are removed.

- ✔ **Local cache:** If you'd like to cache some data rather than store it persistently, the internal data directory is where you should create the cache. You should use the `getCacheDir()` method (which is available on the `Activity` or `Context` objects in Android). Note that if you store data here and the system gets low on internal storage space, Android may delete these files to reclaim space. You should stay within a reasonable limit of space consumed of around 1MB.

- ✔ **External storage:** Every Android device supports shared external storage that you can use to store files. This can either be the removable storage such as a Secure Digital Card (SD Card) or nonremovable internal storage. Files saved to external storage are public — meaning that anyone or any application can alter these files. No security is enforced upon external files. The files can be modified by the user either through a file-manager application or by connecting the user's device to a computer through a USB cable and mounting the device as external storage. Before you work with external storage, check the current state of the external storage with the `Environment` object, using a call to `getExternalStorageState()` to check whether the media is available.

  In Android 2.2, a new set of methods was introduced to handle external files. The main method is a call on the `Context` object — `getExternal-FilesDir()`. This call takes a string parameter as a key to help define what kind of media you are going to save, such as ringtones, music, photos, and so on. For more information, view the external data storage examples and documents here: `http://d.android.com/guide/topics/data/data-storage.html#filesExternal`.

✔ **SQLite database:** Android supports the full use of SQLite databases. An SQLite database is a lightweight SQL (Structured Query Language) database implementation that is available across various platforms including Android, iPhone, Windows, Linux, Mac, and various other embedded devices. You can create tables and perform SQL queries against the tables accordingly. I will be implementing an SQLite database in this chapter to handle the persistence of the tasks in the Task Reminder application.

✔ **Network connection:** Last but definitely not least is network storage, also known as remote storage. This can be any remote data source that you have access to. For example, Flickr exposes an API that allows you to store images on its servers. Your application could work with Flickr to store your images. Your application may also be an Android application for a popular tool on the Internet, such as Twitter, Facebook, or Basecamp. Your app would communicate through HTTP (or any other protocol you deem necessary) to send information to the third-party APIs to store the data.

Choosing a storage option

The various different locations offer up quite the palette of data storage options. However, it's important to figure out which one you want to use. At times, you want to use multiple storage mechanisms.

For example, if you have an application that communicates with a third-party remote API such as Twitter, you may want to keep a local copy of all the data since your last update with the server because network communication is slow and is not 100 percent reliable. This allows the application to remain usable (in some fashion) until the next update can be made. You could store the data in a local copy of an SQLite database, and then when the user initiates an update, the new updates would refresh the SQLite database with the new data.

 If your application relies solely on network communication for retrieval and storage of information, you may want to consider using the SQLite database (or any other storage mechanism) to keep the application usable when the user is not able to connect to a network (most developers know this as *offline mode*). You'd be surprised how often this happens. If your application doesn't function when a network connection is unavailable, you will most likely receive negative reviews in the Android Market (as well as a lot of feature requests to make it work offline). While this does introduce quite a bit of extra work into your application development process, it's worth it tenfold in user experience.

Asking the User for Permission

You wouldn't want your next-door neighbor storing his holiday decorations in your storage shed without clearing it through you first, would you? I didn't think so! Android is no different — storing data anywhere on the device requires some sort of permission from the user. But that's not the only thing that requires some sort of permission.

Seeing how permissions affect the user experience

When users install applications from the Android Market, the application's manifest file is inspected for required permissions that the application needs to operate. Anytime your application needs access to sensitive components such as external storage, access to the Internet, phone device info, and so on, the user is notified that the application would like to access these components. It is then up to the user to decide whether she would like to install the application.

If your application requests a lot of unnecessary permissions, the user will most likely question why the application is requesting the various permissions and might not install the application. Imagine if the Silent Mode Toggle application (built previously in this book) was requesting your current GPS location, needed access to the Internet, and wanted to know information about the device (such as hardware info). The Silent Mode Toggle application has no need for those permissions — therefore, the user is most likely going to be wary of installing an application that is overzealously requesting permissions.

Through the many different applications that I've published, I've found that the fewer number of permissions your application requests, the more likely the user is to install your application. If your application does not need the permission, yank the permission out of the application.

Setting requested permissions in the AndroidManifest.xml file

When you need to request permissions, you need to add them to the `AndroidManifest.xml` file in your project. No permission is necessary to work with an SQLite database; therefore, I'm going to add two permissions to the Task Reminder application that will be required when I add the alarm manager code in Chapter 13:

    ✔ `android.permission.RECEIVE_BOOT_COMPLETED`

    ✔ `android.permission.WAKE_LOCK`

These permissions do look a bit odd. The `RECEIVE_BOOT_COMPLETED` permission allows the application access to know when the phone reboots. The `WAKE_LOCK` permission allows the phone to keep the phone awake while it's performing some background processing. These items are covered in detail, along with the `AlarmManager`, in Chapter 13.

The permissions mentioned previously are quite unique and are not used in most applications — therefore I'll outline a couple of the most common permissions and describe how to set them. A lot of applications require access to the Internet to operate. Some applications also need to write data to the SD Card. If you need either of these, you need to add the following permissions:

    ✔ **Internet:** `android.permission.INTERNET`

    ✔ **SD Card:** `android.permission.WRITE_EXTERNAL_STORAGE`

You can add permissions to the `AndroidManifest.xml` file in one of two ways:

    ✔ Through the `AndroidManifest.xml` Permissions Editor. Choose Add⇨Uses Permission, and then choose the permission from the drop-down list.

    ✔ Through manually editing the XML file. This is how I prefer to do it. You need to add a `uses-permission` element to the manifest `element`. The XML permission request looks like this:

```
<uses-permission android:name="android.permission.WAKE_LOCK" />
```

If you have not done so already, add the `WAKE_LOCK` and `RECEIVE_BOOT_COMPLETED` permissions to the Task Reminder application. To view a full list of available permissions, view the Android permission documentation here: `http://d.android.com/reference/android/Manifest.permission.html`.

If you do not declare the permissions your application needs and a user installs your application on his device, your application will not function as expected; sometimes run-time exceptions will be thrown and crash your application. Always be sure to check that your permissions are present. Most likely, they will be because the app will not work on a device or emulator if they are not.

Creating Your Application's SQLite Database

The Task Reminder application needs a place to store and retrieve your tasks, and the best place for this kind of information is inside an SQLite database. Your application needs to read, create, update, and delete tasks from the database.

The Create, Read, Update, and Delete actions are known as CRUD operations — each letter standing for its respective action.

Understanding how the SQLite database will work

The two activities in the Task Reminder application need to perform various duties to operate. ReminderEditActivity needs to do the following:

1. Create a new record.

2. Read a record so that it can display the details for editing.

3. Update the existing record.

The ReminderListActivity needs to perform these duties:

1. Read all the tasks to show them on the screen.

2. Delete a task by responding to the click event from the context menu after a user has long-pressed an item.

To work with an SQLite database, you must communicate with SQLite through classes in the android.database package. It is very common to abstract as much of the database communication away from the Activity objects as possible. The database mechanisms are placed into another Java file (and usually a package if the database portion is quite large) to help separate the application into layers of functionality. Therefore, if you need to alter code that affects the database, you know that you only need to change the code in one location to do so. I will follow that approach in the sections that follow.

Creating a Java file to hold the database code

The first thing to do is create a Java file in your Android project that will house all the database-centric code. I am going to name my file `RemindersDbAdapter.java`. The name `RemindersDbAdapter` was chosen because this is a simple implementation of the *adapter* software engineering pattern.

The adapter pattern is simply a wrapper class that allows incompatible classes to communicate with each other. Think of the adapter pattern as the wires and ports behind your television and DVD player. The cables plug into ports that are essentially adapters that allow devices to communicate that normally couldn't. They share a common interface. By creating an adapter to handle the database communication, you can communicate with this class via the programming language of Java while this adapter class does the translation and adapts certain Java requests into SQLite-specific commands.

Defining the key elements

Before you open and create your database, I need to define a few key fields. Type the code from Listing 12-1 into your `RemindersDbAdapter` class.

Listing 12-1:   The Constants, Fields, and Constructors of the `RemindersDbAdapter` Class

```
private static final String DATABASE_NAME = "data";                    → 1
private static final String DATABASE_TABLE = "reminders";              → 2
private static final int DATABASE_VERSION = 1;                         → 3


public static final String KEY_TITLE = "title";                        → 5
public static final String KEY_BODY = "body";
public static final String KEY_DATE_TIME = "reminder_date_time";
public static final String KEY_ROWID = "_id";                          → 8


private DatabaseHelper mDbHelper;                                       → 11
private SQLiteDatabase mDb;                                            → 12
```

(continued)

Listing 12-1 *(continued)*

```
    private static final String DATABASE_CREATE =                → 14
            "create table " + DATABASE_TABLE + " ("
                    + KEY_ROWID + " integer primary key autoincrement, "
                    + KEY_TITLE + " text not null, "
                    + KEY_BODY + " text not null, "
                    + KEY_DATE_TIME + " text not null);";

private final Context mCtx;                                      → 21

public RemindersDbAdapter(Context ctx) {                         → 23
        this.mCtx = ctx;
    }
```

Each line is explained in detail here:

→ **1** This is the physical name of the database that will exist in the Android file system.

→ **2** This is the name of the database table that will hold the tasks. I cover the table and how to set it up in the SQL Table section that follows.

→ **3** This is the version of the database. If you were to update the schema of your database, you would increment this and provide an implementation of the onUpgrade() method of the DatabaseHelper. I create the database helper in the "Creating the database table," section later in this chapter.

→ **5** – → **8** These lines define the column names of the table that is described in the "Visualizing the SQL table" section that follows.

→ **11** This is the classwide DatabaseHelper instance variable. The DatabaseHelper is an implementation of the SQLiteOpen-Helper class in Android. The SQLiteOpenHelper class helps with the creation and version management of the SQLite database.

→ **12** This is the class-level instance of the SQLite database object that allows you to create, read, update, and delete records.

→ **14** This line defines the create script for the database. I'm concatenating the various values from the previous lines to create the various columns. Each component of the script is explained in the "Visualizing the SQL table," section that follows.

→ **21** This is the Context object that will be associated with the SQLite database object.

→ **23** The Context object is set via the constructor of the class.

The SQL database is now ready to be created with the DATABASE_CREATE script as defined previously.

Visualizing the SQL table

The table object in SQL is the construct that holds the data that you decide to manage. Visualizing a table in SQLite is similar to looking at a spreadsheet. Each row consists of data, and each column represents the data inside the row. In Listing 12-1 on lines 5–8, I defined the column names for the database. These column names would equate to the header values in a spreadsheet, as shown in Figure 12-1. Each row contains a value for each column, which is how your data is stored in SQLite (conceptually). The real data is stored as 1s and 0s, so I thought a picture and a high-level explanation might help you better understand what's happening than having you binary-decode 010010000110100100100001 and explain that.

_id	title	body	reminder_date_time
1	Order Flight Tickets	Go to travel site and order ti…	2010-11-15 16:15
2	Schedule Time Off	Email manager at work to …	2010-11-17 15:00
3	Take Vacation	YES! Finally take that much n…	2010-12-10 14:30
4	Pay Bills	Pay the bills through bill pay.	2010-11-10 12:15

Starting on line 14, I assemble the database create script. This script concatenates various constants from within the file to create a database create script. When I run this script in SQLite, SQLite creates a table by the name of reminders in a database called data. The columns and how they're built in the create script are described as follows:

- ✔ create table DATABASE_TABLE: This portion of the script informs SQLite that you would like to create a database table with the name of reminders.

- ✔ ROW_ID: This property acts as the identifier for the task. This column has the integer primary key autoincrement attributes applied to it. The integer attribute specifies that the row is an integer. The primary key attribute states that the ROW_ID is the primary identifier for a task. The autoincrement attribute informs SQLite that each time a new task is inserted, simply automatically increment the ROW_ID to the next available integer. For example, if rows 1, 2, and 3 existed and you inserted another record, the value of the ROW_ID column in the next row would be 4.

- ✔ KEY_TITLE: This is the title of the task that the user provides, such as "Schedule Vacation." The text attribute informs SQLite that you are working with a text column. The not null attribute states that the value of this column cannot be null — you must provide a value.

✔ KEY_BODY: This is the body or description of the task. The attributes for this column are the same as for KEY_TITLE.

✔ KEY_DATE_TIME: This is where the date and time of the reminder are stored. The attributes are the same as the prior two columns. Wait! You're probably thinking, "This is a date field; why is he storing it as text?" This is because SQLite does not have a storage class associated with storing dates or times.

For more information on dates and times in SQLite, view the documentation at www.sqlite.org/datatype3.html#datetime.

Creating the database table

You're now ready to create your first table. To do so, you'll provide an implementation of SQLiteOpenHelper. In the RemindersDbAdapter class type, the code is shown in Listing 12-2. This creates a nested Java class inside the RemindersDbAdapter class.

Listing 12-2: Creating Your First Database Table

```
private static class DatabaseHelper extends SQLiteOpenHelper {      → 1
    DatabaseHelper(Context context) {
        super(context, DATABASE_NAME, null, DATABASE_VERSION);       → 3
    }

    @Override
    public void onCreate(SQLiteDatabase db) {                         → 7
        db.execSQL(DATABASE_CREATE);                                  → 8
    }

    @Override
    public void onUpgrade(SQLiteDatabase db, int oldVersion,
            int newVersion) {                                        → 12
        // Not used, but you could upgrade the database with ALTER
        // Scripts
    }
}
```

The code lines are explained here:

→ **1**   The implementation of your SQLiteOpenHelper.

→ **3**   The call made to the base SQLiteOpenHelper constructor. This call creates, opens, and/or manages a database. The database is not actually created or opened until `getReadableDatabase()` or `getWriteableDatabase()` is called on the `SQLiteOpenHelper` instance — in this case, it would be the `mDbHelper` variable.

→ **7**   The `onCreate()` method, which is called when the database is created for the first time.

→ **8**   This is where all the magic happens. This line of code creates your database and your database table. The `execSQL()` method accepts an SQL script string as a parameter. This is the SQL that the SQLite database executes to create the database table.

→ **12**   The `onUpgrade()` method is used when you need to upgrade an existing database.

You now create the database by calling the `getReadableDatabase()` or `getWritableDatabase()` method on the `DatabaseHelper` object. To do this, type the following code anywhere into your `RemindersDbAdapter` class:

```
public RemindersDbAdapter open() throws android.database.SQLException {
        mDbHelper = new DatabaseHelper(mCtx);
        mDb = mDbHelper.getWritableDatabase();
        return this;
}
```

The `open()` method opens (and creates if necessary) the database using the `DatabaseHelper()` class that was just created. This class then returns itself through the `this` Java keyword. The reason that the class is returning itself is because the caller (`ReminderEditActivity` or `ReminderListActivity`) needs to access data from this class and this method returns an instance of the `RemindersDbAdapter`.

Closing the database

A database is an expensive resource and should be closed when not in use. To close the database, type the following method anywhere into your `RemindersDbAdapter` class:

```
public void close() {
     mDbHelper.close();
}
```

This method closes the database when called. You call this from within the `ReminderEditActivity` when the user cancels the activity by using the Back button on the device.

Upgrading your database

When would you upgrade your database? Consider the following situation: You have released your application and 10,000 users have installed the application and are actively using it. Not only are they using it, but they also love it! Some users are even sending in feature requests. You decide that you want to implement one of the feature requests; however, it requires you to change the database schema. You would want to perform SQL `ALTER` statements inside the `onUpgrade()` call to update your database. Other examples on the Internet demonstrate the upgrading of databases through dropping the existing database and then creating a new one. You do not want to do this because performing a database drop will delete all the user's data! Imagine updating your favorite Task Reminder application to then find out that the upgrade erased all your preexisting tasks! That would be a major bug.

Creating and Editing Tasks with SQLite

The first thing you need to do is create a task. To do that, you need to insert a record. After that, you need to list the task(s) on the `Reminder-ListActivity`, which in turn allows you to tap one to edit a task, or long-press one to delete it. These user interactions cover the create, read, update, and delete operations that I discuss previously.

Inserting your first task entry

Inserting tasks is a fairly easy process after you get the hang of it. The path of inserting your first task into the SQLite database includes the following steps:

1. **Set up the required local variables.**

2. **Build the Save button click listener.**

3. **Retrieve values from `EditText` views.**

4. **Interact with the `RemindersDbAdapter` class.**

5. **Open and close the database.**

Upon inserting your first task, you should have a good enough grasp on the `SQLiteDatabase` class interaction to perform some more tasks. Therefore, I'll introduce you to the entire implementation of `RemindersDbAdapter`, which outlines the CRUD operations previously covered.

Saving values from the screen to the database

When the user creates a task, it takes place in the `ReminderEditActivity`. To create the task, you need to create a class-level `RemindersDbAdapter` variable that is instantiated in the `onCreate()` method. After it is instantiated, I open the database with a call to the `RemindersDbAdapter`'s `open()` method in the `onResume()` method. (Type this code into your `RemindersEditActivity` class now.)

```
@Override
protected void onCreate(Bundle savedInstanceState) {
            super.onCreate(savedInstanceState);

        mDbHelper = new RemindersDbAdapter(this);

            setContentView(R.layout.reminder_edit);
            // ... the remainder of the onCreate() method
```

At this point, you have a reference to the `RemindersDbAdapter` that allows you to call into the `RemindersDbAdapter` class to create a task. To add the task, you need the title, description, reminder date, and time. To gain access to the title and description, you need to add three class-level variables to `ReminderEditActivity`. Two of them are `EditText` type variables that reference the `EditText` values in the layout for the `ReminderEditActivity`. The remaining class-level variable is the Save button that you will click when you are ready to save the task to the SQLite database. I have included these variables at the top of my `ReminderEditActivity` file like this. Include these declarations in your file as well:

```
private EditText mTitleText;
private Button mConfirmButton;
private EditText mBodyText;
```

You need to instantiate those in the `onCreate()` method call like this:

```
mConfirmButton = (Button) findViewById(R.id.confirm);
mTitleText = (EditText) findViewById(R.id.title);
mBodyText = (EditText) findViewById(R.id.body);
```

You already have a `Calendar` object that was populated from the `DatePicker` and `TimePicker`; therefore, you do not need to create anything in regard to those values. The only thing left is to provide the ability to save the task after you type values into the `EditText` fields (title and description) by pressing the Save button on the screen. To do that, you need to attach a click listener to the Save button by typing the following code into the `registerButtonListenersAndSetDefaultText()` method:

```
mConfirmButton.setOnClickListener(new View.OnClickListener() {
        public void onClick(View view) {
                saveState();                                            → 3
                setResult(RESULT_OK);                                   → 4
                Toast.makeText(ReminderEditActivity.this,               → 5
                getString(R.string.task_saved_message),
                  Toast.LENGTH_SHORT).show();
                finish();                                               → 7
        }
});
```

This code is explained as follows:

→ **3**   Calls the `saveState()` method.

→ **4**   Sets the result of the `ReminderEditActivity`. Remember, the `ReminderEditActivity` started from the call from `start-ActivityForResult()` inside the `ReminderListActivity`. Setting a result of `RESULT_OK` within `setResult()` informs the `ReminderListActivity` that everything went as planned when the `ReminderEditActivity` `finish()` method runs on line 7. The `RESULT_OK` constant is a member of the parent `Activity` class. This result code can be inspected on `ReminderListActivity` in the `onActivityResult()` method. Your application can return any number of results to the caller to help you logically figure out what to do in the application next.

→ **5**   Creates a Toast message to the user, letting him know that the task saved. You need to create a string resource by the name of `task_saved_message`. I have chosen the value of the resource to be "Task saved."

→ **7**   This line of code calls the `finish()` method, which closes the `ReminderEditActivity`.

You need to create the `saveState()` method in the `ReminderEditActivity`, as shown in Listing 12-3. This method communicates with the `RemindersDb-Adapter` to save the task.

Listing 12-3:   The `saveState()` Method

```
private void saveState() {
        String title = mTitleText.getText().toString();                → 2
        String body = mBodyText.getText().toString();                  → 3

        SimpleDateFormat dateTimeFormat = new
                SimpleDateFormat(DATE_TIME_FORMAT);                     → 5
        String reminderDateTime =
```

```
                    dateTimeFormat.format(mCalendar.getTime());              → 6

        long id = mDbHelper.createReminder(title, body, reminderDateTime);   → 8

    }
```

The lines of code are explained as follows:

→ **2 –** → **3**   These lines of code retrieve the text from the
EditText views.

→ **5**   This line of text defines a SimpleDateFormat that you will use
to store the date and time inside the SQLite database. The DATE_
TIME_FORMAT constant is used. You need to create this at the top
of your class file. The code for the constant is as follows:

```
public static final String DATE_TIME_FORMAT = "yyyy-MM-dd kk:mm:ss";
```

This defines a date and time format that could be demonstrated
as 2010-11-02 12:34:21. This is a good way to store the date and
time in an SQLite database.

→ **6**   This line gets the date and time and places them into a local variable.

→ **8**   This line of code creates a reminder through the create-
Reminder() method on the ReminderDbAdapter class-level
variable — mDbHelper. You need to create that method in the
ReminderDbAdapter class, as shown on line 38 in Listing 12-4
(see the next section).

The task is created by taking the values from the EditText fields and the local
Calendar object and calling the createReminder() on the ReminderDb-
Adapter class. Following the adapter pattern has allowed you to wrap the
SQLite logic behind a Java class, which allows the ReminderEditActivity
to have no knowledge of the inner workings of the SQLite database.

The entire RemindersDbAdapter implementation

Have you ever bought a car after only seeing pictures of the door handle,
hood, and then maybe a seat? Probably not! You'd probably never buy a car
from someone who never showed you pictures of the whole thing first! Heck,
you probably wouldn't even go look at it! Sometimes it's best to see everything all at once instead of piecemealed together. Working with SQLite in the
RemindersDbAdapter class is no different.

Trying to explain everything to you piece by piece first would not make a
lot of sense; therefore, I'm going to show you the entire implementation of
the RemindersDbAdapter in Listing 12-4 so that you can get a feel for what
you're working with. Then, I explain each new area, and I cross-reference it
throughout the rest of this chapter. Hopefully, this will help everything gel
inside that Android brain of yours.

Listing 12-4: The Full Implementation of RemindersDbAdapter

```
public class RemindersDbAdapter {

    private static final String DATABASE_NAME = "data";
    private static final String DATABASE_TABLE = "reminders";
    private static final int DATABASE_VERSION = 1;

    public static final String KEY_TITLE = "title";
    public static final String KEY_BODY = "body";
    public static final String KEY_DATE_TIME = "reminder_date_time";
    public static final String KEY_ROWID = "_id";

    private DatabaseHelper mDbHelper;
    private SQLiteDatabase mDb;

    private static final String DATABASE_CREATE =
            "create table " + DATABASE_TABLE + " ("
                    + KEY_ROWID + " integer primary key autoincrement, "
                    + KEY_TITLE + " text not null, "
                    + KEY_BODY + " text not null, "
                    + KEY_DATE_TIME + " text not null);";

    private final Context mCtx;

    public RemindersDbAdapter(Context ctx) {
        this.mCtx = ctx;
    }

    public RemindersDbAdapter open() throws SQLException {
        mDbHelper = new DatabaseHelper(mCtx);
        mDb = mDbHelper.getWritableDatabase();
            return this;
    }

    public void close() {
        mDbHelper.close();
    }

    public long createReminder(String title, String body, String
            reminderDateTime) {                                           → 38
        ContentValues initialValues = new ContentValues();
        initialValues.put(KEY_TITLE, title);
        initialValues.put(KEY_BODY, body);
        initialValues.put(KEY_DATE_TIME, reminderDateTime);

        return mDb.insert(DATABASE_TABLE, null, initialValues);          → 44
    }

    public boolean deleteReminder(long rowId) {                          → 47
      return
        mDb.delete(DATABASE_TABLE, KEY_ROWID + "=" + rowId, null) > 0;    → 48
    }
```

```
public Cursor fetchAllReminders() {                              → 51
    return mDb.query(DATABASE_TABLE, new String[] {KEY_ROWID, KEY_TITLE,
            KEY_BODY, KEY_DATE_TIME}, null, null, null, null, null);
}

public Cursor fetchReminder(long rowId) throws SQLException {     → 55
    Cursor mCursor =
            mDb.query(true, DATABASE_TABLE, new String[] {KEY_ROWID,
                    KEY_TITLE, KEY_BODY, KEY_DATE_TIME}, KEY_ROWID + "=" +
            rowId, null,
                    null, null, null, null);                     → 56
    if (mCursor != null) {
        mCursor.moveToFirst();                                   → 57
    }
    return mCursor;

}

public boolean updateReminder(long rowId, String title, String body, String
        reminderDateTime) {                                      → 63
    ContentValues args = new ContentValues();                    → 64
    args.put(KEY_TITLE, title);
    args.put(KEY_BODY, body);
    args.put(KEY_DATE_TIME, reminderDateTime);

 return
  mDb.update(DATABASE_TABLE, args, KEY_ROWID + "=" + rowId, null) > 0; → 69
}

        // The SQLiteOpenHelper class was omitted for brevity
        // That code goes here.
}
```

→ **38** On line 38, the `createReminder()` method is created. Directly below the declaration, the `ContentValues` object is used to define the values for the various columns in the database row that you will be inserting.

→ **44** On line 44, the call to `insert()` is made to insert the row into the database. This method returns a long, which is the unique identifier of the row that was just inserted into the database. In the `ReminderEditActivity`, this is set to a local variable that is used in Chapter 13 to help the `AlarmManager` class figure out which task it's working with. The use of the `insert` method and its parameters are explained in detail in the following section.

→ **47** Here, the `deleteReminder()` method is defined — this method accepts one parameter, the `rowId` of the task to delete.

→ **48** Using the `rowId`, I make a call to the `delete()` method on the SQLite database to delete a task from the database. The usage and parameters of the `delete()` method are described in detail in the "Understanding the delete operation" section, later in this chapter.

→ **51** On this line, I define the `fetchAllReminders()` method, which utilizes the `query()` method on the SQLite database to find all the reminders in the system. The `Cursor` object is utilized by the calling application to retrieve values from the result set that was returned from the `query()` method call. The `query()` method usage and its parameters are explained in detail in the "Understanding the query (read) operation" section, later in this chapter.

→ **55** On this line, I define the `fetchReminder()` method, which accepts one parameter — the `row Id` of the task in the database to fetch.

→ **56** This line utilizes the SQLite `query()` method to return a `Cursor` object. The `query()` method usage and its parameters are explained in detail in the "Understanding the query (read) operation" section, later in this chapter.

→ **57** The `Cursor` object can contain many rows; however, the initial position is not on the first record. The `moveToFirst()` method on the cursor instructs the cursor to go to the first record in the result set. This method is only called if the cursor is not null. The reason the cursor is not immediately positioned on the first record is because it's a result set. Before you can work with the record, you must navigate to it. Think of the result set like a box of items: You can't work with an item until you take it out of the box.

→ **63** On this line, I define the `updateReminder()` method which utilizes the `update()` method. The `update()` method is responsible for updating an existing task with new information. The `update()` method usage and parameters are explained in detail in the "Understanding the update operation" section, later in this chapter.

→ **64** The `ContentValues` object is created. This object stores the various values that need to get updated in the SQLite database.

→ **69** This line updates the database record with new values that were provided by the end user of the application. The `update()` method usage and its parameters are explained in detail in the "Understanding the update operation" section, later in this chapter.

The previous code listing outlines the various CRUD routines. Each accepts a variety of different parameters that are explained in detail in the "Understanding the insert operation," "Understanding the query (read) operation," "Understanding the update operation," and "Understanding the delete operation" sections.

Understanding the insert operation

The insert operation is a fairly simple operation because you are simply inserting a value into the database. The `insert()` method accepts the following parameters:

✔ table: The name of the table to insert the data into. I'm using the DATABASE_TABLE constant for the value.

✔ nullColumnHack: SQL does not allow inserting a completely empty row, so if the ContentValues parameter (next parameter) is empty, this column is explicitly assigned a NULL value. I'm passing in null for this value.

✔ values: This parameter defines the initial values as defined as a ContentValues object. I'm providing the initialValues local variable as the value for this parameter. This variable contains the key-value pair information for defining a new row.

Understanding the query (read) operation

The query operation is also known as the read operation because most of the time, you will be *reading* data from the database with the query() method. The query method is responsible for providing a result set based upon a list of criteria that you provide. This method returns a Cursor that provides random read-write access to the result set returned by the query. The query method accepts the following parameters:

✔ distinct: I want each row to be unique. I don't want any copies. I'm providing true for this value.

✔ table: The name of the database table to perform the query against. The value I'm providing is coming from the DATABASE_TABLE constant.

✔ columns: A list of columns to return from the query. Passing null returns all columns, which is normally discouraged to prevent reading and returning data that is not needed. If you need all columns, it's valid to pass in null. I'm providing a string array of columns to return.

✔ selection: A filter describing what rows to return formatted as an SQL WHERE clause (excluding the WHERE itself). Passing a null returns all rows in the table. Depending on the situation, I provide either the rowId of the task that I would like to fetch or I provide a null to return all tasks.

✔ selectionArgs: You may include question marks (?) in the selection. These marks will be replaced by the values from selectionArgs in the order that they appear in the selection. These values are bound as string types. I do not need selectionArgs; therefore, I am passing in null.

✔ groupBy: A filter describing how to filter rows formatted as an SQL GROUP BY clause (excluding the GROUP BY). Passing null causes the rows not to be grouped. I am passing a null value because I do not care how the results are grouped.

✔ having: This is a filter that describes row groups to include in the cursor, if row grouping is being used. Passing null causes all row groups to be included, and is required when row grouping is not being used. I'm passing in a null value.

✔ orderBy: How to order the rows, formatted as an SQL ORDER BY clause (excluding the ORDER BY itself). Passing null uses the default sort order, which may be unordered. I'm passing in a null value because I'm not concerned with the order in which the results are returned.

✔ limit: Limits the number of rows returned by the query by utilizing a LIMIT clause. Passing null states that you do not have a LIMIT clause. I do not want to limit the number of rows returned; therefore, I'm passing in null to return all the rows that match my query.

Understanding the update operation

Updating a record in a database simply takes the incoming parameters and replaces them in the destination cell inside the row specified (or in the rows if many rows are updated). As with the following delete operation, the update can affect many rows. It is important to understand the update method's parameters and how they can affect the records in the database. The update() method accepts the following parameters:

✔ table: The table to update. The value that I'm going to use is provided by the DATABASE_TABLE constant.

✔ values: The ContentValues object, which contains the fields to update. I'm using the args variable, which I constructed on line 64 of Listing 12-4.

✔ whereClause: The WHERE clause, which restricts which rows should get updated. Here I am informing the database to update the row whose ID is equal to rowId by providing the following string value: KEY_ROWID + "=" + rowId.

✔ whereArgs: Additional WHERE clause arguments. Not used in this call; therefore, null is passed in.

Understanding the delete operation

When using the delete() method, various parameters are used to define the deletion criteria in the database. A delete statement can affect none or all of the records in the database. It is important to understand the parameters of the delete call to ensure that you do not mistakenly delete data. The parameters for the delete() method are as follows:

✔ table: The table to delete the rows from. The value of this parameter is provided by the DATABASE_TABLE constant.

✔ whereClause: This is the optional WHERE clause to apply when deleting rows. If you pass null, all rows will be deleted. This value is provided by manually creating the WHERE clause with the following string: KEY_ROWID + "=" + rowId.

✔ whereArgs: The optional WHERE clause arguments. Not needed in this call because everything is provided through the WHERE clause itself. I am passing in a null value because I do not need to use this parameter.

Returning all the tasks with a cursor

You can create a task, but what good is it if you can't see the task in the task list? None, really. Therefore, I'm going to show you how to list the tasks that currently exist in the database in the `ListView` in the `ReminderListActivity`.

Listing 12-5 outlines the entire `ReminderListActivity` with the new code that can read the list of tasks from the database into the `ListView`.

Listing 12-5:   The Entire `ReminderListActivity` with Connections to SQLite

```
public class ReminderListActivity extends ListActivity {
    private static final int ACTIVITY_CREATE=0;
    private static final int ACTIVITY_EDIT=1;

    private RemindersDbAdapter mDbHelper;                            → 5

    /** Called when the activity is first created. */
    @Override
    public void onCreate(Bundle savedInstanceState) {
        super.onCreate(savedInstanceState);
        setContentView(R.layout.reminder_list);
        mDbHelper = new RemindersDbAdapter(this);
        mDbHelper.open();
        fillData();                                                 → 14
        registerForContextMenu(getListView());

    }

    private void fillData() {
        Cursor remindersCursor = mDbHelper.fetchAllReminders();     → 20
        startManagingCursor(remindersCursor);                       → 21

        // Create an array to specify the fields we want (only the TITLE)
        String[] from = new String[]{RemindersDbAdapter.KEY_TITLE}; → 24

        // and an array of the fields we want to bind in the view
        int[] to = new int[]{R.id.text1};                           → 27

        // Now create a simple cursor adapter and set it to display
        SimpleCursorAdapter reminders =
                new SimpleCursorAdapter(this, R.layout.reminder_row,
                        remindersCursor, from, to);                 → 30
        setListAdapter(reminders);                                  → 31
    }

    // Menu Code removed for brevity

    @Override
    protected void onListItemClick(ListView l, View v, int position, long id) {
```

(continued)

Listing 12-5 *(continued)*

```
        super.onListItemClick(l, v, position, id);
        Intent i = new Intent(this, ReminderEditActivity.class);
        i.putExtra(RemindersDbAdapter.KEY_ROWID, id);                    → 40
        startActivityForResult(i, ACTIVITY_EDIT);
    }

    @Override
    protected void onActivityResult(int requestCode, int resultCode, Intent
            intent) {
        super.onActivityResult(requestCode, resultCode, intent);
        fillData();                                                      → 48
    }

    @Override
    public boolean onContextItemSelected(MenuItem item) {                → 52
        switch(item.getItemId()) {
            case R.id.menu_delete:
                AdapterContextMenuInfo info =
                    (AdapterContextMenuInfo)           item.getMenuInfo(); → 55
                mDbHelper.deleteReminder(info.id);                        → 56
                fillData();                                               → 57
                return true;
        }
        return super.onContextItemSelected(item);
    }
}
```

The code for reading the list of tasks is explained as follows:

→ **5**   This line of code defines a class-level `RemindersDbAdapter` instance variable. The variable is instantiated in the `onCreate()` method.

→ **14**   The `fillData()` method is called, which loads the data from the SQLite database into the `ListView`.

→ **20**   When I'm inside the `fillData()` method, I fetch all the reminders from the database, as shown on line 51 of Listing 12-4.

→ **21**   This line uses the manage `startManagingCursor()` method, which is present on the `Activity` class. This method allows the activity to take care of managing the given `Cursor`'s life cycle based on the activity's life cycle. For example, when the activity is stopped, the activity automatically calls `deactivate()` on the `Cursor`, and when the activity is later restarted, it calls `requery()` for you. When the activity is destroyed, all managed `Cursors` are closed automatically.

→ **24**   On this line, I am defining the selection criteria for the query. I am requesting that the task title be returned.

→ **27** On this line, I'm defining the array of views that I want to bind to as the view for the row. Therefore, when I'm showing a task title, that title will correspond to a particular task ID. This is why the variable in line 24 is named `from` and the variable on this line is named `to`. The values from line 24 map to the values on line 27.

→ **30** On this line, I am creating a `SimpleCursorAdapter` that maps columns from a `Cursor` to `TextViews` as defined in an layout XML file. Using this method you can specify which columns you want to display and the XML file that defines the appearance of these views. The use of a `SimpleCursorAdapter` and the associated parameters is described in the following section.

→ **31** The `SimpleCursorAdapter` is passed as the adapter parameter to the `setListAdapter()` method to inform the list view where to find its data.

→ **40** This line of code places the `ID` of the task to be edited into the intent. The `ReminderEditActivity` inspects this intent, and if it finds the `ID`, it attempts to allow the user to edit the task.

→ **48** The `fillData()` method is called when the activity returns from another activity. This is called here because the user might have updated or added a new task. Calling this method ensures that the new task is present in the list view.

→ **52** This line defines the method that handles the user context menu events that occur when a user selects a menu item from the context menu after a long press on the task in the list view.

→ **55** This line of code utilizes the `getMenuInfo()` method of the item that was clicked to obtain an instance of `AdapterContextMenuInfo`. This class exposes various bits of information about the menu item and item that was long-pressed in the list view.

→ **56** This line of code calls into the `RemindersDbAdapter` to delete the task whose ID is retrieved from the `AdapterContextMenu-Info` object's `id` field. This `id` field contains the ID of the row in the list view. This ID is the rowId of the task in the database.

→ **57** After the task has been deleted from the system, I call `fillData()` to repopulate the task list. This refreshes the list view, removing the deleted item.

Understanding the SimpleCursorAdapter

In line 30 of Listing 12-5, I created a `SimpleCursorAdapter`. I'll now explain in more detail what each of these parameters means. The `SimpleCursor-Adapter` does a lot of the hard work for you when you want to bind data from a `Cursor` object to a list view. To set up a `SimpleCursorAdapter`, you need to provide the following parameters:

✔ `this: Context`: The context that is associated with the adapter.

✔ `R.layout.reminder_row - layout`: The layout resource identifier that defines the file to use for this list item.

✔ `reminderCursor - c`: The database `Cursor`.

✔ `from - from`: An array of column names that are used to bind data from the cursor to the view. This is defined on line 24.

✔ `to - - to`: An array of view IDs that should display the column information from the from parameter. The To field is defined on line 27.

✔ The to and from parameters create a mapping informing the `SimpleCursorAdapter` how to map data in the cursor to views in the row layout.

Now, when you start the application, you see a list of items that you have created. These items are being read from the SQLite database. If you do not see a list of items, create one by pressing the menu and selecting the menu item that allows you to add a new task.

Deleting a task

To the end user, deleting a task is as simple as long-pressing an item in the `ReminderListActivity` and selecting the delete action, but to actually delete the task from the database, you need to use the `delete()` method on the SQLite database object. This method is called in Listing 12-4 on line 48.

The `RemindersDbAdapter deleteReminder()` method is called from within the `onContextSelectedItem()` method call on line 56 of Listing 12-5. The one item that is needed prior to deleting the task from the database is the `rowId` of the task in the database. To obtain the `rowId`, you must use the `Adapter-ContextMenuInfo` object, which provides extra menu information. This information is provided to the context menu selection when a menu is brought up for the `ListView`. Because I'm loading the list with a database cursor, the `ListView` contains the `rowId` that I'm looking for — yes, it's that simple! On line 55 of Listing 12-5, I obtain the `AdapterContextMenuInfo` object, and on line 56, I call the `delete()` method with the `rowId` as a parameter. Afterward, I call the `fillData()` method to reload the tasks to the screen. You can now create, list (read), and delete the task. The only thing left is updating the task.

Updating a task

When it comes down to it, updating a task is a fairly trivial process. However, it can get a bit tricky because I'm using the same activity for updating a task as I am for creating the task. Therefore, logic has to be put into place to determine whether I am editing an existing task or creating a new one.

This logic is based on the intent that was used to start the activity. In the `ReminderListActivity`, when an item is tapped, the following activity is started:

```
Intent i = new Intent(this, ReminderEditActivity.class);
i.putExtra(RemindersDbAdapter.KEY_ROWID, id);
startActivityForResult(i, ACTIVITY_EDIT);
```

This code informs Android to start the `ReminderEditActivity` with the i parameter (the intent), which contains extra information — the row id of the task that you would like to edit. On the `ReminderEditActivity` side, I inspect the receiving intent to determine whether it contains the extra id information. If it does, I then consider this an edit action and load the task information into the form to allow the user to edit the information. If the extra information is not there (which would happen if the user elected to add a new task from the menu), I present the user with an empty form to fill out to create a new task.

See Listing 12-6 for an implementation of the previously described logic. The bolded sections outline the new code.

Listing 12-6: The `ReminderEditActivity` That Supports Inserting and Updating a Task

```
public class ReminderEditActivity extends Activity {

    // Other Class level variables go here. Removed for brevity
    private Long mRowId;

    @Override
    protected void onCreate(Bundle savedInstanceState) {
        super.onCreate(savedInstanceState);

        mDbHelper = new RemindersDbAdapter(this);


        setContentView(R.layout.reminder_edit);

        mCalendar = Calendar.getInstance();
        mTitleText = (EditText) findViewById(R.id.title);
        mBodyText = (EditText) findViewById(R.id.body);
        mDateButton = (Button) findViewById(R.id.reminder_date);
        mTimeButton = (Button) findViewById(R.id.reminder_time);

        mConfirmButton = (Button) findViewById(R.id.confirm);

        mRowId = savedInstanceState != null                           → 22
            ? savedInstanceState.getLong(RemindersDbAdapter.KEY_ROWID)
            : null;
        registerButtonListenersAndSetDefaultText();
```

(continued)

Listing 12-6 *(continued)*

```
    }

    private void setRowIdFromIntent() {                              → 28
        if (mRowId == null) {
            Bundle extras = getIntent().getExtras();
            mRowId = extras != null
                ? extras.getLong(RemindersDbAdapter.KEY_ROWID)
                : null;
        }
    }

    @Override
    protected void onPause() {
        super.onPause();
        mDbHelper.close();                                           → 40
    }

    @Override
    protected void onResume() {                                      → 44
        super.onResume();
        mDbHelper.open();                                            → 46
        setRowIdFromIntent();                                        → 47
        populateFields();                                            → 48
    }

    // Date picker, button click events, and buttonText updating, createDialog
    // left out for brevity
    // they normally go here ...

    private void populateFields()  {                                → 55
        if (mRowId != null) {
            Cursor reminder = mDbHelper.fetchReminder(mRowId);      → 57
            startManagingCursor(reminder);                          → 58
            mTitleText.setText(reminder.getString(
        reminder.getColumnIndexOrThrow(RemindersDbAdapter.KEY_TITLE)));  → 60
                mBodyText.setText(reminder.getString(
            reminder.getColumnIndexOrThrow(RemindersDbAdapter.KEY_BODY)));  → 61
            SimpleDateFormat dateTimeFormat =
                    new SimpleDateFormat(DATE_TIME_FORMAT)          → 63
            Date date = null;                                       → 64
            try {
                String dateString =    reminder.getString(
                    reminder.getColumnIndexOrThrow(
                            RemindersDbAdapter.KEY_DATE_TIME));     → 67
                date = dateTimeFormat.parse(dateString);            → 68
                mCalendar.setTime(date);                            → 69
            } catch (ParseException e) {                            → 70
                Log.e("ReminderEditActivity", e.getMessage(), e);  → 71
            }
        }

        updateDateButtonText();
```

```
        updateTimeButtonText();
    }

    @Override
    protected void onSaveInstanceState(Bundle outState) {
        super.onSaveInstanceState(outState);
        outState.putLong(RemindersDbAdapter.KEY_ROWID, mRowId);      → 82
    }

    private void saveState() {
        String title = mTitleText.getText().toString();
        String body = mBodyText.getText().toString();

        SimpleDateFormat dateTimeFormat = new SimpleDateFormat(DATE_TIME_
            FORMAT);
            String reminderDateTime =
                    dateTimeFormat.format(mCalendar.getTime());

        if (mRowId == null) {                                        → 94
            long id = mDbHelper.createReminder(title, body, reminderDateTime);
                → 95
            if (id > 0) {                                            → 96
                mRowId = id;                                         → 97
            }
        } else {
            mDbHelper
                .updateReminder(mRowId, title, body, reminderDateTime);  → 100
        }
    }
}
```

Each line of code is explained as follows:

→ **22**   The instance state is checked to see whether it contains any values for the mRowId. The instance state is set on line 84.

→ **28**   This method sets the mRowId from the intent that started the activity. If the Intent object does not contain any extra information, the mRowId object is left null. Note that I'm using a Long (with a capital *L*). This is a reference-type long — meaning that this object can be null or it can contain a long value.

→ **40**   Before the activity is shut down or when it's paused, the database is closed.

→ **44**   The onResume() method is called as part of the normal activity life cycle. This life cycle is explained in Chapter 5 and visualized in Figure 5-1.

→ **46**   The database is opened so that I can use it in this activity.

→ **47**   This method call sets the mRowId object from the intent that started the activity.

→ **48**   The `populateFields()` method is called to populate the form.

→ **55**   This method populates the form if the `mRowId` object is not null.

→ **57**   This line of code retrieves a `Cursor` from the SQLite database based on the `mRowId`. The `fetchReminder()` call is made on line 55 of Listing 12-4.

→ **58**   Starts the activity management of the `Cursor`.

→ **60**   Sets the text of the title using the `Cursor`. To retrieve values from the cursor, you need to know the index of the column in the cursor. The `getColumnIndexOrThrow()` method on the `Cursor` object provides the column index when given the column name. After the column index is retrieved, you can obtain the column value by calling `getString()` with the column index as a parameter. After the value is retrieved, I set the text of the `mTitleText` `EditText` view.

→ **61**   Retrieves and sets the value for the `mBodyTest` `EditText` view using the same method as described in line 60, but this time using a different column name and index.

→ **63**   Because SQLite does not store actual date types, they are stored as strings. Therefore, I need to create a `SimpleDateFormat` to parse the date. This is the `SimpleDateFormat` that parses the date from the database.

→ **64**   This line instantiates a new `Date` object from the `java.util.Date` package.

→ **67**   Retrieves the date as a string from the `Cursor`.

→ **68**   Parses the date into a `Calendar` object.

→ **69**   This line sets the calendar object's date and time from the date and time that was parsed from the database.

→ **70**   Catching any parse exceptions that may occur due to incorrect string formats that are passed into the `SimpleDateFormat` parsing. The `ParseException` that is caught here is from the `java.text.ParseException` package.

→ **71**   Prints the error message to the system log.

→ **82**   Saves the `mRowId` instance state. The `onSaveInstanceState()` method is called so that you may retrieve and store activity-level instance states in a `Bundle`. This method is called before the activity is killed so that when the activity comes back in the future, it can be restored to a known state (as done in the on-`Resume()` method). On line 22, I check to see whether a `row Id` is present in the `savedInstanceState` object prior to checking the intent for incoming data. I'm doing this because there may be a point in time when Android kills the activity for some reason while you're using the app. Such instances include, but are not limited to, a phone call coming in, using the Maps feature, playing music, and so on. At a later time, when you finally return to the app, the savedInstanceState can be inspected to see whether the activity can resume what it was doing before. Storing the mRowId in this object allows me to resume working with the activity in a predetermined state.

→ **94**   In the saveState() method, I have to determine whether I am going to save a new task or update an existing one. If the mRowId is null, that means that no row Id could be found in the saved-InstanceState or in the incoming intent; therefore, the task is considered new.

→ **95**   A new task is created in the database.

→ **96**   Checking to make sure that the ID returned from the insert is greater than zero. All new inserts return their ID, which should be greater than zero.

→ **97**   Setting the local mRowId to the newly created ID.

→ **100**   This line updates the task. I am passing in the row Id to update the title, the body, and the reminder date and time to update the task with.

When you fire up the application in the emulator, you can now create, read, update, and delete tasks! The only things left to build are the reminders' status bar notifications!

Chapter 13

Reminding the User with AlarmManager

*M*any tasks need to happen on a daily basis, right? Wake up, take a shower, eat breakfast, and so on — I'm sure they all sound familiar. That is the majority of everyone's Monday-through-Friday prework morning routine (or some variance of it). You maybe have an internal clock and get up every day on time, but I have to set alarms to wake up on time to ensure that I get to work on time! At work I have a calendar that reminds me of upcoming events that I need to attend — such as meetings and important server upgrades. Reminders and alarms are part of everyone's everyday routine, and we all rely on them in one way or another.

If you had to build your own scheduled task system it would be a pain. Thankfully Windows has scheduled tasks, Linux has cron, and Android has the `AlarmManager` class. Though Android is based on Linux, you do not have access to cron; therefore, you have to set up your scheduled actions through the Android `AlarmManager`.

Seeing Why You Need AlarmManager

The Task Reminder application has one key word in the application name — *Reminder*. The user needs to be able to set a task title, description, and reminder date and time of when to be reminded of said task. To be reminded of the task, you need a way to tell Android when to remind you of the task. Take the following scenario into consideration: You add a couple tasks in the Task Reminder application — all due later today. You put your device in your pocket and you go about your business. If you were not reminded about the tasks, you might forget about them; therefore, you need some way to be reminded of what should happen. This is where the AlarmManager class comes into play.

The AlarmManager class allows you to schedule a point in time when your application should be run in the future. When an alarm goes off, an intent is broadcast by the system. Your application then responds to that broadcast intent and performs some type of action, such as opening the application, notifying the user via a status bar notification (which I do in Chapter 14), or performing some other type of action.

The AlarmManager holds a CPU wake lock as long as the alarm receiver's onReceive() method is executing. This guarantees that the phone will not sleep until you have finished working with the broadcast. This is why I needed the WAKE_LOCK permission that was set up in the previous chapter.

Waking Up a Process with AlarmManager

To wake up a process with the AlarmManager, you have to set the alarm first. In the Task Reminder application, the best place to do that is right after you save your task in the saveState() method. Before you add that code, however, you need to add four class files to your project:

✔ ReminderManager.java: This class is responsible for setting up reminders using the AlarmManager. The code for this class is shown in Listing 13-1 (see the next section in this chapter).

✔ OnAlarmReceiver.java: This class is responsible for handling the broadcast when the alarm goes off. The code for this class is shown in Listing 13-2 (see the section "Creating the OnAlarmReceiver class," later in this chapter). You need to add the following line of code to the application element in your AndroidManifest.xml file for your application to recognize this receiver:

```
<receiver android:name=".OnAlarmReceiver" />
```

The leading period syntax informs Android that the receiver is in the current package — the one that is defined in the application element of the ApplicationManifest.xml file.

✔ WakeReminderIntentService.java: This abstract class is responsible for acquiring and releasing the wake lock. The code for this class is shown in Listing 13-3 (see the section "Creating the WakeReminderIntentService class," later in this chapter).

✔ `ReminderService.java`: This class is an implementation of the `WakeReminderIntentService` that handles the building of the notification as shown in Chapter 14. The code for this class is shown in Listing 13-4 (see the section "Creating the ReminderService class," later in this chapter).

You need to add the following line of code to the application element in the `AndroidManifest.xml` file for your application to recognize this service:

```
<service android:name=".ReminderService" />
```

Creating the ReminderManager class

As stated previously, the `ReminderManager` class is responsible for setting up alarms using the `AlarmManager` class in Android. I am placing all actions that pertain to setting alarms from the `AlarmManager` into this class.

Add the following code to the end of the `saveState()` method in the `ReminderEditActivity` class to add an alarm for that task:

```
new ReminderManager(this).setReminder(mRowId, mCalendar);
```

This line of code instructs the `ReminderManager` to set a new reminder for the task with a row ID of `mRowId` at the particular date and time as defined by the `mCalendar` variable.

Listing 13-1 shows the code for the `ReminderManager` class.

Listing 13-1: `ReminderManager` Class

```
public class ReminderManager {

private Context mContext;
private AlarmManager mAlarmManager;
public ReminderManager(Context context) {                              → 6
    mContext = context;
    mAlarmManager =
        (AlarmManager)context.getSystemService(Context.ALARM_SERVICE);  → 9
}

public void setReminder(Long taskId, Calendar when) {                  → 12
    Intent i = new Intent(mContext, OnAlarmReceiver.class);            → 13
    i.putExtra(RemindersDbAdapter.KEY_ROWID, (long)taskId);            → 14

    PendingIntent pi =
```

(continued)

Listing 13-1 *(continued)*

```
PendingIntent.getBroadcast(mContext, 0, i,
                    PendingIntent.FLAG_ONE_SHOT);                    → 16

mAlarmManager.set(AlarmManager.RTC_WAKEUP, when.getTimeInMillis(), pi);  → 17
        }
}
```

Each numbered line of code is explained as follows:

→ **6**   The `ReminderManager` class is instantiated with a `context` object.

→ **9**   An `AlarmManager` is obtained through the `getSystem-Service()` call.

→ **12**   The `setReminder()` method is called with the database ID of the task and the `Calendar` object of when the alarm should fire.

→ **13**   A new `Intent` object is created. This intent object is responsible for specifying what should happen when the alarm goes off. In this instance, I am specifying that the `OnAlarmReceiver` receiver should be called.

→ **14**   The `Intent` object is provided with extra information — the ID of the task in the database.

→ **16**   The `AlarmManager` operates in a separate process, and for the `AlarmManager` to notify an application that an action needs to be performed, a `PendingIntent` must be created. The `Pending-Intent` contains an `Intent` object that was created on line 13. On this line, a `PendingIntent` is created with a flag of `FLAG_ONE_SHOT` to indicate that this `PendingIntent` can only be used once.

→ **17**   The `AlarmManager`'s `set()` method is called to schedule the alarm. The `set()` method is provided with the following parameters:

- type: `AlarmManager.RTC_WAKEUP`: Wall-clock time in UTC. This parameter wakes up the device when the specified `trig-gerAtTime` argument time elapses.

- triggerAtTime: `when.getTimeInMillis()`: The time the alarm should go off. The `Calendar` object provides the `get-Time-InMillis()` method, which converts the time into long value, which represents time in units of milliseconds.

- operation: `pi`: The pending intent to act upon when the alarm goes off. The alarm will now go off at the time requested.

If an alarm is already scheduled with a pending intent that contains the same signature, the previous alarm will first be canceled and a new one will be set up.

Creating the OnAlarmReceiver class

The OnAlarmReceiver class (see Listing 13-2) is responsible for handling the intent that is fired when an alarm is raised. This class acts as a hook into the alarm system because it is essentially a simple implementation of a BroadcastReceiver — which can react to broadcast events in the Android system.

Listing 13-2:   OnAlarmReceiver Class

```
public class OnAlarmReceiver extends BroadcastReceiver {
       @Override
       public void onReceive(Context context, Intent intent) {
           long rowid =
               intent.getExtras().getLong(RemindersDbAdapter.KEY_ROWID);      → 4

               WakeReminderIntentService.acquireStaticLock(context);           → 6

               Intent i = new Intent(context, ReminderService.class);          → 8
               i.putExtra(RemindersDbAdapter.KEY_ROWID, rowid);                → 9
               context.startService(i);                                        → 10

       }
}
```

Each numbered line is explained as follows:

→ **4**   I am retrieving the database ID of the task from the intent after the receiver has started handling the intent.

→ **6**   Here, I inform the WakeReminderIntentService to acquire a static lock on the CPU to keep the device alive while work is being performed.

→ **8**   This line defines a new Intent object that will start the ReminderService.

→ **9**   On this line, I am placing the ID of the task into the intent that will be used to start the service that will do the work. This gives the ReminderService class the ID of the task that it needs to work with.

→ **10**   This line starts the ReminderService.

This is the first entry point for the alarm you set. In this BroadcastReceiver, you would not want to let the device go back to sleep during your processing because your task would never complete and could possibly leave your application in a broken state through data corruption with the database.

When an alarm goes off, the pending intent that was scheduled with the alarm is broadcast through the system, and any broadcast receiver that is capable of handling it will handle it.

Because this is your second foray into the BroadcastReceiver object, you're probably still a bit fuzzy about how they work. A BroadcastReceiver is a component that does nothing but receive and react to system broadcast messages. A BroadcastReceiver does not display a user interface; however, it starts an activity in response to the broadcast. The OnAlarmReceiver is an instance of a BroadcastReceiver.

When the AlarmManager broadcasts the pending intent, the OnAlarm-Receiver class responds to the intent — because it is addressed to that class as shown on line 13 of Listing 13-1. This class then accepts the intent, locks the CPU, and performs the necessary work.

Creating the WakeReminder-IntentService class

The WakeReminderIntentService class is the base class for the ReminderService class, as shown in Listing 13-3. This class handles the management of acquiring and releasing a CPU wake lock. A CPU wake lock keeps the device on (but not necessarily the screen) while some work takes place. After the work is complete, this class releases the wake lock so that the device may return to sleep.

Listing 13-3: **WakeReminderIntentService** Class

```
public abstract class WakeReminderIntentService extends IntentService
        {    abstract void doReminderWork(Intent intent);
        →2

    public static final String
        LOCK_NAME_STATIC="com.dummies.android.taskreminder.Static";    →3
    private static PowerManager.WakeLock lockStatic=null;            →4

    public static void acquireStaticLock(Context context) {
        getLock(context).acquire();                                  →5
    }

    synchronized private static PowerManager.WakeLock
                            getLock(Context context) {               →8
        if (lockStatic==null) {
            PowerManager
                mgr=(PowerManager)context
                    .getSystemService(Context.POWER_SERVICE);        →10

        lockStatic=mgr.newWakeLock(PowerManager.PARTIAL_WAKE_LOCK,
```

```
                          LOCK_NAME_STATIC);                    → 12
         lockStatic.setReferenceCounted(true);                 → 13
    }

         return(lockStatic);                                   → 15
    }

    public WakeReminderIntentService(String name) {            → 18
         super(name);
    }

    @Override
    final protected void onHandleIntent(Intent intent) {       → 23
        try {
             doReminderWork(intent);                           → 25
        } finally {
             getLock(this).release();                          → 27
        }

    }
}
```

Each numbered line is explained as follows:

→ **2** This abstract method is implemented in any children of this class — such as in the child ReminderService as shown on line 7 of Listing 13-4.

→ **3** This is the tag name of the lock that I will use to acquire the CPU lock. This tag name assists in debugging.

→ **4** This is the private static wake lock variable, which is referenced and set later in this class.

→ **5** This calls the getLock() method, as described on line 8. After that call is returned, the acquire() method is called to ensure that the device is on in the state that you requested, a partial wake lock. This wake lock prevents the device from sleeping, but it doesn't turn on the screen.

→ **8** This line defines the getLock() method that returns the Power-Manager.WakeLock, which lets you inform Android that you would like the device to stay on to do some work.

→ **10** This line retrieves the PowerManager from the getSystem-Service() call. This is used to create the lock.

→ **12** This creates a new WakeLock using the newWakeLock() method call. This method accepts the following parameters:

   • flags: PowerManager.PARTIAL_WAKE_LOCK: You can provide numerous tags to this call; however, I am only providing this single tag. The PARTIAL_WAKE_LOCK tag informs Android that you need the CPU to be on, but the screen does not have to be on.

- tag: LOCK_NAME_STATIC: The name of your class name or another string. This is used for debugging purposes. This is a custom string that is defined on line 3.

→ **13** This line informs the PowerManager that this reference has been counted.

→ **15** This returns the WakeLock to the caller.

→ **18** This is the constructor with the name of the child instance that has created it. This name is used for debugging only.

→ **23** This is the onHandleIntent() call of the IntentService. As soon as the service is started, this method is called to handle the intent that was passed to it.

→ **25** The service attempts to perform the necessary work by calling doReminderWork().

→ **27** Regardless of whether the call to doReminderWork() is successful, I want to make sure that I release the WakeLock. If I do not release the WakeLock, the device could be left in an On state until the phone is rebooted. This is very undesirable because it would drain the battery. This is why the release() method is called in the final portion of the try-catch block. The final portion of the try-catch block is always called, regardless of whether the try succeeds or fails.

Although no implementation for the doReminderWork() exists in the ReminderService just yet, the Task Reminder application responds to alarms. Feel free to set up multiple tasks and to set break points in the debugger to watch the execution path break in the ReminderService doReminderWork() method.

The AlarmManager does not persist alarms. This means that if the device gets rebooted, the alarms must be set up again. Each time the phone is rebooted, the alarms need to be set up again.

The previous code demonstrates what is necessary to perform work on a device that might be asleep or locked. This code acquires the wake lock, and while the device is locked into a wakeful state, I call into doReminder-Work(), which is implemented in the ReminderService.

Creating the ReminderService class

The ReminderService class (see Listing 13-4) is responsible for doing the work when an alarm is fired. The implementation in this chapter simply creates a shell for work to take place. I will be implementing the status bar notification in Chapter 14.

Listing 13-4: `ReminderService` Class

```
public class ReminderService extends WakeReminderIntentService {          → 1
    public ReminderService() {
        super("ReminderService");
    }

    @Override
    void doReminderWork(Intent intent) {                                   → 7
        Long rowId = intent.getExtras()
            .getLong(RemindersDbAdapter.KEY_ROWID);                        → 8

        // Status bar notification Code Goes here.
    }
}
```

Each numbered line of code is explained as follows:

→ **1**   This line defines the `ReminderService` class by inheriting from the `WakeReminderIntentService`.

→ **7**   The abstract method `doReminderWork()` in the `WakeReminder-IntentService` is implemented here.

→ **8**   On this line, I'm retrieving the task ID that was inside the `Intent` object that passed in this class.

As noted before, this class contains no implementation — other than retrieving the ID of the task from the intent.

Rebooting Devices

I admit, after a long day and a good night's rest, I forget things from time to time. I'm only human, right? I usually have to be reminded of certain things when I wake up; that's just the way it is. The Android `AlarmManager` is no different. The `AlarmManager` does not persist alarms; therefore, when the device reboots, you must set up the alarms all over again. Although it's not a huge pain in the butt, it's something worth knowing.

If you do not set up your alarms again, they simply will not fire, because to Android they do not exist.

Creating a boot receiver

In the last chapter, I had you set up the RECEIVE_BOOT_COMPLETED permission. This permission allows your application to receive a broadcast notification from Android when the device is done booting and is eligible to be interactive with the user. Because the Android system can broadcast a message when this event is complete, you need to add another BroadcastReceiver to your project. This BroadcastReceiver is responsible for handling the boot notification from Android. When the broadcast is received, the receiver needs to connect to SQLite through the RemindersDbAdapter and loop through each task and schedule an alarm for it. This ensures that your alarms don't get lost in the reboot.

Add a new BroadcastReceiver to your application. For the Task Reminder application, I'm giving it a name of OnBootReceiver. You also need to add the following lines of code to the application element in the AndroidManifest.xml file:

```
<receiver android:name=".OnBootReceiver">
    <intent-filter>
        <action android:name="android.intent.action.BOOT_COMPLETED" />
    </intent-filter>
</receiver>
```

This informs Android that the OnBootReceiver should receive boot notifications for the BOOT_COMPLETED action. In laymen's terms — let OnBootReceiver know when the device is done booting up.

The full implementation of OnBootReceiver is shown in Listing 13-5.

Listing 13-5: `OnBootReceiver`

```
public class OnBootReceiver extends BroadcastReceiver {                    →1

    @Override
    public void onReceive(Context context, Intent intent) {               →4
        ReminderManager reminderMgr = new ReminderManager(context);       →6
        RemindersDbAdapter dbHelper = new RemindersDbAdapter(context);
        dbHelper.open();
        Cursor cursor = dbHelper.fetchAllReminders();                     →11
        if(cursor != null) {
            cursor.moveToFirst();                                         →14

            int rowIdColumnIndex = cursor.getColumnIndex(RemindersDbAdapter.
                KEY_ROWID);
              int dateTimeColumnIndex =
              cursor.getColumnIndex(RemindersDbAdapter.KEY_DATE_TIME);

              while(cursor.isAfterLast() == false) {                      →19
                Long rowId = cursor.getLong(rowIdColumnIndex);
```

```
        String dateTime = cursor.getString(dateTimeColumnIndex);

        Calendar cal = Calendar.getInstance();
        SimpleDateFormat format = new
            SimpleDateFormat(ReminderEditActivity.DATE_TIME_FORMAT);

    try {
            java.util.Date date = format.parse(dateTime);              → 27
            cal.setTime(date);                                         → 28

            reminderMgr.setReminder(rowId, cal);                       → 30
    } catch (ParseException e) {
            Log.e("OnBootReceiver", e.getMessage(), e);                → 32
    }

    cursor.moveToNext();                                               → 35
    }
    cursor.close() ;                                                   → 37
    }

    dbHelper.close();                                                  → 40
    }
}
```

Each numbered line is explained in detail as follows:

→ **1**   This is the definition of the `OnBootReceiver`.

→ **4**   This is the `onReceive()` method that is called when the receiver receives an intent to perform an action.

→ **6**   This sets up a new `ReminderManager` object that allows me to schedule alarms.

→ **11**   This obtains a cursor with all the reminders from the `Reminders-DbAdapter`. This is the same call that is used to load the `ListView` in the `ReminderListActivity`.

→ **14**   This moves to the first record in the `Cursor`. Because a cursor can contain many records, you can advance the cursor to the next record upon request. That is what I am doing here.

→ **19**   This sets up a `while` loop. This `while` loop checks to see whether the cursor is moved past the last record. If it equals false, this means that I am still working with a valid record. I move the cursor to the next record on line 35. If this value were true, it would mean that no more records were available to utilize in the cursor.

→ **27**   The date is parsed from the string retrieved from the database.

→ **28**   After the date is retrieved from the cursor, the `Calendar` variable needs to be updated with the correct time. This line formats the parsed date value into the local `Calendar` object.

→ **30**   This schedules a new reminder with the row ID from the database at the time defined by the recently built `Calendar` variable.

→ **32**   This prints any exceptions to the system log.

→ **35**   This line moves to the next record in the cursor. If no more records exist in the cursor, the call to `isAfterLast()` returns true, which means that the `while` loop will exit. After this line executes, the loop processes again by returning execution to line 19 and continuing the process until no more database records are left.

→ **37**   This closes the cursor because it is no longer needed. When I previously worked with the `Cursor` object, you may have noticed that I never had to close the cursor. This is because the `Activity` object was managing the cursor for me. Because I'm in a broadcast receiver, I do not have access to the `Activity` class because it is not in scope and is not valid in this instance.

→ **40**   This closes the `RemindersDbAdapter`, which in turn closes the database because it is no longer needed.

If you were to start the application, create a few reminders, and then reboot the device, you would now see that the reminders persisted. If you decide to debug the application, be sure to set the debuggable attribute to true in the application manifest.

Checking the boot receiver

If you're not sure whether the `OnBootReceiver` is working, you can place log statements into the `while` loop like this:

```
Log.d("OnBootReceiver", "Adding alarm from boot.");
Log.d("OnBootReceiver", "Row Id Column Index - " + rowIdColumnIndex);
```

This prints messages to the system log that are viewable through DDMS. You can then shut down the emulator (or device) and then start it again. Watch the messages stream through in DDMS, and look for the `OnBootReceiver` messages. If you have two tasks in your database, you should see two sets of messages informing you of the system adding an alarm from boot. Then the next message should be the row ID column index.

Chapter 14

Updating the Android Status Bar

Throughout this book, I've covered various ways to grab the user's attention through dialog boxes, toasts, and new activities. While these techniques work well in their respective situations, at other times, you need to inform the user of something, yet you do not want to steal his attention from the current activity. Therefore, you need a way to inform the user that something needs his attention, when he has time to tend to the matter. This is exactly what the status bar is for.

Deconstructing the Status Bar

Resorting to the age-old saying of a picture is worth a thousand words, the best way to describe the status bar is to show it to you via Figure 14-1.

Viewing status bar icons

In Figure 14-1, the first icon at the upper left is a calendar notification informing me that I have an appointment with a coworker today. The second icon is telling me that the device is connected to another device (a computer) via USB, and the third icon informs me that USB debugging is enabled. I can press and slide the status bar down and receive more information, as shown in Figure 14-2.

In Figure 14-2, you can see that each notification has an expanded view that gives you more information about each icon. The user can select the expanded view that interests her — which starts the requested action.

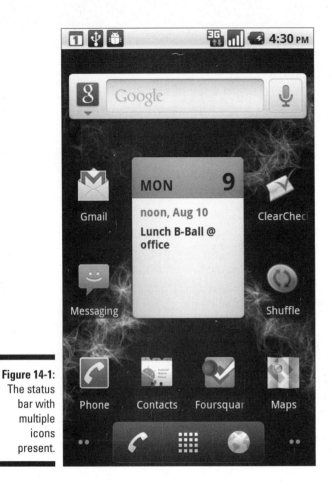

Figure 14-1:
The status
bar with
multiple
icons
present.

As a developer, you have access to modify the contents of the status bar.

Using status-bar tools to notify the user

The status bar provides various tools for you to notify the user. Simple icons floating at the top of the screen in the notification area are not your only options. You can augment your notification by providing the notification with additional flags (which I cover later in this chapter) during the notification process. Some of these options are as follows:

Status bar dragged down

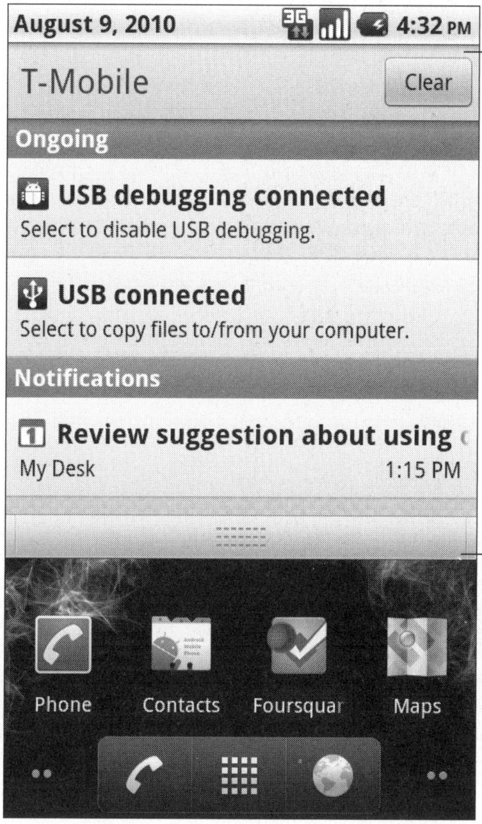

Figure 14-2:
Opening the
status bar.

✔ **Vibration:** You can vibrate the device when a notification occurs. This is useful when the user has the device in his or her pocket.

✔ **Sound:** Sound some type of alarm when the notification occurs, such as a ringtone or prerecorded tone that you install with your application. This is useful if the user has the notification sound level cranked up.

✔ **Lights:** Many devices contain an LED that you have programmatic access to. You can tell the light to flash at a given interval with a specific color that you program. If the LED only supports one color (such as white), it will flash white, ignoring your color requirement. If the user has the device set to silent, using lights provides an excellent cue that something needs attention.

Adding these various options to your notification arsenal can help immensely because they let the user know that something has happened on the device.

The status bar is a very powerful tool because it can be used to provide valuable feedback to the user throughout the lifetime of an application. While icons, vibration, lights, and sound might sound like a golden jackpot, that's not the end of the rainbow, Mr. Leprechaun. Notifications also allow you to provide scrolling information to the user. This is the information that shows when the notification first arrives. After that, the user needs to slide down the status bar to see the expanded view.

The status bar framework can be used to inform users of various activities such as device state, new mail notifications, and even progress downloads, as shown in Figure 14-3.

Different notifications can contain different views.

Figure 14-3:
The progress
loader in the
status bar.

As a developer, you have programmatic access to provide custom expanded views. The expanded view is the view that is present when the user slides the status bar down.

Using the Notification Manager

The notification manager allows you to interface with Android's notification mechanism. Notifications appear in the status bar at the top of the device screen. Working with the NotificationManager is as simple as asking the current context for it. If you are within an activity, the code is as follows:

```
NotificationManager mgr = (NotificationManager)getSystemService(NOTIFICATION_
        SERVICE);
```

This line of code obtains the NotificationManager object from the getSystemService() call.

Creating your first notification

The Task Reminder application needs a way to notify the user that a task needs attention. This would happen when the alarm goes off for that particular task. To set this notification in the status bar, you need to use the NotificationManager.

In the doReminderWork() method of the ReminderService class, type the code as shown in Listing 14-1.

Listing 14-1:   Implementation of `doReminderWork()`

```
Long rowId = intent.getExtras().getLong(RemindersDbAdapter.KEY_ROWID);     → 1

NotificationManager mgr =
            (NotificationManager)getSystemService(NOTIFICATION_SERVICE);   → 3

Intent notificationIntent = new Intent(this, ReminderEditActivity.class);  → 5
notificationIntent.putExtra(RemindersDbAdapter.KEY_ROWID, rowId);          → 6

PendingIntent pi = PendingIntent.getActivity(this, 0, notificationIntent,
            PendingIntent.FLAG_ONE_SHOT);                                  → 8

Notification note=new Notification(android.R.drawable.stat_sys_warning,
            getString(R.string.notify_new_task_message),
                System.currentTimeMillis());                               → 10
```

(continued)

Listing 14-1 *(continued)*

```
note.setLatestEventInfo(this, getString(R.string.notifiy_new_task_title),
        getString(R.string.notify_new_task_message), pi);              → 12

note.defaults |= Notification.DEFAULT_SOUND;                           → 14
note.flags |= Notification.FLAG_AUTO_CANCEL;                           → 15

// An issue could occur if user ever enters over 2,147,483,647 tasks. (Max int
        value).
// I highly doubt this will ever happen. But is good to note.
int id = (int)((long)rowId);                                          → 19
mgr.notify(id, note);                                                 → 20
```

The various lines of Listing 14-1 are explained as follows:

→ **1**   The intent that started the `ReminderService` contains the row ID of the task that I'm currently working with. I need this ID because I will set this as part of the `PendingIntent` for the status. When the notification is selected from the status bar, I want the `ReminderEditActivity` to start with the row ID as part of the pending intent. That way, the `ReminderEdit-Activity` will open, read the data about that particular row ID, and display it to the user.

→ **3**   Get an instance of the `NotificationManager`.

→ **5**   I am building a new intent and setting the class to `ReminderEdit-Activity`. This is the activity that I would like to start when the user selects the notification.

→ **6**   Put the row ID into the intent.

→ **8**   Set up a pending intent to be used by the notification system. Because the notification system runs in another process, a `PendingIntent` is required. The `FLAG_ONE_SHOT` flag is used to indicate that this pending intent can only be used once.

→ **10** This line builds the `Notification` that shows up in the status bar. The `Notification` class accepts the following parameters:

- `icon`: `android.R.drawable.stat_sys_warning`: The resource ID of the icon to place in the status bar. This icon is a small triangle with an exclamation point in the middle. Because this is a built-in Android icon, I do not have to worry about providing small-, medium-, or high-density graphics — they are already built into the platform.

- `tickerText`: `getString(R.string.notify_new_task_message)`: The text that flows by when the notification first activates.

- `when`: `System.currentTimeMillis()`: The time to show in the time field of the notification.

→ **12** This line sets the content of the expanded view with that standard Latest Event layout as provided by Android. For example, you could provide a custom XML layout to display. In this instance, I am not providing a custom layout; I'm simply providing the stock notification view. The `setLatestEventInfo()` method accepts the following parameters:

- `context: this`: The context to associate with the event info

- `contentTitle: getString(R.string.notifiy_new_task_title)`: The title that goes into the expanded view

- `contextText: getString(R.string.notify_new_task_message)`: The text that goes into the expanded view

- `contentIntent: pi`: The intent to launch when the expanded view is selected

→ **14** A bitwise-ored in setting the `Notification` object to include sound during the notification process. This forces the default notification sound to be played if the user has the notification volume on.

→ **15** A bitwise-ored in setting the `Notification` object flag's property that cancels the notification after it is selected by the user.

→ **19** Casting the ID to an integer. The ID stored in the SQLite database is long; however, I am casting it to an integer. A loss of precision is happening. However, I highly doubt that this application would ever have more than 2,147,483,647 tasks set up (which is the maximum number that an integer can store in Java). Therefore, this casting should be okay. The casting to an integer is necessary because the code on line 20 only accepts an integer as the ID for the notification.

→ **20** Raises the notification to the status bar. The `notify()` call accepts two parameters:

- `id: id`: An ID that is unique within your application.

- `Notification: note`: A `Notification` object that describes how to notify the user.

Viewing the workflow

The previous code allows the following workflow to occur:

✔ The user is active in another application, such as e-mail.

✔ A task is due and therefore the alarm fires. The notification is created in the status bar.

✔ The user can elect to slide down the status bar and select the notification or ignore it for now.

If the user chooses to slide open the status bar and select an item, the pending intent within the notification will be activated. This in turn causes the `ReminderEditActivity` to open with the given row ID of the task.

✔ The notification is removed from the status bar.

✔ The task information is retrieved from the database and displayed on the form in the `ReminderEditActivity`.

Adding string resources

You may notice that you need to add the following two string resources:

✔ `notify_new_task_message`: I have set the value of this to "A task needs to be reviewed!" This message is used as the message in the expanded view and is used as the ticker text when the notification first arrives.

✔ `notify_new_task_title`: I have set the value of this to "Task Reminder." This message is used as the title for the expanded view.

Updating a Notification

At some time, you might need to update the view of your notification. Consider the following situation: You have some code that runs in the background to see whether the tasks have been reviewed. This code checks to see whether any notifications are overdue. You decide that after the two-hour mark passes, you want to change the icon of the notification to a red-colored exclamation point and flash the LED quickly with a red color. Thankfully, updating the notification is a fairly simple process.

If you call one of the `notify()` methods with an ID that is currently active in the status bar, and with a new set of notification parameters, the notification is updated in the status bar. Therefore, you would simply create a new `Notification` object with the red icon as a parameter and call `notify()` — which would update the notification.

Clearing a Notification

Users are by far the most unpredictable group — because they could be anywhere in the world! They could be first-time users, advanced power users, and so on. Each user utilizes the device in his or her own special way. At some point, your user sees a notification and decides to open the app the manual/long way — via the app launcher.

If the user decides to open your application via the app launcher while a notification is active, your notification will persist. Even if the user looks at the task at hand, the notification will still persist on the status bar. While this is not a big deal, your application should be able to recognize the state of the application and should take the appropriate measures to cancel any existing notifications that might be present for the given task. However, if the user opens your app and reviews a different task that does not have an active notification, you should not clear any notifications. Only clear the notification for which the user is reviewing.

The `NotificationManager` makes it real simple to cancel an existing notification with the `cancel()` method. The `cancel()` method accepts one parameter — the ID of the notification. Remember how I used the ID of the task as the ID for the note? This is why I did that. The ID of the task is unique to the Task Reminder application. By doing this, I can easily open a task and cancel any existing notification by calling the `cancel()` method with the ID of the task.

At some point, you might also need to clear all previously shown notifications. To do this, simply call the `cancelAll()` method on the `NotificationManager`.

Chapter 15

Working with Android's Preference Framework

. . . .

In This Chapter

▶ Seeing how preferences work in Android

▶ Building a preference screen

▶ Working with preferences programmatically

. . . .

1 would consider myself a power user of computer software, and I'm sure that you're a power user as well. I know that most programs can be configured to suit my needs (for the most part), and I usually go out of my way to find the settings or preferences to set up my favorite configuration for a given program. Allowing your users to do the same in your Android application gives your application an advantage in regard to usability. Thankfully creating and providing a mechanism to edit preferences in Android are fairly easy processes.

Out of the box, Android provides a robust preference framework that allows you to declaratively as well as programmatically define preferences for your application. Android stores preferences as persistent key-value pairs of primitive data types for you. You are not required to store the values in a file, database, or any other mechanism. The Android preference framework takes the values you provide and commits them to internal storage on behalf of your application. You can use the preference framework to store booleans, floats, ints, longs, and strings. The data persists across user sessions as well — meaning that if the user closes the app and reopens it later, the preferences are saved and can be utilized. This is true even if your application is killed.

In this chapter, I delve into the Android preference framework and describe how to incorporate it into your applications. I demonstrate how to utilize the built-in `PreferenceActivity` to create and edit preferences. I also demonstrate how to read and write preferences from code within your application. At the end of the chapter, you will have fully integrated preferences into the Task Reminder application.

Understanding Android's Preference Framework

One of the great things about the Android preference framework is the simplicity of developing a screen that allows the user to modify preferences. Most of the heavy lifting is done for you by Android, because developing a preference screen is as simple as defining a preference screen in XML that is located in the res/xml folder of your project. While these XML files are not the same as layout files, they are specific XML definitions that define screens, categories, and actual preferences. Common preferences that are built into the framework include the following:

- EditTextPreference: A preference that can store plain text as a string

- CheckBoxPreference: A preference that can store a boolean value

- RingtonePreference: A preference that allows the user to store a preferred ringtone from those available on the device

- ListPreference: A preference that allows the user to select a preferred item from a list of items in the dialog box

If the built-in preferences do not suit your needs, you can create your own preference by deriving from the base Preference class or Dialog-Preference. A DialogPreference is the base class for preferences that are dialog box-based. When clicked, these preferences open a dialog box showing the actual preference controls. Examples of built in Dialog-Preferences are EditTextPreference and ListPreference.

Android also provides a PreferenceActivity in which you can derive from and load the preference screens in the same manner that you would load a layout for a basic Activity class. This base class allows you to tap into the PreferenceActivity events and perform some advanced work, such as setting an EditTextPreference to accept only.

Understanding the PreferenceActivity Class

The responsibility of the PreferenceActivity class is to show a hierarchy of Preference objects as lists, possibly spanning multiple screens, as shown in Figure 15-1.

A preference screen with various preferences listed

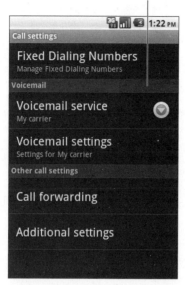

Figure 15-1:
The
preference
screen for
the call
settings in
Android.

When preferences are edited, they are stored using an instance of `Shared-Preferences`. The `SharedPreferences` class is an interface for accessing and modifying preference data returned by `getSharedPreferences()` from any `Context` object.

A `PreferenceActivity` is a base class that is very similar to the `Activity` base class. However, the `PreferenceActivity` behaves a bit differently. One of the most important features that the `PreferenceActivity` handles is the displaying of preferences in the visual style that resembles the system preferences. This gives your application a consistent feel across the board in regard to Android user interface components. You should use the `Preference-Activity` when dealing with preference screens in your Android applications.

Persisting preference values

Because the Android framework stores preferences in the `Shared-Preferences`, which automatically stores the preference data in internal storage, it is easy for you to create a preference. When a user edits a preference, the value is automatically saved for you — that's right, you don't have to do any persisting yourself!

I'm sure this sounds like a little bit of black magic, but I assure you it's not! In Figure 15-2, I am editing an `EditTextPreference` that will be used in the Task Reminder application. After I select OK, Android takes the value I provided and persists it to `SharedPreferences` — I don't need to do anything else. Android does all the heavy lifting in regard to persisting the preference values.

Figure 15-2:
Setting a
preference.

Laying out preferences

Working with layouts in Android can sometimes be, well, a painstaking process of alignment, gravity, and so on. Building layouts is almost like building a Web site with various tables all over the place. Sometimes it's easy; sometimes it's not. Thankfully, laying out Android preferences is much simpler than defining a layout for your application screen.

Android preference screens are broken into the following categories:

✔ `PreferenceScreen`: Represents a top-level preference that is the root of a preference hierarchy. You can use a `PreferenceScreen` in two places:

• In a `PreferenceActivity`: The `PreferenceScreen` is not shown because it only shows the containing preferences within the `PreferenceScreen` definition.

- In another preference hierarchy: When present in another hierarchy, the PreferenceScreen serves as a gateway to another screen of preferences. Think of this as nesting PreferenceScreen declarations inside other PreferenceScreen declarations. While this might seem confusing, think of this as XML. In XML you can declare an element, and any element can contain the same parent element. At that point, you're nesting the elements. The same goes for the PreferenceScreen. By nesting them, you are informing Android that it should show a new screen when selected.

✔ PreferenceCategory: This preference is used to group preference objects and provide a title above the group that describes the category.

✔ Preference: A preference that is shown on the screen. This preference could be any of the common preferences or a custom one that you define.

By laying out a combination of the PreferenceScreen, Preference-Category, and Preference in XML, you can easily create a preference screen that looks similar to Figure 15-1.

Creating Your First Preference Screen

Creating preferences using the PreferenceActivity and a preference XML file is a fairly straightforward process. The first thing you do is create the preference XML file, which defines the layout of the preferences and the string resource values that show up on the screen. These string resources are presented as TextViews on the screen to help the user determine what the preference is for.

The PreferenceScreen I am building is for the Task Reminder application. I want to be able to give my users the chance to set the default time for a reminder (in minutes) and a default title for a new task. As the application stands right now, the default title is empty and the default reminder time is set to the current time. These preferences will allow the user to save a couple of steps while building new tasks. For example, if the user normally builds tasks with a reminder time of 60 minutes from now, the user can now set that in the preferences. This new value becomes the value of the reminder time when the user creates a new task.

Building the preferences file

To build your first preference screen, you need to create a res/xml folder in your project. Inside the res/xml folder, create an XML file — I'm naming mine task_preferences.xml. Listing 15-1 outlines what should be in the file.

Listing 15-1: The `task_preferences.xml` File

```xml
<?xml version="1.0" encoding="utf-8"?>
<PreferenceScreen                                                          → 2
  xmlns:android="http://schemas.android.com/apk/res/android">
        <PreferenceCategory                                                → 4
            android:key="@string/pref_category_task_defaults_key"          → 5
            android:title="@string/pref_category_task_defaults_title">     → 6
        <EditTextPreference                                                → 7
            android:key="@string/pref_task_title_key"                      → 8
            android:dialogTitle="@string/pref_task_title_dialog_title"     → 9
            android:dialogMessage="@string/pref_task_title_message"        → 10
            android:summary="@string/pref_task_title_summary"              → 11
            android:title="@string/pref_task_title_title" />               → 12
        </PreferenceCategory>
        <PreferenceCategory                                                → 13
            android:key="@string/pref_category_datetime_key"               → 14
            android:title="@string/pref_category_datetime_title">          → 15
            <EditTextPreference                                            → 16
                android:key="@string/pref_default_time_from_now_key"       → 17
    android:dialogTitle="@string/pref_default_time_from_now_dialog_title"  → 18
    android:dialogMessage="@string/pref_default_time_from_now_message"     → 19
    android:summary="@string/pref_default_time_from_now_summary"           → 20
    android:title="@string/pref_default_time_from_now_title" />            → 21
    </PreferenceCategory>
</PreferenceScreen>
```

Quite a few string resources are introduced in Listing 15-1. They will be listed in Listing 15-2. Each numbered line of code is explained as follows:

→ **2**   This is the root-level `PreferenceScreen`. It is the container for the screen itself. All other preferences live below this declaration.

→ **4**   This is a `PreferenceCategory` that defines the category for task defaults, such as title or body. As you may have noticed, on line 13, I am declaring another `PreferenceCategory` for the default task time. Normally I would have placed these two items into the same category, but I separated them in this instance to demonstrate how to use multiple `PreferenceCategory` elements on one screen.

→ **5**   This line defines the key that is used to store and retrieve the preference from the `SharedPreferences`. This key must be unique.

→ **6**   This line defines the category title.

→ **7**   This line contains the definition of the `EditTextPreference`, which is responsible for storing the preference for the default title of a task.

→ **8**   This line contains the key for the default title text `EditTextPreference`.

→ **9**   The `EditTextPreference` is a child class of `DialogPreference`, which means that when you select the preference, you will receive a dialog box similar to what's shown in Figure 15-2. This line of code defines the title for that dialog box.

→ **10**   This line defines the message that appears in the dialog box.

→ **11**   This line defines the summary text that is present on the preferences screen, as shown in Figure 15-1.

→ **12**   This line defines the title of the preference on the preference screen.

→ **13**   This line defines the `PreferenceCategory` for the default task time.

→ **14**   This line defines the category key.

→ **15**   This line defines the title of the category.

→ **16**   This line is the start of the definition of the `EditTextPreference`, which stores the default time in minutes (digits) that the task reminder time will default to from the current time.

→ **17**   This line defines the key for the default task time preference.

→ **18**   This line defines the title of the dialog box that presents when the preference is selected.

→ **19**   This line defines the message that will be present in the dialog box.

→ **20**   This line defines the summary of the preference that is present on the main preference screen, as shown in Figure 15-1.

→ **21**   This line defines the title of the preference on the preference screen.

Adding string resources

For your application to compile, you need the string resources for the preferences. In your `res/values/strings.xml` file, add the following values:

```xml
<!-- Preferences -->
<string name="pref_category_task_defaults_key">task_default_category</string>
<string name="pref_category_task_defaults_title">Task Title Default</string>
<string name="pref_task_title_key">default_reminder_title</string>
<string name="pref_task_title_dialog_title">Default Reminder Title</string>
<string name="pref_task_title_message">The default title for a reminder.</string>
<string name="pref_task_title_summary">Default title for reminders.</string>
<string name="pref_task_title_title">Default Reminder Title</string>
<string name="pref_category_datetime_key">date_time_default_category</string>
<string name="pref_category_datetime_title">Date Time Defaults</string>
```

```
<string name="pref_default_time_from_now_key">time_from_now_default</string>
<string name="pref_default_time_from_now_dialog_title">Time From Now</string>
<string name="pref_default_time_from_now_message">The default time from now (in
          minutes) that a new reminder should be set to.</string>
<string name="pref_default_time_from_now_summary">Sets the default time for a
          reminder.</string>
<string name="pref_default_time_from_now_title">Default Reminder Time</string>
```

You should now be able to compile your application.

Defining a preference screen was fairly simple — provide the values to the attributes needed and you're done. While the preference screen may be defined in XML, simply defining it in XML does not mean that it will show up on the screen. To get your preference screen to display on the screen, you need to create a PreferenceActivity.

Working with the PreferenceActivity Class

The PreferenceActivity shows a hierarchy of preferences on the screen according to a preferences file defined in XML — such as the one you just created. The preferences can span multiple screens (if multiple PreferenceScreen objects are present and nested). These preferences automatically save to SharedPreferences. As an added bonus, the preferences shown automatically follow the visual style of the system preferences, which allows your application to have a consistent user experience in conjunction with the default Android platform.

To inflate and display the PreferenceScreen you just built, add an activity that derives from PreferenceActivity to your application. I am going to name mine TaskPreferences. The code for this file is shown in Listing 15-2.

Listing 15-2:   The `TaskPreferences` File

```
public class TaskPreferences extends PreferenceActivity {              → 1
      @Override
      protected void onCreate(Bundle savedInstanceState) {
          super.onCreate(savedInstanceState);
          addPreferencesFromResource(R.xml.task_preferences);          → 5

          EditTextPreference timeDefault = (EditTextPreference)
    findPreference(getString(R.string.pref_default_time_from_now_key));  → 6
  timeDefault.getEditText().setKeyListener(DigitsKeyListener.getInstance()); → 7
    }
}
```

Yes, that's it! That's all the code that is needed to display, edit, and persist preferences in Android! Each numbered line of code is explained as follows:

→ **1**   The `TaskPreferences` class file is defined by inheriting from the `PreferenceActivity` base class.

→ **5**   The call to `addPreferencesFromResource()` method is provided with the resource ID of the `task_preferences.xml` file stored in the `res/xml` directory.

→ **6**   I am retrieving the `EditTextPreference` for the default task reminder time by calling the `findPreference()` method and providing it with the key that was defined in the `task_preferences.xml` file.

→ **7**   On this line, I am obtaining the `EditText` object, which is a child of the `EditTextPreference`, using the `getEditText()` method. From this object, I set the key listener, which is responsible for listening to key-press events. I set the key listener through the `setKeyListener()` method, and by providing it with an instance of `DigitsKeyListener`, the `EditTextPreference` only allows digits to be typed into the `EditTextPreference` for the default reminder time. This is because I do not want users to type in string values such as `foo` or `bar` into the field because it is not a valid integer value. Using the `DigitsKeyListener` ensures that the only values passed into the preferences are digits.

At this point, the activity is ready to be used. This `PreferenceActivity` allows users to edit and save their preferences. As you can see, this implementation required very little code. The next step is getting the preference screen to show up by adding a menu item for it.

Don't forget! You also need to add your new `PreferenceActivity` to your `AndroidManifest.xml` file with the following line of code:

```
<activity android:name=".TaskPreferences" android:label="@string/app_name" />
```

Opening the PreferenceActivity class

To open this new activity, you need to add a menu item to the `Reminder-ListActivity`. To add a new menu item, you need to add a new menu definition to the `list_menu.xml` file located in the `res/menu` directory. Updating this file updates the menu on the `ReminderListActivity`. The updated `list_menu.xml` file is shown as follows with the new entry bolded:

```
<?xml version="1.0" encoding="utf-8"?>
<menu
    xmlns:android="http://schemas.android.com/apk/res/android">
    <item android:id="@+id/menu_insert"
        android:icon="@android:drawable/ic_menu_add"
        android:title="@string/menu_insert" />
        <item android:id="@+id/menu_settings"
            android:icon="@android:drawable/ic_menu_preferences"
            android:title="@string/menu_settings" />
</menu>
```

The last item adds a menu item for settings, which uses the built-in Android settings icon and a string resource called `menu_settings`. You need to add a new string resource called `menu_settings` with a value of `Settings` in your string resources.

Handling menu selections

Now that you have your menu updated, you need to be able to respond to when the menu item is tapped. To do so, you need to add code to the `onMenuItem Selected()` method in the `ReminderListActivity`. The code to handle the settings menu selection is bolded:

```
@Override
public boolean onMenuItemSelected(int featureId, MenuItem item) {
        switch(item.getItemId()) {
            case R.id.menu_insert:
                createReminder();
                return true;
            case R.id.menu_settings:
                Intent i = new Intent(this, TaskPreferences.class);
                startActivity(i);
                return true;
            }
        return super.onMenuItemSelected(featureId, item);
    }
}
```

The bolded code here simply creates a new `Intent` object with a destination class of `TaskPreferences`. When the user selects the Settings menu item, he is now shown the preferences screen, where he can edit the preferences. If you start the app and select Settings, you should see something similar to Figure 15-3.

Figure 15-3:
The
preferences
screen.

Working with Preferences in Your Activities at Run Time

While setting preferences in a PreferenceActivity is useful, in the end, it provides no actual value unless you can read the preferences from the SharedPreferences object at run time and utilize them in your application. Thankfully Android makes this a fairly simple process as well.

In the Task Reminder application, you need to read these values in the ReminderEditActivity to set the default values when a user creates a new task. Because the preferences are stored in SharedPreferences, you can access the preferences across various activities in your application.

Retrieving preference values

Open the ReminderEditActivity and navigate to the populateFields() method. This method determines whether the task is an existing task or a new task. If the task is new, I am going to pull the default values from

`SharedPreferences` and load them into the activity for the user. If for some reason the user has never set the preferences, they will be empty strings, and at that point, I will ignore the defaults. In short, I am only going to utilize the preferences if the user has set them.

To retrieve the preference values, you need to utilize the `Shared-Preferences` object, as shown in Listing 15-3. In the `populateFields()` method, add the bolded code as shown in Listing 15-3.

Listing 15-3: Retrieving Values from `SharedPreferences`

```
private void populateFields()  {
    if (mRowId != null) {
        Cursor reminder = mDbHelper.fetchReminder(mRowId);
        startManagingCursor(reminder);
        mTitleText.setText(reminder.getString(
        reminder.getColumnIndexOrThrow(RemindersDbAdapter.KEY_TITLE)));
        mBodyText.setText(reminder.getString(
        reminder.getColumnIndexOrThrow(RemindersDbAdapter.KEY_BODY)));

        SimpleDateFormat dateTimeFormat = new
            SimpleDateFormat(DATE_TIME_FORMAT);
        Date date = null;
        try {
            String dateString =
                reminder.getString(reminder.getColumnIndexOrThrow(
                    RemindersDbAdapter.KEY_DATE_TIME));
            date = dateTimeFormat.parse(dateString);

            mCalendar.setTime(date);
        } catch (IllegalArgumentException e) {
            e.printStackTrace();
        } catch (ParseException e) {
            e.printStackTrace();
        }
    } else {                                                              → 21
    SharedPreferences prefs =
        PreferenceManager.getDefaultSharedPreferences(this);             → 22
        String defaultTitleKey = getString(R.string.pref_task_title_key); → 23
        String defaultTimeKey =
                getString(R.string.pref_default_time_from_now_key);       → 24

        String defaultTitle = prefs.getString(defaultTitleKey, "");      → 26
        String defaultTime = prefs.getString(defaultTimeKey, "");        → 27
        if("".equals(defaultTitle) == false)
            mTitleText.setText(defaultTitle);                            → 30
        if("".equals(defaultTime) == false)
            mCalendar.add(Calendar.MINUTE, Integer.parseInt(defaultTime)); → 33
    }

    updateDateButtonText();
    updateTimeButtonText();                                              → 37
}
```

Each new line of code is explained as follows:

→ **21**   I have added the `else` statement to handle the logic for a new task.

→ **22**   This line retrieves the `SharedPreferences` object from the static `getDefaultSharedPreferences()` call on the `PreferenceManager` object.

→ **23**   On this line, I'm retrieving the key value for the default title preference from the string resources. This is the same key that is used in Listing 15-1 to define the preference.

→ **24**   On this line, I'm retrieving the key value for the default time offset, in minutes, from the preferences (a different key but the same process as line 23).

→ **26**   On this line, I'm retrieving the default title value from the preferences with a call to `getString()` on the `SharedPreferences` object. The first parameter is the key for the preference, and the second parameter is the default value if the preference does not exist (or has not been set). In this instance, I'm requesting that the default value be `""` (an empty string) if the preference does not exist.

→ **27**   On this line, I'm retrieving the default time value from the preferences, using the same method as described on line 26 with a different key.

→ **30**   On this line, I'm setting the text value of the `EditText` view — which is the title of the task. I'm only setting this value if the preference was not equal to an empty string.

→ **33**   On this line, I'm incrementing time on the local `Calendar` object by calling the `add()` method with the parameter of `Calendar.MINUTE` if the value from the preferences was not equal to an empty string. The `Calendar.MINUTE` constant informs the `Calendar` object that the next parameter should be treated as minutes and the value should get added to the calendar's minute field. If the minutes force the calendar into a new hour or day, the calendar object updates the other fields for you. For example, if the calendar was originally set to 2010-12-31 11:45 p.m. and you added 60 minutes to the calendar, the new value of the calendar would be 2011-01-01 12:45 a.m. Because the `EditTextPreference` stores all values as strings, I'm casting the string minute value to an integer with the `Integer.parseInt()` method. By adding time to the local `Calendar` object, the time picker and button text associated with opening the time picker are updated as well.

→ **37**   On this line, I'm updating the time button text to reflect the time that was added to the existing local `Calendar` object.

When you start the application, now you can set the preferences and see them reflected when you choose to add a new task to the list. Try clearing the preferences and then choosing to create a new task. Notice that the defaults no longer apply. Wow, that was easy!

Setting preference values

While not used in the Task Reminder application, at times you might need to update preference values through code. Consider the following case: You develop a help desk ticket system application that requires the user to enter his or her current department. You have a preference for the default department, but the user never utilizes the preferences screen. Therefore, the user repeatedly enters the department by hand into your application. Through logic that you define and write, you determine that the user is entering the same department for each help desk ticket (assume that it's the Accounting department). Therefore, you prompt the user and ask her whether she would like to set the default department to Accounting. If the user chooses Yes, you would programmatically update the preferences for her. I'm going to show you how to do that now.

To edit preferences programmatically, you need an instance of Shared-Preferences. You can obtain that through the PreferenceManager, as shown in Listing 15-4. After you obtain an instance of SharedPreferences, you can edit various preferences by obtaining an instance of the preference Editor object. After the preferences are edited, you need to commit them. This is also demonstrated in Listing 15-4.

Listing 15-4:   Programmatically Editing Preferences

```
SharedPreferences prefs =
    PreferenceManager.getDefaultSharedPreferences(this);       → 1
Editor editor = prefs.edit();                                  → 2
editor.putString("default_department", "Accounting");          → 3
editor.commit();                                               → 4
```

Each numbered line of code is explained as follows:

→ **1** An instance of SharedPreferences is retrieved from the PreferenceManager.

→ **2** An instance of the preferences Editor object is obtained by calling the edit() method on the SharedPreferences object.

→ **3** On this line, I am editing a preference with the key value of default_department by calling putString() method on the Editor object. I am setting the value to "Accounting". Normally, the key value would be retrieved from the string resources and the value of the string would be retrieved through your program or user input. The code snippet is kept simple for brevity.

→ **4**   After changes are made to any of the preferences, you must call the commit() method on the Editor object to persist them to SharedPreferences. The commit call automatically replaces any value that is currently stored in SharedPreferences with the key given in the putString() call.

If you do not call commit() on the Editor object, your changes will not persist and your application will not function as you expect.

By adding a preference screen to your application, you've given your application configurability, which will make the application more useful to end users. It's fairly simple to add new preferences through code or through an XML preference declaration, so you have no excuse not to add them! Making the app more configurable can give your power users the extra features that they are looking for.

Part IV
The Part of Tens

In this part . . .

Part IV consists of some of the best secret-sauce-covered Android nuggets that you acquire only after having been in the development trenches for quite some time. First, I list some of the best sample applications that can help springboard you on your way to creating the next hit application. These applications range from database-oriented apps to interactive games to applications that interact with third-party Web application programming interfaces (APIs).

I close Part IV with a list of professional tools and libraries that can help streamline and improve the productivity of your application development process and make your life as a developer much easier.

Chapter 16

Ten Great Free Sample Applications and SDKs (With Code!)

During your career as an Android developer, you may run into various roadblocks, many of which may be Android code based. Perhaps the functionality you're after is communicating with a third-party API that returns JSON, or maybe you need to know how to perform collision detection in a game. When I run into such a circumstance, I usually end up searching the Web for sample code. Chances are that someone else has already written the code I'm after! I can then review that code, alter it as needed, and continue with development.

Sample code is great, but it's just that — sample code. It's not production ready. While I agree with this statement, I would like to add that reviewing sample code has an added side effect: It is a learning enhancer. A good way to find out how to program for Android is to look at the sample code! Sure, sample code comes with the Android SDK — such as the API demos I mention in Chapter 2. But the real cool stuff is the plethora of real-world application code that is freely available on the Web! You can find plenty of good-quality open-source applications that serve as great examples that are available on the Internet thanks to the open-source nature of Android.

Telling you to find them yourself would be rather rude, now wouldn't it? To help speed your learning process, this chapter presents ten really cool open-source applications and samples for you to check out and benefit from. Most of the source code examples that follow are real-world Android applications that you can install from the Android Market. I would advise you to download the application on your device and interact with it. Then crack open the source code and see how the gears are turning each application.

The Official Foursquare App

Foursquare is all the rage right now. The location-based, check-in, social-networking app allows users to see where everyone is on a map and also claim statuses at various locations throughout the world. An example of this would be becoming the virtual mayor of your neighborhood. Do the inner workings of an Android social networking app interest you? If so, check out Foursquare's source code on Google Code. Do you need to know how to communicate with a third-party API that returns XML or JSON? If so, I can't think of a better way to start discovering than to review this proven working application source code! Isn't this open-source mind-set thing just awesome! This source has a ton of examples that use Android features, including the following:

- ✔ Asynchronous tasks
- ✔ XML parsing
- ✔ Multiple activities
- ✔ User authentication with OAuth
- ✔ Google Maps and Map Layers
- ✔ GPS
- ✔ Third-party Web API integration (the Foursquare API)

Not only do you find a lot of source code to learn from, but everything is also broken up and organized into various packages; this makes it easy to locate the examples that you're looking for. Source code: `http://code.google.com/p/foursquared`.

LOLCat

This is a great example if you are interested in image manipulation with Android. You find out how to take a picture using the device's camera, add captions to it, and then save the resulting file on the SD card. You also discover how to create various intents, which allow you to send the image as an MMS (multi-media message) image or as an e-mail attachment. Source code: `http://code.google.com/p/apps-for-android`.

Amazed

Amazed is a fun game that can demonstrate the use of the device's built-in accelerometer to control a 2D marble through various obstacles inside increasingly difficult maze levels. If you are interested in accelerometer-based applications, reviewing this application source code can help you immensely. Not only does the application show you how to use the accelerometer, it also demonstrates other game development fundamentals such as collision detection and the game loop principle. Source code: `http://code.google.com/p/apps-for-android`.

APIDemos

The Android SDK provides various sample applications, one of which is the API Demos application. This application demonstrates how to use the various Android APIs through small, digestible, working examples. You find tons of simple straight-to-the-point examples in the API Demos source code. Perhaps you're interested in incorporating animation into your project, or you want to play an audio file inside your app — that's easy because the API Demos provide examples of both! If you have a lot of ideas but not a lot of time, you should definitely check out these cool examples. I recommend installing this demo app on your device and playing with each of the numerous examples to see exactly what they can do. Source code: In your Android SDK, in the `samples` folder.

MultipleResolutions Example

If you want your app to run well on all screen sizes, the Multiple Resolution example in the Android SDK is a must read. I wish this example existed when I started supporting multiple screens because it would have saved me hours of debugging and positioning UI views. Android has provided a working sample app that shows you how to support multiple screen sizes and resolutions without breaking a sweat. The sample demonstrates the proper way to size your resources and position your views to eliminate messy workarounds with very little code. I highly recommend reading through the sample code before you develop your first app because it can save you headaches later on. Source code: In your Android SDK, in the `samples` folder.

Last.fm App Suite

Are you the next up-and-coming Internet radio sensation? If so, you might want to find out how to stream music by using the Last.fm API as an example. To run and test the app, you need a Last.fm API key that can be obtained by visiting this URL: www.last.fm/api/account. You also need a paid account to stream music; however, a paid account isn't necessary to review the code. You don't need to apply for a key or pay for an account if you simply want to review the source code. This example can help you understand the fundamentals of streaming music from a remote location. Source code: http://github.com/mxcl/lastfm-android.

Hubroid

Git is a popular open-source Distributed Version Control System (DVCS), and actually, all the code and documents written for this book were stored in various Git repositories during the writing! Hubroid is a GitHub.com-based application for Android that allows you to view all your favorite Git repositories located on GitHub.com from the palm of your hand. Hubroid demonstrates how to use the GitHub API. If you want to work with the GitHub API, this code is a great resource on how to "Git 'er done." Source code: http://github.com/eddieringle/hubroid.

Facebook SDK for Android

Are you feeling ambitious? If so, you might want to tackle the task of creating the next best Facebook application, but maybe you don't know where to begin. The Facebook Android SDK enables you to integrate Facebook functionality into your application easily. You can use it to authorize users, make API requests, and much more! Integrate all the Facebook goodness without breaking a sweat. Source code: http://github.com/facebook/facebook-android-sdk.

Replica Island

Perhaps you want to make a side-scrolling game but have no clue how to get started. Well, it's your lucky day because Replica Island is a very cool side-scrolling game that features none other than the little green robot that we know and love — the Android. Not only is it a popular free game on the Android Market, it's also completely open source and a great learning tool for game developers! This truly is a great example of a 2D game for the Android platform. Source code: `http://code.google.com/p/replicaisland`.

Notepad Tutorial

If you're interested in learning how to use the basics of SQLite without all the other fluff of services, background tasks, and so on, this app is for you. Although simple in its execution and usage, the source code and tutorial that go along with it help you understand the basics of SQLite. Source code and tutorial: `http://d.android.com/guide/tutorials/notepad/index.html`.

Chapter 17

Ten Tools That Make Your Developing Life Easier

As a developer, you inherently will build tools to help yourself become more productive. I have created various helper methods to assist in asynchronous communication, XML and JSON parsing, date and time utilities, and much more. Before you write a ton of helper classes or frameworks to handle items for you, I advise you to look on the Internet for tools that already exist. I've compiled a list of ten tools and utilities that can make your developer life much easier by increasing your productivity and ensuring that your app is up to snuff.

droid-fu

droid-fu is an open-source library with a handful of methods that can karate-chop your development time drastically. droid-fu is comprised of utility classes that do all the mundane heavy lifting for you, such as handling asynchronous background requests, retrieving images from the Web, and most amazingly, enhancing the application life cycle. Never worry about state changes because droid-fu handles all of it and much more. Don't just sit there. Start earning your black belt in droid-fu today! Source code: `http://github.com/kaeppler/droid-fu`.

RoboGuice

No, it's not the latest and greatest energy drink marketed to developers. RoboGuice is a framework that uses Google's Guice library to make dependency injection a breeze. Dependency injection handles initializing your variables at the right time so that you don't have to. This really cuts down the amount of code you have to write overall, and it makes maintaining your application a breeze in the future. Source code: `http://code.google.com/p/roboguice`.

DroidDraw

DroidDraw is a graphical user interface (GUI) tool that helps you create layouts for your Android application by dragging and dropping controls onto a designer-like surface. I use it when I am designing the first version of UIs or for mockup purposes because it's the only way to visualize your user interface without compiling your app. After you design your view in DroidDraw, you can save it and use it in your application. Please note that this application is in beta at the time of writing and may change when released. Site: `www.droiddraw.org`.

Draw 9-patch

Draw 9-patch is a utility that enables you to easily create scalable images for Android. While Draw 9-patch images were not discussed in this book, you can find more detail here: `http://d.android.com/guide/developing/tools/draw9patch.html`.

You use this utility to embed instructions in your image to tell the OS where to stretch your images so that they display as crisp and clean as possible regardless of the size or resolution of the device screen.

Hierarchy Viewer

Working with various views inside your layout file to create a UI isn't always as straightforward as you would like it to be. The Hierarchy Viewer, located in the Android SDK `tools` directory, lets you see exactly how your widgets are laid out on the screen in a graphical representation. This format allows you to clearly see each widget's boundaries so that you can determine what's going on inside your layout. This is the ultimate tool to make pixel-perfect UIs. The

Hierarchy Viewer also lets you magnify the display in the pixel-perfect view to make sure that your images and UIs will display flawlessly on all screen sizes and densities. You can read all about it at `http://developer.android.com/guide/developing/tools/hierarchy-viewer.html`.

UI/Application Exerciser Monkey

Don't worry — this monkey doesn't need to be fed bananas to remain happy! You use Exerciser Monkey to stress-test your application. It simulates random touches, clicks, and other user events to make sure that abnormal usage won't make your app explode. The Monkey can be used to test your apps either on your emulator or on your own device. For more info, see `http://developer.android.com/guide/developing/tools/monkey.html`.

zipalign

zipalign aligns all uncompressed data in your APK. Running zipalign minimizes memory consumption during run time. If you're using the ADT in Eclipse, your application always gets zip-aligned when you export a signed application, as demonstrated in Chapter 8. More info can be found at `http://developer.android.com/guide/developing/tools/zipalign.html`.

layoutopt

layoutopt is a command-line tool that analyzes your layouts and reports any problems or inefficiencies. This is a great tool to run against all your layouts and resource directories because it identifies problems that may slow down your app and cause problems later on. Check out `http://developer.android.com/guide/developing/tools/layoutopt.html`.

Git

Git is a super-fast, free, and open-source-distributed version-control system. Git manages repositories quickly and efficiently, making it painless to back up your work in a cinch. Don't let a system crash ruin your day by not having a version-control system for your next spectacular app! Git makes working with branching very simple and effective and integrates into your workflow very easily. Eclipse plug-ins exist to help manage your Git repository from within the Eclipse IDE. Although Git is distributed, you will most likely want a remote location where the Git repository is stored. You can obtain a free private Git repository from Projectlocker.com or Unfuddle.com. If your code is open source, you can create free repositories on Github.com. More info can be found at `http://git-scm.com`.

Paint.NET and GIMP

You will be working with images at some point in your Android development career. Most professionals use Adobe Photoshop, but not all of us can shell out that much money for an image-editing program. Therefore, you have two free alternatives: Paint.NET and GIMP.

Paint.NET is a free image-manipulation program written on top of the .NET Framework. Paint.NET works great and is used by many developers around the world. This application is targeted for Windows. Get Paint.NET here: `www.getpaint.net`.

The GIMP application is an open-source program that is similar to Photoshop. GIMP can be installed on Windows, Linux, or the Mac. See `www.gimp.org`.

Index

● E ●

Notes

Notes

Notes

Internet

Blogging For Dummies,
3rd Edition
978-0-470-61996-4

eBay For Dummies,
6th Edition
978-0-470-49741-8

Facebook For Dummies,
3rd Edition
978-0-470-87804-0

Web Marketing
For Dummies,
2nd Edition
978-0-470-37181-7

WordPress
For Dummies,
3rd Edition
978-0-470-59274-8

Language & Foreign Language

French For Dummies
978-0-7645-5193-2

Italian Phrases
For Dummies
978-0-7645-7203-6

Spanish For Dummies,
2nd Edition
978-0-470-87855-2

Spanish
For Dummies,
Audio Set
978-0-470-09585-0

Math & Science

Algebra I
For Dummies,
2nd Edition
978-0-470-55964-2

Biology For Dummies,
2nd Edition
978-0-470-59875-7

Calculus For Dummies
978-0-7645-2498-1

Chemistry For Dummies
978-0-7645-5430-8

Microsoft Office

Excel 2010 For Dummies
978-0-470-48953-6

Office 2010 All-in-One
For Dummies
978-0-470-49748-7

Office 2010 For Dummies,
Book + DVD Bundle
978-0-470-62698-6

Word 2010 For Dummies
978-0-470-48772-3

Music

Guitar For Dummies,
2nd Edition
978-0-7645-9904-0

iPod & iTunes For
Dummies, 8th Edition
978-0-470-87871-2

Piano Exercises
For Dummies
978-0-470-38765-8

Parenting & Education

Parenting For Dummies,
2nd Edition
978-0-7645-5418-6

Type 1 Diabetes
For Dummies
978-0-470-17811-9

Pets

Cats For Dummies,
2nd Edition
978-0-7645-5275-5

Dog Training For Dummies,
3rd Edition
978-0-470-60029-0

Puppies For Dummies,
2nd Edition
978-0-470-03717-1

Religion & Inspiration

The Bible For Dummies
978-0-7645-5296-0

Catholicism For Dummies
978-0-7645-5391-2

Women in the Bible
For Dummies
978-0-7645-8475-6

Self-Help & Relationship

Anger Management
For Dummies
978-0-470-03715-7

Overcoming Anxiety
For Dummies,
2nd Edition
978-0-470-57441-6

Sports

Baseball
For Dummies,
3rd Edition
978-0-7645-7537-2

Basketball
For Dummies,
2nd Edition
978-0-7645-5248-9

Golf For Dummies,
3rd Edition
978-0-471-76871-5

Web Development

Web Design
All-in-One
For Dummies
978-0-470-41796-6

Web Sites
Do-It-Yourself
For Dummies,
2nd Edition
978-0-470-56520-9

Windows 7

Windows 7
For Dummies
978-0-470-49743-2

Windows 7
For Dummies,
Book + DVD Bundle
978-0-470-52398-8

Windows 7 All-in-One
For Dummies
978-0-470-48763-1

Wherever you are in life, Dummies makes it easier.

From fashion to Facebook®, wine to Windows®, and everything in between, Dummies makes it easier.

Visit us at Dummies.com